MOST DESERVING OF DEATH?

The role of capital punishment in America has been criticised by those for and against the death penalty, by the judiciary, academics, the media and by prison personnel. This book demonstrates that it is the inconsistent and often incoherent jurisprudence of the United States Supreme Court which accounts for a system so lacking in public confidence. Using case studies, Kenneth Williams examines issues such as jury selection, ineffective assistance of counsel, the role of race and claims of innocence which affect the Court's decisions and how these decisions are played out in the lower courts, often an inmate's last recourse before execution. Discussing international treaties and their lack of impact on capital punishment in America, this book has international appeal and makes an important contribution to legal scholarship. It also provides a unique understanding of the dynamics of an alarmingly problematic system and will be valuable to those interested in human rights and criminal justice.

D1602658

Most Deserving of Death?
An Analysis of the Supreme Court's
Death Penalty Jurisprudence

KENNETH WILLIAMS
South Texas College of Law, USA

Routledge
Taylor & Francis Group

LONDON AND NEW YORK

First published 2012 by Ashgate Publishing

2 Park Square, Milton Park, Abingdon, Oxon OX14 4RN
711 Third Avenue, New York, NY 10017, USA

Routledge is an imprint of the Taylor & Francis Group, an informa business

First issued in paperback 2016

British Library Cataloguing in Publication Data
Williams, Kenneth.
  Most deserving of death? : an analysis of the Supreme
  Court's death penalty jurisprudence. -- (Law, justice and
  power series)
  1. United States. Supreme Court. 2. Capital punishment--
  United States. 3. Due process of law--United States.
  4. Discrimination in capital punishment--United States.
  5. Discrimination in criminal justice administration--
  United States.
  I. Title II. Series
  345.7'30773-dc23

Library of Congress Cataloging-in-Publication Data
Williams, Kenneth (Kenneth A.), 1961-
  Most deserving of death? : an analysis of the Supreme Court's death
penalty jurisprudence / by Kenneth Williams.
    p. cm.
  Includes bibliographical references and index.
  ISBN 978-0-7546-7885-4 (hardback)
  1. Capital punishment--United States. 2. United States. Supreme
Court--Cases. 3. Due process of law--United States. 4. Discrimination in
capital punishment--United States. 5. Discrimination in criminal justice
administration--United States. I. Title.
  KF9227.C2W55 2012
  345.73'0773--dc23
                                                                    2011041811

ISBN 978-0-7546-7885-4 (hbk)
ISBN 978-1-138-26040-5 (pbk)

Contents

List of Tables

Acknowledgments

There are many people I would like to thank for their assistance in bringing this project to fruition. First, I want to thank Professors Susan Rozelle, Laurent Sacharoff, and Andrew Taslitz for reading the manuscript and providing valuable input during our roundtable discussion at the Law and Society Association meeting in San Francisco. Second, I would like to thank Professors Jonathan Miller and Mary Pat Truethart for reading parts of the book and providing helpful comments. Third, I would like to thank South Texas College of Law and Southwestern Law School for providing financial and institutional support for this project. Finally, I would like to thank my many colleagues and friends for listening to me talk about the book and for sharing their insights.

Introduction

The death penalty continues to be one of the most divisive issues in the United States. Past disputes, such as slavery and racial segregation, have been largely resolved. Yet, the debate over capital punishment persists. Proponents and opponents of capital punishment disagree over whether it is just, whether it deters, whether it is racist, and just about every other issue associated with the death penalty. Even the Bible is inconclusive on the question of capital punishment; both sides regularly cite its passages in making their cases. Both sides, however, seem to have reached a consensus about one thing: the system is broken.

Opponents have argued for years that the arbitrariness and unfairness of the death penalty alone are reasons why it should be abolished. They have been joined in their criticisms more recently by proponents of the death penalty. New Mexico Governor Bill Richardson, a supporter of capital punishment, decided to sign a bill repealing the death penalty in his state. According to Richardson, he did so because he came to the conclusion that "regardless of my personal opinion about the death penalty, I do not have confidence in the criminal justice system as it currently operates to be the final arbiter when it comes to who lives and who dies for their crimes."[1] Another proponent, Governor Pat Quinn of Illinois, signed into law his state's repeal of capital punishment. During most of Justice Harry Blackmun's tenure on the United States Supreme Court, he consistently voted to uphold the death penalty because he believed that "on their face, [the] goals of fairness, reasonable consistency, and absence of error appear to be attainable."[2] Prior to leaving the Court, however, Justice Blackmun announced that he felt "morally and intellectually obligated simply to concede that the death penalty experiment has failed."[3] Justice Blackmun found that despite efforts to make the system work, the death penalty "remains fraught with arbitrariness, discrimination and caprice, and mistake"[4] and that "the basic question – does the system accurately and consistently determine which defendants 'deserve' to die cannot be answered in the affirmative."[5] Former Illinois Governor George Ryan, also a supporter of capital punishment, commuted the death sentences of every death row inmate

---

1   Governor Bill Richardson Signs Repeal of the Death Penalty, available at http://www.deathpenaltyinfo.org/documents/richardonstatement.pdf.
2   *Callins v. Collins*, 510 U.S. 1141, 1144 (1994) (Bluckmun, J., dissenting).
3   *Id.* at 1145.
4   *Id.* at 1144.
5   *Id.* at 1145.

while he was governor and also imposed a moratorium on executions.[6] He did so as a result of the fact that his state had wrongly convicted and sentenced to death more inmates than it had executed.[7] Conservative activist Richard Viguerie believes that his fellow conservatives should oppose capital punishment because "conservatives have every reason to believe that the death penalty system is no different from any politicized, costly, inefficient, bureaucratic, government run operation, which we conservatives know are rife with injustice."[8] Other prominent conservatives, such as George Will and Pat Robertson, have also been critical of the system. Because of the flaws in the administration of the death penalty – the mistakes that can lead to the execution of innocent people – George Will has concluded that "the ultimate punishment makes reason ... ultimately turn away."[9] Pat Robertson indicated that he favored a moratorium on executions because "we cannot have a culture that discriminates against African-Americans and the poor, and that's what's happening."[10]

The American criminal justice system is acknowledged as a model for criminal procedure worldwide. The death penalty, however, is one of the system's biggest flaws. How did we end up with a system that both supporters and opponents of the death penalty would agree has become dysfunctional? It is the thesis of this book that the United States Supreme Court, through its inconsistent and often incoherent jurisprudence, bears primary responsibility. This may seem to be an unfair accusation in light of the fact that the Court has spent an enormous amount of time on the death penalty over the past four decades. The Court began to regulate the death penalty in 1972 with its decision in *Furman v. Georgia.* Although the Court later upheld the death penalty against constitutional attack in its 1976 *Gregg v. Georgia* decision, the Court signaled that it would continue to regulate the process. Thus began the modern era of attempting to identify those offenders "most deserving of death."[11]

In its endeavor to limit the death penalty to the worst offenders, the Court began by limiting the crimes punishable by death. The Court immediately outlawed the death penalty for rapists and in doing so signaled that it would allow only murderers to be executed.[12] The Court later indicated that even someone who rapes a child does not deserve to die.[13] The Court also limited the class of individuals who can

---

6   See R. Warden, *Illinois Death Penalty Reform*, 95 J. Crim. L. & Criminology 381, 382, and n. 6 (2005).

7   *Id.*

8   R. Viguerie, When Governments Kill, available at http://www.sojo.net/index.cfm?action=magazine.article&issue=soj0907&article=whengovernments-kill.

9   G. Will, The Ultimate Punishment, available at http://townhall.com/columnists/GeorgeWill/2003/10/30/the_ultimate_punishment.

10   Transcript William & Mary Speech on the Role of Religion and the Death Penalty, available at http://www.deathpenaltyinfo.org/PRobertsonWMSpeech.pdf.

11   See *Roper v. Simmons*, 543 U.S. 551, 568 (2005).

12   See *Coker v. Georgia*, 433 U.S. 584 (1977).

13   See *Kennedy v. Louisiana*, 128 S. Ct. 2641 (2008).

be executed. The Court has held that the deterrent and retributive functions of the death penalty are not properly served by the execution of juveniles,[14] individuals who are mentally retarded,[15] and those who become insane as a result of their long, solitary confinement.[16] Because "death is different" the Court has also adopted procedures unique to capital cases. For instance, defendants in capital cases are allowed to seek mercy from the sentencer and, as a result, have the right to present "as a mitigating factor, any aspect of a defendant's character or record or any circumstances of the offense that the defendant proffers as a basis for a sentence less than death."[17]

The purpose of this book is not to make the case for or against abolition. Rather, the book is written to provide the reader with a better understanding of the death penalty: when it is sought, why it is sought, and to understand some of the problems that have been encountered in carrying it out. A further goal of the book is to outline and critique the Supreme Court's role in the system: how it has alleviated some problems but exacerbated others. The foremost goal of the book is to determine whether the Supreme Court has achieved its goal of reserving the death penalty for the worse offenders – those who are "most deserving of death."

---

14   See *Roper v. Simmons*, 543 U.S. 551 (2005).
15   See *Atkins v. Virginia*, 536 U.S. 304 (2002).
16   See *Ford v. Wainwright*, 477 U.S. 399 (1986).
17   *Lockett v. Ohio*, 438 U.S. 586, 604 (1978).

Chapter 1

History of Capital Punishment
in the United States

History of Capital Punishment

Societies have used death to punish criminals for their transgressions since the fifth century BC. The first formal death penalty laws were established in the eighteenth century BC, when the Code of King Hammurabi of Babylon codified the death penalty for 25 different crimes. Murder was the primary offense that subjected an individual to the death penalty but there were many others. Individuals were also sentenced to death for marrying a Jew, not confessing to a crime, treason, uttering blasphemy, cursing a parent, publishing libels and insulting songs, and making disturbances in the city at night. Executions were carried out by burning at the stake, hanging, beheading, boiling in oil, crucifying, drawing, quartering and disemboweling, and decapitation.

English common law recognized eight capital crimes: treason, petty treason (the killing of a husband by a wife), murder, larceny, robbery, burglary, rape, and arson. However, the number of capital crimes in Britain increased dramatically between the seventeenth and nineteenth centuries. By 1820, there were more than 200 capital crimes in Britain. In addition to the common law capital crimes, individuals could also be executed for many property crimes, such as theft of a pocket handkerchief, and forgery. The late nineteenth century saw a marked decline in crimes punishable by death, due largely to the refusal of British jurors to convict if the offense was not serious. After 1863, murder was the primary offense for which people were executed until England abolished the death penalty in 1965.

English settlers brought the common law, including the death penalty, with them when they came to America. The first recorded American execution occurred in 1608. Captain George Kendall was executed in the Jamestown colony of Virginia for being a spy for Spain. Death penalty laws varied considerably among the colonies. Massachusetts' capital crimes derived from the Bible: idolatry, witchcraft, blasphemy, murder, manslaughter, poisoning, bestiality, sodomy, adultery, man stealing, false witness in a capital trial, and rebellion. In contrast, Pennsylvania and South Jersey were settled by Quakers and they limited the death penalty to murder and treason. As the population of the colonies began to grow, they expanded the number of capital crimes as a means of maintaining public order.

The writing of Italian jurist Cesare Beccaria and others influenced the death penalty in the United States. Beccaria believed that the state had no justification for taking human life, that the death penalty was a barbarity, and that it did not deter crime. These writings led to the creation of an abolitionist movement and significant reforms. For instance, Thomas Jefferson introduced legislation that would make only murder and treason capital crimes. Dr Benjamin Rush, a signatory of the Declaration of Independence, was also influenced and as a result launched the first movement to abolish capital punishment in the United States. He did not believe the death penalty to be a deterrent and that it actually increased criminal conduct. The most significant reform was the division of murder into degrees. This led some states to limit the death penalty to first degree murder. Another significant reform was providing juries with sentencing discretion. Southern states were first in enacting this reform, in all likelihood so that all-white jurors would have discretion to be lenient in sentencing white defendants.

The framers of the Constitution and the Bill of Rights did not prohibit capital punishment in 1791. In fact, many of the provisions seemed to endorse it. The Fifth Amendment provides that "no person shall be held to answer for a *capital*, or otherwise infamous crime, unless on a presentment or indictment of a Grand Jury."[1] The Fifth Amendment further provides that no person can be "subject for the same offence to be twice put in jeopardy of *life*," and that no one can be "deprived of *life*" without due process of law. The only provision of the Bill of Rights that could arguably be interpreted as prohibiting capital punishment is the Eighth Amendment, which outlaws "cruel and unusual punishments."[2] However, such a reading would be inconsistent with the other provisions of the Bill of Rights which seem to clearly authorize capital punishment. Furthermore, capital punishment was widely practiced when the Constitution and Bill of Rights were written, and the fact that the framers did not specifically condemn capital punishment was not an oversight. The Eighth Amendment was understood at the time to prohibit some of the more egregious forms of executions such as burning at the stake and crucifixion. Following the Civil War, Congress enacted the Fourteenth Amendment in order to protect the newly freed slaves. This Congress was obviously aware of the fact that slaves were frequently executed. The Fourteenth Amendment, however, does not prohibit capital punishment, and in fact seems to endorse its continued use. Like the Fifth Amendment, the Fourteenth Amendment prohibits the states from depriving "any person of *life*, liberty, or property without due process of law."[3]

Capital punishment has always been more widely used in the south. Before the Civil War, it was used as a means of controlling the slave population. Many southern states explicitly punished a slave with death for committing certain offenses, while whites who committed the same offense were not punished nearly as harshly. Virginia, for instance, required the death penalty for any slave convicted of a crime punishable by three or more years' imprisonment for whites. In Georgia, the death penalty was required for a slave convicted of raping a white woman,

---

1   U.S. Const. amend. V.
2   U.S. Const. amend. VIII.
3   U.S. Const. amend. XIV.

whereas a white man convicted of raping a white female could be sentenced to prison for as little as two years. After the Civil War, the death penalty continued to be used to control black Americans. Blacks were not allowed to participate in the criminal justice system, except as defendants. As a result, blacks were often sentenced to death following perfunctory trials. Lynchings were also an extralegal means of keeping black people "in their place." State officials often participated in these lynchings, or at least turned a blind eye to them.

Supreme Court Regulation before 1972

There have been 14,489 legal executions in the United States between 1608 and 1972. Despite the fact that the death penalty was widely practiced and disproportionately employed against blacks, the Supreme Court provided very limited oversight over the administration of the death penalty prior to 1972. On occasion, the Court overturned death sentences due to some procedural irregularity during the defendant's trial.[4] However, the Court made only two broad pronouncements regarding capital punishment prior to 1972. In *Powell v. Alabama*,[5] the defendants were young African American men described by the court as "ignorant and illiterate" and they had been charged with raping two white women.[6] The community was so hostile towards the defendants that the state militia had to be called in to assist in guarding them. The trial judge appointed all the members of the bar for the purpose of arraigning the defendants. No specific attorney was named to represent them until the very morning of trial. As a result, no investigation of the facts occurred. Not surprisingly, the defendants were convicted and sentenced to death. The Court held "that in a capital case, where the defendant is unable to employ counsel, and is incapable adequately of making his own defense because of ignorance, feeble mindedness, illiteracy, or the like, it is the duty of the court, whether requested or not, to assign counsel for him."[7] The Court also held that the appointment of counsel must be made well before trial so that counsel would have the opportunity to investigate and prepare for trial. Thus, in 1932, the Court held that counsel had to be appointed for every indigent defendant facing the death penalty.[8]

---

4   The Court reversed convictions based on prosecutorial misconduct, see, e.g., *Alcorta v. Texas*, 355 U.S. 28 (1957); coerced confessions, see, e.g., *Brown v. Mississippi*, 297 U.S. 278 (1936); and ambiguous jury instructions, see *Andres v. United States*, 333 U.S. 740 (1948).

5   287 U.S. 45 (1932).

6   *Id.* at 71.

7   *Id.*

8   The right of defendants charged with non-capital crimes to counsel was not established until 31 years later in *Gideon v. Wainwright*, 372 U.S. 335 (1963).

The Supreme Court's only other broad pronouncement addressed jury selection in capital cases. An Illinois state statute provided that: "In trials for murder it shall be a cause for challenge of any juror who shall, on being examined, state that he has conscientious scruples against capital punishment, or that he is opposed to the same."[9] This statute allowed prosecutors to remove any juror who "might hesitate to return a verdict inflicting [death]."[10] In *Witherspoon v. Illinois*, after the judge said "let's get these conscientious objectors out of the way, without wasting any time on them,"[11] 47 potential jurors were successfully challenged for cause based on their attitudes toward the death penalty. Only five of the 47 explicitly indicated that they would not vote for the death penalty under any circumstance. Potential jurors who may have been opposed to capital punishment but who nonetheless might be willing to impose such a penalty were automatically eliminated. Thus, Witherspoon's jury was composed solely of individuals who supported capital punishment. The Supreme Court held that "a jury composed exclusively of such people cannot speak for the community"[12] given the fact that a large percentage of the community opposes the death penalty. The Court went on to state that:

> a State may not entrust the determination of whether a man should live or die to a tribunal organized to return a verdict of death. Specifically, we hold that a sentence of death cannot be carried out if the jury that imposed or recommended it was chosen by excluding veniremen for cause simply because they voiced general objections to the death penalty or expressed conscientious or religious scruples against its infliction.[13]

The Court was confronted with two systemic challenges to the death penalty prior to 1972, both of which it rejected. The first was a series of challenges to the methods by which executions were carried out. In *Wilkerson v. Utah*,[14] after the defendant was convicted of murder and sentenced to death, the trial judge ordered that he be shot to death. The Supreme Court held that because soldiers convicted of desertion or other capital military offenses were frequently shot, this manner of execution was not cruel and unusual punishment. *In Re Kemmler*[15] involved a challenge to New York's practice of imposing death by electrocution. The Supreme Court declared that although the death penalty per se was not cruel, punishments

---

9　*Witherspoon v. Illinois*, 391 U.S. 510, 513 (1968).

10　*Id.*

11　*Id.* at 514.

12　*Id.* at 520.

13　*Id.* at 522. This decision was later modified in *Wainwright v. Witt*, 469 U.S. 412 (1985). The Court held that potential jurors with conscientious or religious scruples against the death penalty could be excluded if their views substantially impair their ability to perform as jurors.

14　99 U.S. 130, 135 (1879).

15　136 U.S. 436 (1890).

are cruel when they involve torture or a lingering death. However, the Court deferred to the New York state courts in their interpretation that electrocution was the most humane form of execution and that it produced an instantaneous and painless death. A newspaper account described Kemmler's subsequent execution as follows:

> After the first convulsion there was not the slightest movement of Kemmler's body ... Then the eyes that had been momentarily turned from Kemmler's body returned to it and gazed with horror on what they saw. The men rose from their chairs impulsively and groaned at the agony they felt. "Great God! He is alive!" someone said: "Turn on the current," said another ... Again came that click as before, and again the body of the unconscious wretch in the chair became as rigid as one of bronze. It was awful, and the witnesses were so horrified by the ghastly sight that they could not take their eyes off it. The dynamo did not seem to run smoothly. The current could be heard sharply snapping. Blood began to appear on the face of the wretch in the chair. It stood on the face like sweat ... An awful odor began to permeate the death chamber, and then, as though to cap the climax of this fearful sight, it was seen that the hair under and around the electrode on the head and the flesh under and around the electrode at the base of the spine was singeing. The stench was unbearable.[16]

Finally, the Supreme Court rejected Willie Francis's request that Louisiana not be allowed to attempt to electrocute him again after the first attempt failed. Francis was sentenced to death after being convicted of murder.[17] On the day of his scheduled execution, he was placed in the electric chair. The executioner threw the switch but Francis did not die. Francis was returned to his cell. The state sought and obtained a new death warrant. Francis claimed that it would be cruel and unusual punishment for the state to attempt to electrocute him again. Specifically he argued that the first attempt obviously did not produce instantaneous death and the second constitutes lingering punishment. The Supreme Court held that the state could attempt to execute Francis again since there was no purpose on its part to inflict unnecessary pain. The dissent felt that the lack of intent on the state's part was immaterial. The dissenters believed that repeated application of electrical currents into the body fails to produce a painless death.

The second systemic challenge was to the unfettered discretion that states gave to jurors in deciding whether a person should live or die. In *McGautha v. California*,[18] the Court considered challenges to both California and Ohio laws in which "the decision whether the defendant should live or die was left to the

---

16 D. Denno, *Is Electrocution an Unconstitutional Method of Execution? The Engineering of Death Over the Century*, 35 Wm & Mary L. Rev. 551, 600 n. 322 (1994).

17 *Louisiana Ex Rel. Francis v. Resweber*, 329 U.S. 459 (1947).

18 402 U.S. 183 (1971).

absolute discretion of the jury."[19] In both states there were no standards to guide or limit the jurors' discretion. The defendants claimed that this was lawless and violated due process. In support of their claim that the lack of standards produced arbitrary decisions, they asserted that the death penalty is imposed on far fewer than half the defendants found guilty of capital crimes. The Supreme Court held that there was nothing wrong with the states' failure to limit the jury's discretion: "The States are entitled to assume that jurors confronted with the truly awesome responsibility of decreeing death for a fellow human will act with due regard for the consequences of their decision and will consider a variety of factors, many of which will have been suggested by the evidence or by the arguments of defense counsel."[20] The flaw in the Court's rationale was that while the jury may consider factors suggested by the evidence and by defense counsel, we know from history that the likelihood they would consider other factors such as race was great.

The Supreme Court did decide two cases that did not directly involve capital punishment but that set the stage for future successful challenges to certain aspects of the death penalty. In *Weems v. United States*,[21] the Supreme Court found a sentence of 15 years' imprisonment at hard labor plus a lifetime disqualification from many civil rights to be too harsh for falsifying a minor government record. Thus, the Court for the first time established the proposition that a sentence that is so disproportionate to the crime can violate the Eighth Amendment. This rationale was subsequently used by the Court in holding that the death penalty could not be imposed for the crime of rape. In *Trop v. Dulles*,[22] the Court held that the Eighth Amendment would not be confined to its original meaning. According to the Court, "the words of the Amendment are not precise" and "their scope is not static."[23] "The Amendment must draw its meaning from the evolving standards of decency that mark the progress of a maturing society." This evolving standard of decency analysis caused a later Court to conclude that society had come to condemn the death penalty for juveniles and the mentally retarded.

Furman v. Georgia and the Aftermath

In *McGautha,* the Court gave states complete discretion in administering the death penalty. However, only a year later the Court completely changed course. In *Furman v. Georgia*,[24] the Court struck down every death penalty statute in the county. In its 233-page opinion, five justices agreed that the manner in which the death penalty was administered violated the prohibition on cruel and unusual

---

19   *Id.* at 185.
20   *Id.* at 207–8.
21   217 U.S. 349 (1910).
22   356 U.S. 86 (1958).
23   *Id.* at 100–101.
24   408 U.S. 238 (1972).

punishment but they disagreed as to the reasoning. Thus, every member of the Court wrote a separate opinion to articulate their views.

Justice Douglas believed that the death penalty was cruel and unusual punishment because it was selectively applied to disfavored groups such as racial minorities and the poor. Justice Brennan concluded that the death penalty was unusual because of its arbitrary imposition: "Indeed, it smacks of little more than a lottery system."[25] He also believed that the death penalty did not provide any additional deterrent than did imprisonment. Justice Marshall concluded that the death penalty was excessive and unnecessary because it failed to serve the purposes of the criminal law, such as deterrence, any more than imprisonment. He rejected retribution as a valid legislative purpose because he believed it to be incompatible with the Eighth Amendment. In the most controversial section of his opinion, he declared that the American people would reject capital punishment if they were better informed about it: "the question with which we must deal is not whether a substantial proportion of American citizens would today, if polled, opine that capital punishment is barbarously cruel, but whether they would find it to be so in light of all information presently available."[26] According to Justice Marshall, information that would sway an informed public against capital punishment would include the fact that executions are more costly than life imprisonment, the risk of executing the innocent, and the fact that the death penalty is discriminatory in its application.

The concurring opinions of Justices Stewart and White were not nearly as sweeping. They did not categorically reject the death penalty in the abstract. Justice Stewart was bothered by the fact that only a tiny percentage of killers and rapists were sentenced to death. In the most quoted line in the entire 233-page opinion he stated: "these death sentences are cruel and unusual in the same way that being struck by lightning is cruel and unusual."[27] Unlike Justice Marshall, he thought retribution was a legitimate penological goal. Justice White believed that because the death penalty was imposed so infrequently and inconsistently, it served none of the purposes of the criminal law.

President Nixon made a campaign promise to appoint "law and order" justices to the Supreme Court, and all four of his appointees dissented from the Court's ruling in *Furman*. Justice Blackmun acknowledged that he was personally opposed to capital punishment:

> I yield to no one in the depth of my distaste, antipathy, and indeed, abhorrence, for the death penalty, with all its aspects of physical distress and fear and or moral judgment exercised by finite minds. That distaste is buttressed by a belief that capital punishment serves no useful purpose that can be demonstrated. For me, it violates childhood's training and life's experiences, and is not compatible

---

25   *Id.* at 293.
26   *Id.* at 362 (Marshall, J., concurring).
27   *Id.* at 309.

with the philosophical convictions I have been able to develop. It is antagonistic to any sense of "reverence of life."[28]

He added that he would oppose capital punishment were he a legislator. He felt bound, however, by the Court's precedent – including *McGautha*, decided only one year earlier – and the fact that the Court has been "presented with nothing that demonstrates a significant movement of any kind" by the people against the death penalty in this brief time.[29] Justice Powell challenged the notion that society was evolving in opposition to capital punishment. According to Justice Powell, the public's views are best expressed through its legislative bodies and juries. The number of states that retained capital punishment remained steady after World War I. Also, juries in the 1960s returned death sentences at a rate of two per week and the annual rate of death sentences had remained constant over a 10-year period. Chief Justice Burger wrote probably the most important dissent. He pointed out that Justices Stewart and White did not rule that the death penalty violated the Constitution in all circumstances. He provided legislators with a roadmap to satisfy White and Stewart's concerns about arbitrariness. According to Burger, they could do so by providing judges and juries with standards to follow in capital cases or by narrowing the crimes punishable by death. As will be discussed, most legislative bodies heeded Justice Burger's advice.

The *Furman* decision was not well received, probably due to the fact that the Court changed course so abruptly. The Court went from barely regulating the administration of the death penalty to declaring every death penalty statute in the nation unconstitutional. The Court failed to prepare the public for the result in *Furman*, which it could have done had it been regulating the death penalty and exposing its flaws prior to the decision. As a result, the public reaction was overwhelmingly negative. Thirty-five states plus the federal government enacted new capital punishment statutes. Public opinion polls indicated that public support for capital punishment was almost equally divided prior to *Furman* but support for capital punishment actually *increased* after the decision.[30] Despite the backlash, however, *Furman* was the beginning of the Court's attempt to regulate the death penalty and to standardize its procedures.

Gregg v. Georgia

The state of Georgia, along with 34 other states, responded to *Furman* by limiting the crimes punishable by death: murder, kidnapping for ransom or where the victim is harmed, armed robbery, rape, treason, and aircraft piracy. Georgia also

---

28   *Id.* at 405–6.

29   *Id.* at 408.

30   S. Banner, *The Death Penalty: An American History* 268 (Cambridge, Mass.: Harvard University Press, 2002).

provided that a capital defendant's guilt and sentence would be determined in two separate proceedings. Georgia attempted to limit the sentencer's discretion by requiring that the jury find at least one statutory aggravating circumstance in order to sentence the defendant to death. In *Gregg v. Georgia*,[31] the Supreme Court agreed to review Georgia's new death penalty procedures. The *Furman* decision was in peril due to the fact that one of the Justices in the five–four majority had been replaced; and in fact after the Court reviewed Georgia's administration of the death penalty it determined that Georgia's procedures passed constitutional muster. Not only did the newest member of the Court, Justice Stevens, vote to sustain the death penalty but also two members of the *Furman* majority, Justices White and Stewart, concluded that the Georgia death penalty procedures passed constitutional muster.

In *Gregg,* the Court ensured that the constitutionality of the death would not continue to be litigated by declaring that it was "not a form of punishment that may never be imposed, regardless of the circumstances of the offense, regardless of the character of the offender, and regardless of the procedure followed in reaching the decision to impose it."[32] The Court discussed two primary reasons for this conclusion. First, in applying the evolving standards of decency test, the Court found that society continued to endorse the death penalty. The Court cited the legislative response to *Furman.* Thirty-five states and the federal government had enacted new death penalty statutes during a four-year period. Second, the Court found that the death penalty served two penological justifications: deterrence and retribution. According to the Court, if the imposition of the death penalty did not "measurably [contribute] to one or both of these goals, it 'is nothing more than the purposeless and needless imposition of pain and suffering,' and hence an unconstitutional punishment."

The Court also found Georgia's new procedures acceptable. According to the Court, Georgia satisfied its concern about arbitrariness by requiring the jury to consider the circumstances of the crime and the defendant at a separate sentencing procedure. The new statute also limited the sentencer's discretion by providing guidance as to which aggravating circumstances could be considered. The Court also believed that the Georgia statute provided additional safeguards against arbitrariness by requiring automatic appeals of all death sentences to the Georgia Supreme Court.

Justices Brennan and Marshall were the only members of the Court who believed that the death penalty in all circumstances was cruel and unusual punishment, a position they adhered to during their entire careers on the Court. Justice Brennan believed that the death penalty treats "members of the human race as nonhumans, as objects to be toyed with and discarded."[33] Justice Marshall acknowledged that the public accepted the death penalty, as evidenced by the legislative response

---

31   428 U.S. 153 (1976).

32   *Id.* at 187.

33   *Id.* at 230.

to *Furman*. He continued to maintain, however, that this would not be so if the public were fully informed as to the death penalty's many flaws. Justice Marshall also maintained, as he did in *Furman,* that the death penalty was cruel and unusual because it was in fact gratuitous. In his view, society's desire to deter could be satisfied by a less severe sanction – life imprisonment.

Interestingly, three of the five justices who constituted the majority in *Gregg* subsequently renounced their earlier position and adopted Justices Brennan and Marshall's view that the death penalty could not be applied consistent with the Eighth Amendment. Justice Stevens wrote that:

> I have relied on my own experience in reaching the conclusion that the imposition of the death penalty represents 'the pointless and needless extinction of life with only marginal contributions to any discernible social or public purposes'. A penalty with such negligible returns to the State [is] patently excessive and cruel and unusual punishment violative of the Eighth Amendment.[34]

Justice Blackmun declared that he would "no longer tinker with the machinery of death."[35] He expressed his view that the goal of making the death penalty fair "is so plainly doomed to failure that it – and the death penalty – must be abandoned."[36] Finally, after retiring from the Court, Justice Powell was asked whether he would change his vote in any case. He replied that he "would vote the other way in any capital case ... [believing now that] capital punishment should be abolished."[37]

A few states responded to *Furman* by attempting to totally eliminate jury discretion. For instance, North Carolina required that any defendant convicted of first degree murder be sentenced to death. There were two defects with laws like North Carolina's. First, the jury would continue to have discretion. In the event that the jury did not want the defendant to be sentenced to death, the jury could simply acquit. The prosecutor could also continue to exercise discretion in the charging decision. Thus, although the law appeared to eliminate discretion, in fact it had not. A second problem with North Carolina's law was that it did not provide an opportunity for the jury to consider the defendant's humanity. As the Court stated:

> [The shortcoming] is its failure to allow the particularized consideration of relevant aspects of the character and record of each convicted defendant before the imposition upon him of a sentence of death ... A process that accords no significance to [such factors] excludes ... the possibility of compassionate or mitigating factors stemming from the diverse frailties of humankind. It treats

---

34   *Baze v. Rees*, 128 S. Ct. 1520, 1551 (2008) (Stevens, J., concurring).

35   *Callins v. Collins*, 510 U.S.. 1141 (1994) (Blackmun, J., dissenting).

36   *Id.* at 1159.

37   J. Jeffries, Jr., *Justice Lewis F. Powell, Jr.: A Biography*, 465–6 (New York: C. Scribner's Sons, 1994).

all persons convicted of a designated offense not as uniquely human beings, but as members of a faceless, undifferentiated mass to be subjected to the blind infliction of the penalty of death.[38]

The *Gregg* decision set the stage for the modern era of capital punishment. While the Court made it clear that it would not entertain any claims in the near future regarding the constitutionality of the death penalty, the Court also recognized that "death is different." It would begin to regulate the administration of the death penalty as never before, with the goal of creating a system that is fair and accurate in determining those "most deserving of death." Has this goal been realized since the Supreme Court began to regulate the administration of the death penalty? That question will be explored in future chapters.

---

38 *Woodson v. North Carolina*, 428 U.S. 280, 303–4 (1976).

Chapter 2
The Problem of Ineffective Representation

Introduction

Whether one ends up on death row is usually determined not by the heinousness of the crime but by the quality of trial counsel. The public has increasingly been made aware of this fact. There have been stories about sleeping lawyers,[1] lawyers missing filing deadlines,[2] alcoholic and disoriented lawyers,[3] and lawyers who failed to vigorously defend their clients.[4] Several United States Supreme Court justices have acknowledged the problem.[5] The United States Senate held a hearing

---

1 See, e.g., *Burdine v. Johnson*, 262 F.3d 336, 338 (5th Cir. 2001).

2 See, e.g., L. Olsen, *Texas Death Row Lawyers' Late Filings Deadly to Inmates*, Houston Chronicle, March 22, 2009.

3 See, e.g., S. Nesmith, *Jimmy Ryce Case: Defense Attorney Says He Told Boy's Killer To Lie on Stand*, Miami Herald, Jan. 19, 2007 at A1. ("[A lawyer] told his client to lie on the stand because he was on medication and 'disoriented' during the trial").

4 See, e.g., S. Nesmith, *Jimmy Ryce Case: Dad: Boy a Pawn in "Ego Contest" Between Lawyers*, Miami Herald, Jan. 12, 2007 at B5 (assistant public defender accused public defender of hindering accused killer's defense for political reasons).

5 Justice Ruth Bader·Ginsburg remarked, "I have yet to see a death case, among the dozens coming to the Supreme Court on eve of execution petitions, in which the defendant was well represented at trial." Ruth Bader Ginsburg, Assoc. Justice of the Supreme Court of the United States, Remarks at the University of District of Columbia, David A. Clarke School of Law, Joseph L. Rauh Lecture: *In Pursuit of the Public Good: Lawyers Who Care* (Apr. 9, 2001), http://supremecourtus.gov/publicinfo/speeches/sp_04-09-01a.html. Former Justice Sandra Day O'Connor had this to say on the topic: "Serious questions are being raised about whether the death penalty is being fairly administered in this country. Perhaps it's time to look at minimum standards for appointed counsel in death cases and adequate compensation for appointed counsel when they are used." Sandra Day O'Conner, Former Assoc. Justices of the Supreme Court of the United States, Speech to the Minnesota Women Lawyers (July 2, 2001), available at http://www.thejusticeproject.org/national/ problem. In an address to the American Bar Association, former Justice John Paul Stevens said: "[Justice Thurgood Marshall's] rejection of the death penalty rested on principles that would be controlling even if error never infected the criminal process. Since his retirement, with the benefit of DNA evidence, we have learned that a substantial number of death sentences have been imposed erroneously. That evidence is profoundly significant – not only because of its relevance to the debate about the wisdom of continuing to administer capital punishment, but also because it indicates that there must be serious flaws in our administration of criminal justice. Many thoughtful people have quickly concluded that inadequate legal representation explains those errors. It is true, as many have pointed out

on the problem of inadequate counsel in death penalty cases[6] and President Bush even addressed the issue in his 2005 State of the Union address.[7] The public has not been made aware, however, of the fact that very few defendants who receive substandard representation have been successful in overturning their convictions on appeal.

In *Strickland v. Washington*,[8] the Supreme Court held that a defendant seeking to overturn his conviction on grounds of ineffective assistance of counsel must demonstrate not only that his attorney performed deficiently, but also that he was prejudiced as a result of his counsel's performance. Justice Thurgood Marshall was prophetic in his *Strickland* dissent, predicting that very few defendants would be able to meet the burden of providing proof of prejudice and that has in fact been the case.[9] The purpose of this chapter is to outline the problem of incompetent representation in death penalty cases and discuss how the Court's two-part *Strickland* test has exacerbated the problem.

The chapter begins with a discussion of the numerous problems that are created when defendants are not properly represented. Following that is a full discussion of the *Strickland* decision, including Justice Marshall's dissenting opinion and how the prejudice requirement often results in a breakdown in the adversarial system. The next section analyzes three subsequent Supreme Court decisions which were designed to clarify *Strickland*, and presumably, to make it easier for defendants to prove a claim of ineffective assistance of counsel.

In the next section are the results of a survey of circuit court decisions, conducted in order to determine whether there is a disparity in applying *Strickland* and to gauge the impact of the Supreme Court's decision in *Wiggins v. Smith*[10] — the most important of the three decisions the Court issued in an attempt to clarify

---

and as our cases reveal, that a significant number of defendants in capital cases have not been provided with fully competent legal representation." Justice John Paul Stevens, Address to the American Bar Association Thurgood Marshall Awards Dinner Honoring Abner Mikva (Aug. 6, 2005), http:www.supremecourtus.gov/publicinfo/speeches/sp_08-06-05.html.

6   See *The Adequacy of Representation in Capital Cases: Hearing before the Subcommittee on the Constitution of the Committee on the Judiciary*, 110th Cong. (2008), available at http://judiciary.senate.gov/resources/110transcripts.cfm.

7   In his February 2005 State of the Union address, President Bush said: "Because one of the main sources of our national unity is our belief in equal justice, we need to make sure Americans of all races and backgrounds have confidence in the system that provides justice. In America, we must make doubly sure no person is held to account for a crime he or she did not commit, so we are dramatically expanding the use of DNA evidence to prevent wrongful conviction. Soon I will send to Congress a proposal to fund special training for defense counsel in capital cases, because people on trial for their lives must have competent lawyers by their side." *Address before a Joint Session of the Congress on the State of the Union*, 41 Weekly Comp. Pres. Doc. 126, 130 (Feb. 2, 2005).

8   466 U.S. 668 (1984).

9   *Id*. at 710 (Marshall, J., dissenting).

10   539 U.S. 510, 514 (2003).

Strickland. The survey indicates that defendants sentenced to death have not achieved any greater success in obtaining relief on ineffective assistance claims even after the Wiggins decision and that the prejudice prong, as Justice Marshall predicted, continues to be a major impediment for these defendants, including those with viable claims. What follows is a discussion of a case that I litigated in order to demonstrate the impediment that the prejudice prong presents to defendants with legitimate claims. Finally, there is a review of proposals that others have made for improving the prejudice requirement and a discussion of whether eliminating the requirement of proving prejudice is the only viable option available to the Court at this point. The chapter concludes with a synopsis of successful lower court claims of ineffective assistance of counsel.

Although *Strickland* applies to both capital and non-capital cases and the Court's two part test may also adversely impact non-capital defendants' in their pursuit for justice, the focus of this chapter is on *Strickland's* impact on capital cases.

Consequences of Bad Lawyering

Incompetent attorneys create numerous problems for their clients. The most serious problem they create is the risk that their clients will be wrongly convicted. Wrongful convictions have become a systemic problem in the criminal justice system.[11] Wrongful convictions in capital cases are especially problematic because of the risk that an innocent individual will be executed. As will be discussed in greater detail in Chapter 4, there is a strong possibility that at least one individual was executed even though it now appears that he was innocent. The Death Penalty Information Center has identified others who were executed despite serious uncertainty about their guilt.[12] Furthermore, the Death Penalty Information Center has identified 138 individuals in 26 states since 1973 who have been released from death row because strong evidence regarding their innocence emerged after they were convicted and sentenced to death.[13]

Many factors contribute to wrongful convictions. For instance, prosecutorial misconduct, misidentifications, false confessions, jailhouse snitch testimony, and junk science have all been identified as factors. However, nothing causes wrongful convictions more than incompetent legal representation. A competent attorney can

---

11   A more detailed discussion of the problem of wrongful convictions occurs in Chapter IV. For additional information regarding wrongful convictions, see S.R. Gross et al., *Exonerations in the United States, 1989 through 2000*, 95/2 J. Crim. L. & Criminology (2005).

12   Death Penalty Information Center, *Executed but Possibly Innocent*, available at http://www.deathpenaltyinfo.org/node/1935 (last visited October 2010).

13   Death Penalty Information Center, *Innocence: List of Those Freed from Death Row*, available at http://www.deathpenaltyinfo.org/innocence-list-those-freed-death-row (last visited October 2010).

overcome some of the causes of wrongful conviction. A competent attorney will conduct a thorough investigation. They will follow leads, interview witnesses, pursue alibi witnesses, and consult experts. They will put themselves in position to uncover prosecutorial misconduct, to effectively cross-examine witnesses about mistaken identifications to undermine the credibility of questionable jailhouse snitches who may fabricate to curry favor with the prosecution and to challenge the state's expert witnesses. In short, a competent attorney is able to challenge the state's case. When an attorney is able to effectively challenge the state's case, the chance of a wrongful conviction diminishes substantially.

Since the Supreme Court restored capital punishment, it has sought to identify and limit the punishment to those most deserving of death. Bad lawyering, however, makes it more difficult to achieve this objective. For instance, as a result of incompetent counsel, juries often do not learn of mitigating evidence such as an inmate's upbringing and any abuse they suffered as a child. Furthermore, incompetent defense attorneys frequently fail to remove problematic jurors from the venire. These attorneys can also complicate the death row inmate's efforts to obtain appellate relief. The failure of defense counsel to make a timely objection at trial or to follow the state's procedural rules prevents the issue from being considered on appeal in most circumstances.

As will be detailed later, death row inmates are provided three layers of appellate review before they are executed: a direct appeal of their conviction, a state collateral proceeding, and a federal habeas proceeding. They often receive substandard representation during these proceedings. The direct appeal attorney may not raise meritorious issues. The attorney representing the inmate may do likewise in the state proceedings, which precludes the claims from being considered in federal court. A number of death row inmates have been unable to have their claims, including claims of innocence, considered on the merits in federal court because of their attorneys' failure to present the claims during the state court proceedings.[14] Incredibly, some inmates have never had their appeals considered, and were executed as a result of their attorneys' failure to timely file their appeals.[15]

The Supreme Court's Response to the Problem of Incompetent Counsel

In *Powell v. Alabama*,[16] the Supreme Court recognized a right to trial counsel for indigent defendants in capital cases. However, the standard for determining

---

14 See S. Bright, *Elected Judges and the Death Penalty in Texas: Why Full Habeas Corpus Review by Independent Federal Judges is Indispensable in Protecting Constitutional Rights*, 78 Tex. L. Rev. 1805, 1836 (2000).

15 See L. Olsen, *Texas Death Row Lawyers' Late Filings Deadly to Inmates*, Houston Chronicle, March 22, 2009 (reporting that six men were executed after their attorneys missed the deadline for filing their appeals).

16 287 U.S. 45, 71 (1932).

whether counsel performed effectively was extremely low. Some courts adopted a "farce and mockery" standard.[17] As the term implies, counsel's representation passed constitutional muster as long as it did not make a "farce and mockery" of the proceedings. Other courts adopted a "reasonable competence" test, which required counsel's performance to be "within the range of competence demanded of attorneys in criminal cases."[18] The lack of a uniform standard for determining when a defendant's right to an effective advocate had been violated led the Supreme Court to subsequently adopt a two-prong test for the entire nation in *Strickland v. Washington.*[19]

In *Strickland,* the Court held that in order to prevail on a claim of ineffective assistance of counsel, the petitioner has to prove that counsel performed deficiently and that the petitioner suffered prejudice as a result of counsel's deficient performance. Counsel's performance is deficient in the event that counsel failed to perform reasonably under the circumstances. Trial attorneys charged with rendering ineffective assistance often defend their actions by claiming that their decisions were strategic, and the Court indicated that in evaluating the deficient performance prong, reviewing courts should give deference to counsel's strategic decisions. The burden is on the petitioner to demonstrate that counsel's strategic decisions were unreasonable. The Court also made it difficult for petitioners to prevail by requiring that they prove there is a reasonable probability that the outcome of the proceedings would have been different if not for the bad lawyering. This is an especially difficult burden for death-sentenced defendants. The prosecution typically seeks the death penalty in cases involving an abundance of evidence implicating the defendant in the crime and also in cases where there is an abundance of aggravating evidence. The defendant must overcome the abundance of evidence that the prosecution offered during the trial and sentencing phase and prove either that it is unlikely that they would have been convicted or sentenced to death had their attorney performed competently. The Court also instructed reviewing courts that they could resolve claims of ineffective assistance by assessing whether the petitioner had been prejudiced by counsel's performance without even addressing the adequacy of counsel's performance.

Justice Marshall wrote a dissenting opinion in *Strickland* which strongly critiqued the majority's two-prong approach to deciding claims of ineffective assistance of counsel. He felt that the majority's two-prong test would prove to be unhelpful because the deficient performance prong would be "so malleable that, in practice, it will either have no grip at all or will yield excessive variation in the manner in which the Sixth Amendment is interpreted and applied by different courts."[20] He also thought the adoption of more specific and particularized

17 See, e.g., *State v. Pacheco*, 588 P.2d 830, 833 (Ariz. 1978); *Hoover v. State*, 606 S.W.2d 749, 751 (Ark. 1980); *Line v. State*, 397 N.E.2d 975, 976 (Ind. 1979).

18 *McMann v. Richardson*, 497 U.S. 759, 770–71 (1970).

19 466 U.S. 668.

20 *Id.* at 707 (Marshall, J., dissenting).

standards would be a better approach. Justice Marshall was especially critical of the prejudice prong. First, he believed that it would be difficult for a reviewing court to assess the impact of counsel's performance based on a cold record. According to Justice Marshall, prejudice is difficult to assess because "[s]eemingly impregnable cases can sometimes be dismantled by good defense counsel."[21] Justice Marshall certainly would have pointed to the trial of O.J. Simpson and the way in which Simpson's "dream team" of defense lawyers attacked the prosecution's "mountain of evidence" as an illustration.[22] Second, Justice Marshall thought the constitutional guarantee of effective assistance of counsel should prevent the conviction of innocent persons and ensure "that convictions are obtained only through fundamentally fair procedures."[23] He rejected the majority's view "that the Sixth Amendment is not violated when a manifestly guilty defendant is convicted after a trial in which he was represented by a manifestly ineffective attorney."[24]

Justice Marshall's concerns have proven to be valid. As he predicted, there has been "excessive variation in the manner in which the Sixth Amendment is interpreted and applied by different courts." As you will read later, the U.S. Court of Appeals for the Fourth, Fifth, and Eleventh Circuits have interpreted and applied *Strickland* much differently than the Ninth Circuit. The *Strickland* analysis has not worked much better than the tests previously employed, due to the Court's failure to adopt particularized standards. Furthermore, the prejudice prong has proven to be an insurmountable hurdle for most death-sentenced defendants. As a result, the vast majority of claims by death-sentenced individuals of ineffective assistance of counsel have been rejected after *Strickland*, even in cases where counsel's performance was notoriously bad.[25] The two-prong *Strickland* test has been harshly criticized by scholars[26] and even by members of the bench.[27]

---

21   *Id.* at 710.

22   See, e.g., P. Arenella, *Foreword: O.J. Lessons*, 69 S. Cal. L. Rev. 1233, 1234 (1996).

23   *Strickland v. Washington*, 466 U.S. 668, 711 (1984).

24   *Id.*

25   See, e.g., S. Bright, *Counsel for the Poor: The Death Sentence Not for the Worst Crime but for the Worse Lawyer*, 103 Yale L. J. 1835, 1857–66 (1994).

26   See, e.g., S. Bright, *The Politics of Crime and the Death Penalty: Not "Soft on Crime" But Hard on the Bill of Rights*, 39 St. Louis U. L. J. 479, 498 (1995); W. Geimer, *A Decade of Strickland's Tin Horn: Doctrinal and Practical Undermining of the Right to Counsel*, 4 Wm. & Mary Bill Rts. J. 91, 93 (1995); R. Klein, *The Constitutionalization of Ineffective Assistance of Counsel*, 58 Md. L. Rev. 1433, 1446 (1999).

27   Alvin Rubin, a judge on the U.S. Court of Appeals for the Fifth Circuit wrote: "The Constitution, as interpreted by the courts, does not require that the accused, even in a capital cases, be represented by able or effective counsel. It requires representation only by a lawyer who is not ineffective under the standard set by Strickland v. Washington. Proof that the lawyer was ineffective requires proof not only that the lawyer bungled but also that his errors likely affected the result. Ineffectiveness is not measured against the standards set by good lawyers but by the average – 'reasonableness under prevailing norms' – and 'judicial scrutiny of counsel's performance must be highly deferential.' Consequently, accused

The Court has only extended the right to effective assistance of counsel to the representation that has been rendered at trial and on direct appeal. The Court has refused to extend the right to effective assistance of counsel to post-conviction proceedings, which are often the most important stage of a death-sentenced defendant's appeals. Therefore, when an inmate's attorney fails to timely file his writ, as has happened on several occasions in Texas, or when an attorney fails to raise potentially meritorious claims in the inmate's post-conviction writ, the inmate has little recourse to correct this injustice.

Williams, Wiggins, and Rompilla: A Glimmer of Hope?

The Court evidently recognized that the *Strickland* standard was not functioning as intended and moved more toward Justice Marshall's position in several subsequent cases. It sought to clarify *Strickland* in these cases.

Williams v. Taylor[28]

Terry Williams was convicted of capital murder after robbing and killing a neighbor for "a couple of dollars." At his sentencing hearing, the prosecution's two experts testified that "there was a 'high probability' that Williams would pose a serious continuing threat to society."[29] Williams's trial counsel offered the testimony of Williams's mother and neighbors, who described Williams as a "nice boy." The Court noted that "[o]ne of the neighbors had not been previously interviewed by defense counsel, but was noticed by counsel in the audience during the proceedings and asked to testify on the spot."[30] Defense counsel's closing argument was primarily devoted to explaining that it was difficult to find a reason why the jury should spare Williams's life.

Williams's trial attorneys, however, did not present any evidence of the defendant's nightmarish childhood. They did not mention the fact that Williams's parents had been imprisoned for criminal neglect; that his childhood home had feces and urine on the floor; that the children in his household were dirty and without clothing; and that four of the children were found to be under the influence of whiskey. Williams also had been repeatedly beaten by his father, placed in foster care while his parents were in prison, and returned to his parents' custody upon their release – and none of this information was presented to the jury. Trial

---

persons who are represented by 'not-legally-ineffective' lawyers may be condemned to die when the same accused, if represented by effective counsel, would receive at least the clemency of a life sentence." *Riles v. McCotter*, 799 F.2d 947, 955 (5th Cir. 1986) (Rubin, J., concurring).

28   529 U.S. 362 (2000).

29   *Id*. at 368–9.

30   *Id*.

counsel also neglected to present evidence that Williams was borderline mentally retarded. Additionally, they failed to point out that the prosecution experts "believed that Williams, if kept in a 'structured environment,' would not pose a future danger to society."[31]

The Supreme Court found that trial counsel rendered ineffective assistance of counsel. The Court found that counsel performed deficiently by not conducting a reasonable investigation that would have uncovered the mitigating evidence described above. Thus, the Court established for the first time the duty of trial counsel to conduct a reasonable investigation into the defendant's background in search of mitigation evidence. The Court also found that Williams had been prejudiced by counsel's performance because the cumulative effect of Williams's mitigation evidence may have made a difference had it been presented. The Court found prejudice despite significant aggravating evidence in Williams's background – including two assaults on elderly victims, armed robbery, arson, burglary, and grand larceny.

Wiggins v. Smith[32]

This was probably the most important decision after *Strickland*. Kevin Wiggins challenged the adequacy of his representation after he was sentenced to death. Had his trial attorneys investigated Wiggins's background, they would have learned that Wiggins had suffered severe abuse as a child living with an "alcoholic, absentee mother."[33] They also would have learned that Wiggins and his siblings were frequently left alone and forced to "beg for food and to eat paint chips and garbage;"[34] that he was physically tortured and repeatedly raped while in foster care; and that he ran away from the abuse and began living on the streets at a young age. According to the Supreme Court, this is "the kind of troubled history" that is "relevant to assessing a defendant's moral culpability."[35] Wiggins's lawyers, however, chose to "focus their efforts on 'retry[ing] the factual case' and disputing Wiggins's direct responsibility for the murder."[36] The Court found that, although his attorney made a strategic decision to forgo an investigation into Wiggins's background and to focus on his innocence at the sentencing phase, this was not a reasonable decision given the fact that they made this decision without the benefit of having all the information and therefore was not reasonable: "We base our conclusion on the much more limited principle that 'strategic choices made after less than complete investigation are reasonable' only to the extent that 'reasonable professional judgments support the limitations on investigation.'"[37] The Court also found that

---

31   *Id.* at 371.
32   539 U.S. 510 (2003).
33   *Id.* at 535.
34   *Id.* at 516–17.
35   *Id.* at 535.
36   *Id.* at 517.
37   *Id.* at 533 (quoting *Strickland v. Washington*, 466 U.S. 668, 690–91 (1984)).

Wiggins had been prejudiced by counsel's performance. In light of Wiggins's "excruciating life history" and the absence of any record of violent conduct to offset the "powerful mitigating narrative," the Court concluded that there was a reasonable probability that the jury, when it learned of the mitigation evidence, would have returned a different verdict.

Wiggins was important because it firmly established the duty of trial counsel to conduct an investigation into the defendant's background. The Court also made it clear that it would not defer to counsel's decisions simply because they are characterized as strategic. Rather, the Court indicated that it would only give deference to reasonable strategic decisions that are made after counsel has been fully informed of the defendant's background as a result of an investigation.

Rompilla v. Beard[38]

Rompilla also involved a challenge to trial counsel's performance during the sentencing phase of a capital case. Ronald Rompilla's severely alcoholic parents reared him in a slum environment and physically and verbally abused him. Rompilla's parents kept him and his siblings isolated in a filthy home without indoor plumbing, forced him to sleep in an attic with no heat, and did not provide clothing for their children, who were forced to attend school in rags. Rompilla also suffered from organic brain damage and fetal alcohol syndrome. Rompilla's school records showed him to be in the mentally retarded range. Defense counsel failed to discover any of this evidence and, therefore, none of this information was presented to the jury. The Supreme Court held that by failing to investigate Rompilla's background and uncover the significant mitigating evidence his attorneys performed deficiently. The Court made this determination even though Rompilla only provided minimal assistance to his attorneys regarding his background. The Court also held that Rompilla was prejudiced by their failure to discover and present this evidence because it may have influenced the jury's appraisal of Rompilla's culpability.

Florida v. Nixon[39]

Unlike *Williams, Wiggins,* and *Rompilla,* the Supreme Court found that counsel's performance in *Florida v. Nixon* was reasonable under the very unusual circumstances of the case. The prosecution had overwhelming evidence of Nixon's guilt: he confessed to the police, his brother, and his girlfriend that he had kidnapped a stranger, stolen her car, and burned her alive; before the murder, an eyewitness saw Nixon and the victim together at a shopping center; Nixon was seen driving the victim's car after her death; his palm print was found on the trunk of the car; and pawnshop records verified that Nixon had pawned her rings following

---

38 545 U.S. 374 (2005).
39 543 U.S. 175 (2004).

her death. After deposing the state's witnesses, trial counsel decided to concede Nixon's guilt and instead focus on the sentencing phase in order to attempt to save Nixon's life. Trial counsel believed that this strategy would allow him to maintain credibility with the jury. During the sentencing phase, counsel presented extensive evidence that Nixon was "not normal organically, intellectually, emotionally or educationally or in any other way."[40] Nixon never agreed or objected to defense counsel's strategy. After he was sentenced to death, Nixon claimed that counsel was ineffective for failing to obtain his consent to concede guilt and for pursuing such a strategy. The Supreme Court held that, given the strength of the prosecution's case, trial counsel made a reasonable strategic decision in focusing his efforts on trying to prevent his client's execution. Thus, the Court indicated that it would continue to defer to strategic decisions that were reasonable.

Summary

The decisions in *Williams, Wiggins, Rompilla,* and *Nixon* have provided some clarification. First, these decisions make it clear that an attorney has an obligation to conduct a reasonable investigation. In a capital case, that includes not only an investigation into any plausible defenses but also requires an investigation of the defendant's background for mitigating evidence. Second, the Court made it clear that while an attorney's strategic decisions will continue to receive deference, these decisions must be made after a thorough investigation and must also be reasonable. Finally, these decisions make it clear that the American Bar Association Guidelines for the Appointment and Performance of Defense Counsel in Death Penalty Cases are to be referred to in determining whether counsel's performance was deficient.

Despite the Court's efforts to clarify *Strickland,* two problems remain. First, *Strickland* continues to produce inconsistent results. Second, the requirement of proving prejudice is a special challenge for death-sentenced defendants who frequently cannot meet the challenge even in cases in which their attorney's performance was abysmal.

Continuing Problems

Inconsistent Outcomes

The Supreme Court has failed to develop a clear standard for separating those inmates entitled to relief on their claims of ineffective assistance of counsel from those who are not. It is difficult to understand, for instance, why a few defendants obtain relief when their attorneys fail to present evidence of their horrific childhoods to the jury but many others with equally horrible or worse childhoods do not obtain relief. The cases of George Porter, Jr and Robert J. Van Hook, both

---

40 *Id.* at 183.

decided by the Supreme Court and during the same term, perfectly illustrate this point. Porter and Van Hook were both military veterans. Both were convicted and sentenced to death for felony murder: Porter murdered his former girlfriend and her boyfriend during the course of committing burglary, whereas Van Hook murdered and robbed another male during a sexual encounter. The aggravating evidence in both cases was similar. The state's primary aggravating evidence against both men consisted of prior criminal activity: Porter had murdered his former girlfriend's boyfriend; Van Hook had committed previous robberies. Both Porter's and Van Hook's trial attorneys failed to present evidence of their abusive childhoods; they had been repeatedly beaten by their fathers. Their attorneys also did not inform the jury that they had a history of mental illness and that their fathers had beaten their mothers many times in their presence. If there was any significant differences between the two cases it was that Van Hook confessed to the murder – which is typically a mitigating factor – and that Porter stole a friend's gun and told another friend shortly before the murder that she would soon be reading about him in the newspaper. The Supreme Court granted relief to Porter but denied relief to Van Hook. In Porter's case, the Court did something it had never done previously: all nine justices agreed that Porter's trial counsel rendered ineffective assistance of counsel. The Court reasoned that "there exists too much mitigating evidence that was not presented to now be ignored."[41] The Court found that Porter was prejudiced by his trial counsel's performance because the weight of evidence in aggravation was not substantial. The Court even observed that "our nation has a long tradition of according leniency to veterans in recognition of their service."[42] In Van Hook's case, Court held that Van Hook's attorney's performance fell "well within the range of professionally reasonable judgments."[43] The Court also held that Van Hook's mitigation evidence would not have influenced the outcome given the weight of the aggravating evidence offered against him.

If I were teaching these two cases in my criminal procedure class, I would have a difficult time providing to my students a plausible explanation for the different outcomes. Apparently I am not alone. Linda Greenhouse, a commentator for the *New York Times*, wrote about the two cases:

> Setting the Porter and the Van Hook cases side by side, what strikes me is how similarly horrific the two men's childhoods were – indeed, how common such childhoods were among the hundreds of death-row inmates whose appeals I have read over the years and, I have to assume, among the 3,300 people on death row today. It is fanciful to suppose that each of these defendants had lawyers who made the effort to dig up the details and offer these sorry life stories to the jurors who would weigh their fate.

---

41 *Porter v. McCollum*, 130 S.Ct. 447, 455 (2009).
42 *Id.*
43 *Bobby v. Van Hook*, 130 S.Ct. 13, 19 (2009).

I don't make that observation to excuse the crimes of those on death row, but only to underscore the anomaly of the mercy the court bestowed this week on one of that number. Am I glad that a hapless 77-year-old man won't be put to death by the State of Florida? Yes, I am. Am I concerned about a Supreme Court that dispenses empathy so selectively? Also yes.[44]

I conducted a survey of decisions by the most active death penalty circuits: the Fourth, Fifth, Ninth, and Eleventh Circuits.[45] Specifically, I sought to determine the records of these circuits on claims of ineffective assistance of counsel in capital cases during the five years before and after the 2003 *Wiggins* decision. The survey was conducted for two reasons. First, I wanted to determine whether there was a disparity between circuits in their application of *Strickland.* Second, I wanted to determine the impact of *Wiggins* and whether the decision made it easier for death-sentenced inmates to prove claims of ineffective assistance. The Fourth Circuit considered claims of ineffective assistance of counsel in 37 capital cases following *Wiggins* and denied relief on each occasion. During the five years prior to *Wiggins*, the Fourth Circuit considered 40 claims of ineffective assistance of counsel by death row inmates but did not grant relief to a single petitioner. The Fifth Circuit considered 81 ineffective assistance claims by death row inmates after *Wiggins* and granted relief on three occasions. During the five years prior to *Wiggins*, although it considered 41 claims of ineffective assistance of counsel, the Fifth Circuit granted relief to only three death-sentenced defendants. The Eleventh Circuit considered 22 *Strickland* claims of death-sentenced defendants following *Wiggins* and granted relief on one occasion. During the five years prior to *Wiggins,* the Eleventh Circuit considered 35 claims of ineffective assistance of counsel but relief was granted on only three occasions. In contrast to the other circuits, the Ninth Circuit considered 18 ineffective assistance of counsel claims by death-sentenced defendants post *Wiggins* and granted relief in 10 cases. Inmates were also more successful in the Ninth Circuit than in the other circuits during the five years prior to the *Wiggins* decision. The Ninth Circuit held that the representation provided to death row inmates failed to meet constitutional standards in 11 of the 24 cases it considered prior to *Wiggins*. In terms of percentages, the circuits' decisions on successful *Strickland* claims are shown in Table 2.1.

---

44   L. Greenhouse, *Selective Empathy*, December 3, 2009, available at http:// opinionator.blogs.nytimes.com/2009/12/03/selective-empathy.

45   The Fourth Circuit covers Virginia, one of the most active death penalty states; the Fifth has jurisdiction over Texas, which carries out more executions than any other state; the Ninth Circuit has jurisdiction over California, which has the largest death row population in the nation; and the Eleventh Circuit covers Alabama, Florida, and Georgia, all active death penalty states.

Table 2.1   Percentage of successful ineffective assistance claims by circuit, 1998–2008

Jurisdiction	5 years before Wiggins	5 years after Wiggins
4th Circuit	0%	0%
5th Circuit	7.3%	3.8%
9th Circuit	45.8%	52.6%
11th Circuit	8.5%	4.5%

These findings lead to several conclusions. First, there is a tremendous disparity between circuits, which leads to the conclusion that Justice Marshall was prescient when he wrote that the standard for determining ineffective assistance of counsel:

> is so malleable that, in practice, it will either have no grip at all or will yield excessive variation in the manner in which the Sixth Amendment is interpreted and applied by different courts. To tell lawyers and the lower courts that counsel for a criminal defendant must behave "reasonably" and must act "like a reasonably competent attorney" is to tell them almost nothing.[46]

Some may blame the disparity on the liberal bent of the Ninth Circuit, while others may blame the disparity on the hostility of conservative southern judges on the Fourth, Fifth, and Eleventh Circuits. The truth of the matter is that the *Strickland* standard is so flexible that it permits judges to do whatever they may be inclined to do. Second, the Supreme Court's decision in *Wiggins v. Smith* has not made much of an impact as the findings indicate that death-sentenced defendants were no more likely to prevail after the decision than they were prior to the decision. In fact, in two of the circuits, the Fifth and Eleventh, these defendants actually fared slightly worse after *Wiggins*. Third, the defendants who were successful both before and after *Wiggins* were more likely to have their death sentences overturned as opposed to their convictions. This can be explained, in part, by the fact that an appellate court is probably reluctant to overturn a conviction because of the burden on the state of retrying the case after an extensive period of time has elapsed. Because the government tends to rely on prior convictions during the sentencing phase, it is less burdensome for the state to retry that phase of the case. Additionally, the Court made it clear in *Wiggins* that trial counsel must investigate and present compelling mitigation evidence during the sentencing phase and it is easier to conclude that the defendant suffered prejudice when counsel fails to do so. For instance, it is easier to conclude that certain mitigating evidence, such as childhood abuse, could have led a jury to sentence the defendant to life imprisonment than it is to conclude that a defendant would have been acquitted

---

46   *Strickland v. Washington*, 466 U.S. 668, 708–9 (1984 (Marshall, J., dissenting).

had counsel uncovered certain evidence during the guilt–innocence phase when there is evidence implicating the defendant in the crime.

The Prejudice Requirement

Many death-sentenced defendants are unsuccessful because of the requirement that they prove prejudice. In *Strickland,* the Court held that the prejudice prong is satisfied by showing that "there is a reasonable probability that, absent [counsel's] errors, the factfinder would have had a reasonable doubt respecting guilt."[47] Although the Court rejected a sufficiency of the evidence test for determining prejudice, that is exactly the test that has been routinely applied by the lower courts.[48] As long as there is evidence in the record implicating the defendant in the crime, the lower courts will typically excuse counsel's often substandard performance and find that the defendant did not suffer prejudice. In *McFarland v. Scott,*[49] Justice Blackmun provided illustrations of cases in which defendants clearly received substandard representation but still did not prevail because the lower courts determined that they had not suffered prejudice:

> The impotence of the *Strickland* standard is perhaps best evidenced in the cases in which ineffective-assistance claims have been denied. John Young, for example, was represented in his capital trial by an attorney who was addicted to drugs and who a few weeks later was incarcerated on federal drug charges. The Court of Appeals for the Eleventh Circuit rejected Young's ineffective-assistance-of-counsel claim on federal habeas, and this Court denied review. Young was executed in 1985 …

Jesus Romero's attorney failed to present any evidence at the penalty phase and delivered a closing argument totaling 29 words. Although the attorney was later suspended on unrelated grounds, Romero's ineffective-assistance claim was rejected by the Court of Appeals for the Fifth Circuit, and this Court denied certiorari. Romero was executed in 1992. Larry Heath was represented by counsel who filed a six-page brief before the Alabama Court of Criminal Appeals. The attorney failed to appear for oral argument before the Alabama Supreme Court and filed a brief in that court containing a one-page argument and citing a single case. The Eleventh Circuit found no prejudice, and this Court denied review. Heath was executed in Alabama in 1992.[50]

Another illustration is provided by the Eleventh Circuit's decision in *Davis v. Terry.*[51] Troy Davis had been convicted and sentenced to death for shooting a

---

47   *Id.* at 695.
48   See, e.g., *Hartford v. Culliver*, 459 F.3d 1193, 1201 (11th Cir. 2006).
49   512 U.S. 1256 (1994) (Blackmun, J., dissenting) (citations omitted).
50   *Id.* at 159–60.
51   465 F.3d 1249 (11th Cir. 2006).

police officer based solely on eyewitness testimony. There was no confession and no physical evidence implicating him in the crime. The murder weapon was never found. Davis alleged that counsel was ineffective for failing to interview crucial witnesses and for not impeaching some of the prosecution witnesses. In a holding that is fairly representative of the lower court's attitude toward the prejudice requirement, the Eleventh Circuit held that "none of the testimony which Davis asserts counsel should have obtained would overcome the prejudice requirement of *Strickland* in light of the totality of the evidence presented at trial."[52] The Georgia Board of Pardons and Paroles subsequently granted Davis a reprieve on the eve of his execution.

In *Colvin-el v. Nuth*,[53] the defense "put on no proof during the guilt phase of the trial" despite the existence of evidence suggesting the possibility of a different perpetrator, including the "unidentified fingerprint found on the piece of paper in the [victim's] purse, which [was] shown not to have been that of the [defendant]." The Fourth Circuit Court of Appeals held that the defendant was unable to prove prejudice, and denied relief. The Governor of Maryland subsequently commuted the defendant's sentence to life because the Governor "came to the conclusion that [the defendant] was almost certainly guilty of this horrible crime but 'almost certainly' is not strong enough."[54]

In *Anderson v. Quarterman*,[55] appellate counsel only raised three issues on direct appeal because appellate counsel thought that raising other issues was a "waste of time." Although the Fifth Circuit found that appellate counsel's performance was deficient, relief was denied because the Court found that the defendant had not been prejudiced.

As these cases illustrate, the courts tend to resolve claims on ineffective assistance in the government's favor as long as there is evidence implicating the defendant as the assailant even if there was evidence that trial counsel failed to uncover which undermines the government's case. Judge Harry Edwards has identified the serious flaw in using a sufficiency of the evidence approach in determining whether an inmate was harmed by counsel's representation:

> The most serious flaw in the guilt-based approach … is the tendency to undermine our most important legal principles … [A]ny analysis measuring the harmlessness of error according to the weight of the evidence that the prosecution stacks against a defendant erodes the individual rights and liberties that are presumed to elevate our system of justice. A focus on guilt skews the judicial assessment of harmlessness. The values that underlie the individual rights guaranteed by the Constitution, federal statutes, and procedural rules

52   *Id.* at 1256.
53   1999 U.S. App. LEXIS 13293 (4th Cir. 1999).
54   T. Waldron and D. O'Brien, *Glendening Acts to Stop Execution: Death Sentence is Commuted to Life Imprisonment*, Balt. Sun, June 8, 2000, at A1.
55   204 F. App. 402, 410 (5th Cir. 2006).

often are general. Constitutional rights, in particular, often represent broad ideas of individual liberty and human dignity. By contrast, a criminal act appears vivid and almost tangible, so the need to punish the guilty is both immediate and strongly felt. A wrong, often a grievous wrong, has occurred, and the defendant, by all appearances, is responsible. It is, therefore, to be expected that the desire to punish the guilty will frequently prevail over the need to honor individual rights.[56]

Furthermore, as another judge pointed out:

"prejudice" to the defendant may take many forms. The likelihood of acquittal at trial is not the only touchstone against which the consequences of counsel's failures is to be measured. The duties of an attorney extend to many areas not necessarily affecting the outcome of the trial. As the present case highlights, inadequate investigation and preparation may prejudice the defendant not only at trial but *before* trial – in counsel's inability to offer informed, competent advice on whether to plead guilty and whether to demand a jury trial – as well as *after* trial – in providing ineffective representation at sentencing.[57]

A Case Study of the Difficulty of Proving Prejudice

Johnny Ray Conner was convicted of murdering the owner of a Houston, Texas, convenience store during an attempted robbery. Conner did not confess and no murder weapon was ever discovered. Despite that, the government's case against Conner seemed strong, consisting of the testimony of three eyewitnesses and Conner's fingerprint which was found in the store. Six individuals claimed to have seen the assailant and they all agreed that the assailant ran swiftly from the crime scene. That was their only agreement. They gave varying descriptions of the assailant to the police shortly after the crime. One witness described the assailant's height as between 5 feet 10 inches and 6 feet 1 inch; others indicated that the assailant was about 5 feet 7 inches tall. The witnesses also failed to agree about the clothing worn by the assailant: he was described by some as wearing shorts above his knees, while others told the police that the assailant wore long pants below his ankles. Some of the witnesses indicated that the assailant wore a baseball cap, while others indicated that the assailant did not wear a cap. Johnny Ray Conner had a distinctive teardrop tattoo below his eye. However, none of the eyewitnesses indicated to the police that the assailant had a tattoo on his face, including the two

---

56   H. Edwards, *To Err is Human, but Not Always Harmless: When Should Legal Error Be Tolerated?* 70 N.Y.U. L. Rev. 1167, 1194 (1995).

57   *United States v. Decoster*, 624 F.2d 196, 291–3 (D.C. Cir. 1976) (Bazelon, J., dissenting) (emphasis in original).

eyewitnesses who testified that they observed the assailant for an extended period of time at close range.

In addition to the discrepancies in the eyewitness descriptions, the Houston Police Department presented the six eyewitnesses with a photo array, only three of whom identified Conner. In fact, one of the three eyewitnesses who made a positive identification admitted during the trial that she picked Conner out of the photo array because his picture was the only one containing Houston Police Department booking numbers.[58] The state also had what many would believe to be ironclad proof of Conner's guilt: his fingerprints on a juice bottle in the store. The state presented evidence that one of the fingerprints on the bottle was Conner's. The police found another unidentified fingerprint on the bottle – the source of which neither defense counsel nor the police made any effort to ascertain. In addition, Conner was a resident in the neighborhood near the convenience store and it would not have been unusual for his and many other fingerprints to be in the store. Finally, evidence of widespread corruption in the Houston crime lab emerged while Conner's case was pending.

At Conner's trial, trial counsel presented no defense other than cross-examining the prosecution's witnesses. The jury was not informed of most of the weaknesses in the government's case. Most significantly, after Conner was sentenced to death, I discovered that, prior to the crime, Conner had broken his right leg playing football in high school, which resulted in traumatic nerve damage to his right peroneal nerve and the development of a condition known as "foot drop."[59] According to expert testimony, Conner's condition would have made it difficult for him to have run in a normal manner, and it certainly would have been difficult for him to run as swiftly as the witnesses claimed to have seen the assailant run. Conner's condition had been documented in his medical records. Trial counsel, however, never consulted Conner's medical records and, as a result, never investigated the possibility that Conner could not run in the manner in which the eyewitness testimony claimed he ran.

Since actual innocence claims were not cognizable in a habeas proceeding, I brought an ineffective assistance of counsel claim instead. The essence of the claim was that counsel had performed deficiently because of their failure to consult

---

58 Eyewitness Martha Meyers testified as follows:

Q: Isn't it a fact, ma'am, the only particular individual in this particular grouping that has any type of numbers that denotes any type of police record is number five?

A: Yes, sir.

Q: Would that have anything to have done [sic] with you picking out number five?

A: Yes, sir.

Q: Are you absolutely positive about that?

A: Yes, sir.

59 "Foot drop is caused by weakness or paralysis of the muscles on the side of the shinbone, and causes the toes to drag and the foot to hang." K. Williams, *Does Strickland Prejudice Defendants on Death Row?*, *43 U. Rich. L. Rev. 1459, 1483 (2009)*.

Conner's medical records, as the American Bar Association (ABA) Guidelines for the Performance of Defense Counsel in Death Penalty Cases mandate and as a result of their failure to investigate Conner's medical history. Conner was prejudiced as a result of counsel's poor performance given the fact that the eyewitnesses had insisted that the assailant ran so swiftly from the crime scene. There was a reasonable probability that the outcome of Conner's trial would have been different had the jury learned of Conner's gait problem. The federal district court held that Conner satisfied both prongs of *Strickland.* According to the Court, the lead trial counsel decided before trial that he would invest little time and effort into contesting Conner's guilt. As a result of this decision, trial counsel conducted very little investigation into Conner's background, and no investigation into Conner's medical history. The district court held that trial counsel's decision was unreasonable in light of the ABA guidelines:

> In this case, had counsel conduced a prompt and reasonably diligent investigation into any possible mitigating evidence in Conner's medical history, they would have discovered before trial that Conner suffered from foot drop, and they could have used this evidence to further undermine the State's already weak case. Counsel's investigation therefore fell below objective standards of professionally reasonable conduct.[60]

The federal district court also held that trial counsel's deficient performance prejudiced Conner:

> [T]he State's case against Conner was weak. While the testimony of six witnesses all identifying Conner as the gunman may have seemed compelling, the testimony of these witnesses was riddled with inconsistencies. In addition to the explicit inconsistencies, two of the witnesses testified that they saw the gunman's face for an extended period, yet neither testified that the gunman had Conner's distinctive tattoo of a teardrop under his eye – a tattoo about which the prosecution made much ado during the sentencing phase ... Yet, there is significant evidence before this Court that Conner could not run without lifting his entire right leg and throwing his foot forward because of his foot drop – a physical fact that would result in a very distinctive gait, and one discoverable through a review of Conner's medical records. In light of the glaring inconsistencies in the witness identification testimony and the lack of physical evidence against Conner, counsel's failure to discover and present this evidence – evidence that would have cast grave doubt on whether Conner was the person the witnesses actually saw – is sufficient to undermine confidence in the outcome of Conner's trial.[61]

---

60   *Conner v. Dretke,* No. H-024627, slip op. at 2, 16 (S.D. Tex. March 22, 2005).
61   Id. at 17–18.

The Fifth Circuit Court of Appeals reversed the federal district court's grant of habeas relief. The Fifth Circuit did not address trial counsel's performance. Instead, the Fifth Circuit held that Conner was not entitled to relief because he "cannot show prejudice resulting from his counsel's alleged deficiency in not reviewing his medical history."[62] The Fifth Circuit held, without acknowledging the flaws in the evidence – such as the eyewitness inconsistencies – that Conner could not establish prejudice because he "has done nothing to lessen the impact of the other evidence against him."[63] Instead of analyzing whether there should be confidence in a conviction in which trial counsel failed to conduct an investigation into potentially exculpatory evidence and whether confidence is warranted when that conviction is based primarily on flawed testimony, the Fifth Circuit merely weighed the prosecution's evidence and determined that it was sufficient to sustain his conviction. The Supreme Court subsequently denied certiorari over the dissents of Justices Ginsburg and Stevens,[64] and on August 22, 2007, Johnny Ray Conner was executed.

Alternatives to the Prejudice Requirement

One obvious alternative is to adopt the position of Justice Marshall and not require that death-sentenced defendants prove prejudice. There would then be many reversals which would provide states with an incentive to ensure that death-sentenced defendants receive competent legal representation. Judges would also be more proactive in ensuring that defendants receive adequate representation. At the present time, there is no such incentive to provide defendants with better lawyers. Everyone is aware of the difficulty defendants face in proving prejudice and that their chance of prevailing on a claim of ineffective assistance of counsel is minimal. The situation would change if defendants were not required to prove prejudice. They would prevail more frequently and the states would want to avoid the expense and inconvenience of retrials and would, therefore, devote greater resources to ensure that defendants receive competent trial attorneys.

Another alternative is to tinker with the prejudice requirement. In *Strickland*, the Supreme Court placed the burden of proving prejudice on the defendant. It has been suggested that the burden should instead be placed on the government. That is, the government would have to prove that the defendant suffered no prejudice as a result of counsel's poor performance. According to the proponent of this proposal, "To place the burden on the defendant would require him to establish the likelihood of his innocence."[65] The problem with requiring the defendant

---

62   *Conner v. Quarterman*, 477 F.3d 287, 294 (5th Cir. 2007).
63   *Id.* at 294.
64   *Conner v. Quarterman*, 128 S. Ct. 24 (2007).
65   *United States v. Decoster*, 624 F.2d 196, 291 (D.C. Cir. 1976) (Bazelon, J., dissenting).

to prove his innocence is that "[t]he presumption of innocence that cloaks the accused cannot be stripped by a conviction obtained in something less than a constitutionally adequate trial."[66] The question then is whether placing the burden on the government to prove prejudice would make a difference. In all likelihood it would not. Even if the burden is shifted to the government to prove that the defendant did not suffer prejudice, this is still an approach that focuses on guilt and the sufficiency of the evidence. Courts are still likely to find in most instances that the defendant did not suffer prejudice because of their desire to uphold convictions and avoid forcing states to retry cases. For instance, when a defendant proves on direct appeal that one of their other constitutional rights has been violated, the burden is on the government to prove that the defendant was not harmed by the violation. In *People v. Gamache*,[67] during its deliberations the jury viewed a videotape of Gamache confessing to the crime while being interrogated by the police. The videotape had not been admitted into evidence because the statement was obtained in violation of Gamache's rights. Even though the prosecution had the burden of proving that Gamache was not harmed as a result of this serious violation, the government still prevailed because the evidence that Gamache committed the murder was "overwhelming."

Others have suggested that attorney error can be presumed to have prejudiced the defendant under certain circumstances.[68] Presently, defendants are presumed to suffer prejudice when their attorney fails to function during critical stages of the proceedings, for instance, by sleeping while a prosecution witness is testifying;[69] or when their attorney is not licensed to practice law;[70] or when the attorney has an actual conflict of interest.[71] This list could be expanded and prejudice could be presumed in other circumstances, for example, in the event an attorney fails to conduct a reasonable investigation. It would be difficult, however, to delineate those situations when prejudice ought to be presumed from those when the defendant should be required to prove prejudice.

Successful Cases

As the study of circuit courts indicates, some death-sentenced defendants do prevail on claims of ineffective assistance of counsel, especially in certain areas of the country. Who are these defendants and what was exceptional about their cases

---

66   *Id.*

67   227 P.3d 342, 388 (Ca. 2010).

68   See, e.g., J. Kirchmeier, *Drink, Drugs, and Drowsiness: the Constitutional Right to Effective Assistance of Counsel and the Strickland Prejudice Requirement*, 75 Neb. L. Rev. 425, 465–70 (1996).

69   See *Burdine v. Johnson*, 262 F.3d 336, 338 (5th Cir. 2001).

70   See *United States v. Novak*, 903 F.2d 883, 890 (2nd Cir. 1990).

71   See *Cuyler v. Sullivan*, 446 U.S. 335, 349–50 (1980).

that allowed them to prevail when so many others have not? Overwhelmingly, the successful defendants were those whose lawyers failed to investigate and present to the jury significant mitigation evidence that has the effect of reducing the defendant's moral culpability. For instance, in *Dobbs v. Turpin*,[72] counsel was ineffective for failing to pursue and present evidence of Dobbs's unfortunate childhood – which included evidence that his mother often would not let him stay in the house with her, and when she did allow him to stay she ran a brothel where she exposed him to sexual promiscuity, alcohol, and violence. In *Karis v. Calderon*,[73] trial counsel failed to investigate and present evidence that Karis endured brutal violence at the hands of his father and step-father, and that he witnessed similar violent acts committed against his mother by both men. In *Brownlee v. Haley*,[74] trial counsel failed to present evidence of Brownlee's "severe intellectual limitations," which included evidence that he was borderline mentally retarded. In *Douglas v. Woodford*,[75] the jury was not made aware of Douglas's impoverished upbringing at the hands of his abusive foster parents, who would often lock him in a closet for extended periods of time. In *Correll v. Ryan*,[76] the jury did not learn that Correll suffered brain damage as a child as a result of a brick wall falling on his head when he was seven years old. This brain damage caused him to use drugs to self-medicate by the age of 10, which caused him to become a heavy methaphetamine user at the time of the offense, likely causing impulse control problems, judgment impairment, and aggressiveness.

A defendant's chance of prevailing is much greater when his attorney is either ignorant of or misinterprets the law. The attorneys for the death-sentenced defendant in *Lawhorn v. Allen*,[77] waived closing argument at the sentencing phase under the mistaken belief that the prosecutor would be precluded from making a closing argument. Alabama law, however, provides the trial judge with the discretion to permit or deny the prosecution a closing argument. Counsel was deemed to be ineffective for failing to conduct adequate legal research on this point. In *Hoffman v. Arave*,[78] the Ninth Circuit found counsel was ineffective for advising his client to reject a plea bargain under which he could have pled guilty to first degree murder in exchange for the state's withdrawal of the death penalty as a sentencing option. In *Lankford v. Arave*,[79] counsel was found to be ineffective for requesting a jury instruction which relieved the prosecution of its obligation to present evidence to corroborate the accomplice testimony upon which its case

---

72   142 F.3d 1383 (11th Cir. 1998).
73   283 F.3d 1117 (9th Cir. 2002).
74   306 F.3d 1043 (11th Cir. 2002).
75   316 F.3d 1079 (9th Cir. 2003).
76   465 F.3d 1006 (9th Cir. 2006).
77   519 F.3d 1272 (11th Cir. 2006).
78   455 F.3d 926 (9th Cir. 2006).
79   486 F.3d 578 (9th Cir. 2006).

was built. Finally, in *Jennings v. Woodford*,[80] relief was granted as a result of trial counsel's failure to investigate and present available evidence suggesting that as a result of petitioner's long-term methaphetamine use, including on the night of the murder, Jennings lacked he capacity to form the intent necessary for first degree murder.

While the above discussion illustrates that the courts are more likely to grant relief in certain types of cases, it is much less clear why these defendants received relief while many others whose attorneys failed to inform the jury of significant mitigating circumstances or whose attorneys made decisions based on an ignorance or misinterpretation of the law did not receive relief.

Conclusion

There are many problems with the way in which the death penalty is administered. For instance, race often distorts who is sentenced to death, and prospective jurors with moral qualms about the death penalty are often removed. Many of these problems can be remedied or at least minimized at trial if death-sentenced defendants are afforded competent legal representation. However, most defendants do not receive the representation that the Constitution entitles them to, even when their life is on the line. There has been a breakdown in the adversarial system because so many defendants are being convicted and sentenced to death as a result of the substandard representation they are being provided. The Supreme Court's adoption of a prejudice requirement is primarily responsible for the poor representation that death row inmates are receiving. The states and trial judges who preside over capital trials have proven to be either disinterested or ineffectual in ensuring the proper functioning of the adversarial system. Inmates charged with capital crimes lack the political clout to change the situation through the political process. Therefore, only the Supreme Court can ensure that the Sixth Amendment guarantee of effective assistance of counsel is realized, and its insistence on requiring proof of prejudice undermines that right.

---

80   290 F.3d 1006 (9th Cir. 2002).

Chapter 3
Race and the Death Penalty

History

Race has been a factor in who is sentenced to death and executed throughout U.S. history. Before the Civil War, every southern state allowed slaves and free negroes to be sentenced to death for crimes punishable by lesser penalties when whites committed them.[1] After the war, Congress proposed and the states ratified the Fourteenth Amendment – with its guarantee of Equal Protection of the Laws. Senator Howard, who introduced the Fourteenth Amendment in the Senate, said that "This abolishes all class legislation in the States and does away with the injustice of subjecting one caste of persons to a code not applicable to another. It prohibits the hanging of a black man for a crime for which the white man is not to be hanged."[2] In the House, Thaddeus Stevens explained that the Fourteenth Amendment's aim was to ensure that: "Whatever law punishes a white man for a crime shall punish the black man precisely in the same way … Whatever law protects the white man shall afford equal protection to the black man."[3] Formal legal discrimination in all aspects of American life, including the imposition of the death penalty, persisted despite the passage of the Fourteenth Amendment, due in large part to the Supreme Court's failure to enforce the amendment. Instead of using the amendment to eliminate the apartheid that existed in the United States, the Court used the Fourteenth Amendment to protect railroads and other corporate interests.[4]

Even though formal discrimination has ended, one scholar has identified the "Foremost Five Facts" that remain about the death penalty in the United States:

1. African Americans constitute a very high percentage of the persons executed in the United States throughout the past 140 years.
2. The classic observations of Emile Durkheim and Gunnar Myrdal would lead us to predict that in a caste society the harshest penalties will be inflicted upon persons of the lowest caste who dare to commit crimes against persons of the highest caste; somewhat less severe penalties will

---

1 See Stuart Banner, *The Death Penalty: An American History*, 140–42 (Cambridge, Mass.: Harvard University Press, 2002).
2 Cong. Globe, 39th Cong., 1st Sess. 2766 (May 23, 1866).
3 Cong. Globe, 39th Cong. 1st Sess. 2459 (May 8, 1866).
4 James MacGregor Burns, *Packing the Court: The Rise of Judicial Power and the Coming Crisis of the Supreme Court*, 93–113 (New York: The Penguin Press, 2009).

be imposed for crimes against high-caste victims when the perpetrator is also high-caste; relatively lenient punishments will be dispensed to low-caste perpetrators of crimes against low-caste victims; and very lenient or no punishment will be forthcoming when high-caste perpetrators commit crimes against low-caste victims.

3. The findings of David Baldus and his colleagues regarding interracial and intraracial sentencing in the State of Georgia, which were presented to the Supreme Court in the *McCleskey* litigation, displayed precisely this pattern.

4. A wide array of subsequent studies, most of which like the Baldus team's Georgia studies, meticulously controlled for non-racial variables, has consistently found that race alone can explain the observed death-sentencing patterns in state after state, and under every form of capital sentencing procedure.

5. Local knowledge agrees. In every watering hole in every American state and locality, criminal trial lawyers in their cups recite some version of the same *Statement of the Real Law of Homicide*, which goes: "If a black man kill a white man, that be first-degree murder; if a white man kill a white man, that be second-degree murder; if a black man kill a black man, that be mere manslaughter; whereas if a white man kill a black man that be excusable homicide (unless a woman be involved, in which cases the black man died of natural causes)."[5]

The Supreme Court, Race, and Capital Punishment

The Supreme Court and Race

One of the Court's most famous decisions is *Brown v. Board of Education*.[6] In *Brown*, the Court invalidated state-mandated segregation in public schools. This decision helped to create a romantic image of the Supreme Court as the protector of African Americans. The Court's decisions, however – both before and after Brown – do not conform to this image.

Prior to the Civil War, the Court sustained the constitutionality of federal fugitive slave laws;[7] and in one of its worst moments, the Court upheld slavery and declared that blacks "had no rights which the white man was bound to respect."[8] Even after the Civil War ended and Congress enacted the Fourteenth Amendment providing every person in the United States with "equal protection of the laws,"

---

5 Anthony G. Amsterdam, *Opening Remarks: Race and the Death Penalty Before and after McCleskey*, 39 Colum. Hum. Rts. L. Rev. 34, 38–40 (2007–08).

6 349 U.S. 294 (1955).

7 *Prigg v. Pennsylvania*, 41 U.S. 539 (1842).

8 *Dredd Scott v. Sanford*, 60 U.S. 393, 407 (1856).

the Court upheld state mandated segregation.[9] Once legal segregation ended, the Court restricted the states in their attempts to remedy past discrimination. For instance, in *Milliken v. Bradley*,[10] the Court did not allow large, mostly white suburban school districts to be included in efforts to desegregate public schools. In *Washington v. Davis*[11] – a decision which had ramifications for later decisions regarding the death penalty – the Court held that the equal protection clause was not violated, based on a showing that a law simply had a disproportionate burden on a particular racial group. Rather, proof of intentional discrimination was needed in order to prove that the law violated equal protection. Finally, although it has not completely precluded schools and universities from considering race in order to diversify its student body,[12] the Court has made it much more difficult for them to do so.[13]

Given this history, it is not surprising that the Court would refuse to sustain challenges to the death penalty based on the disproportionate number of African Americans who have been sentenced to death and executed.

Racial Disparities in the Imposition of the Death Penalty and the Court's Response

Racism in the imposition of the death penalty is not a relic of America's past. About half of those on death row are racial minorities, and about 80 percent of the victims of death row inmates are white. Justice Brennan described this harsh reality as follows:

> At some point in this case, Warren McCleskey doubtless asked his lawyer whether a jury was likely to sentence him to die. A candid reply to this question would have been disturbing. First, counsel would have had to tell McCleskey that few details of the crime or of McCleskey's past criminal conduct were more important than the fact that his victim was white. Furthermore, counsel would feel bound to tell McCleskey that defendants charged with killing white victims in Georgia are 4.3 times as likely to be sentenced to death as defendants charged with killing blacks. In addition, frankness would compel the disclosure that it was more likely than not that the race of McCleskey's victim would determine whether he received a death sentence: 6 of every 11 defendants convicted of killing a white person would not have received the death penalty if their victims had been black, while, among defendants with aggravating and mitigating

---

9   *Plessy v. Ferguson*, 163 U.S. 537 (1896).
10   418 U.S. 717 (1974).
11   426 U.S. 229 (1976).
12   *Grutter v. Bollinger*, 539 U.S. 306 (2003).
13   *Regents of Univ. of Cal. v. Bakke*, 438 U.S. 265 (1978); *Gratz v. Bollinger*, 539 U.S. 244 (2003); *Parents Involved in Community Schools v. Seattle School District No. 1*, 551 U.S. 701 (2007).

factors comparable to McCleskey's, 20 of every 34 would not have been sentenced to die if their victims had been black. Finally, the assessment would not be complete without information that cases involving black defendants and white victims are more likely to result in a death sentence than cases featuring any other racial combination of defendant and victim. The story could be told in a variety of ways, but McCleskey could not fail to grasp its essential narrative line: there was a significant chance that race would play a prominent role in determining if he lived or died.[14]

The case that Justice Brennan is referring to is *McCleskey v. Kemp*.[15] The Supreme Court was confronted with the issue of racism in the administration of the death penalty in the *McCleskey* case. Warren McCleskey was an African American who had been convicted of killing a white police officer during the course of a robbery. He was sentenced to death by a Fulton County, Georgia jury. On appeal, McCleskey claimed that Georgia's capital sentencing process was administered in a racially discriminatory manner. In support of this claim, he presented a statistical study (the Baldus study, conducted by Professor David Baldus and his colleagues at the University of Iowa Law School) to the Court that purports to show a disparity in the imposition of the death penalty in Georgia based on the race of the murder victim and, to a lesser extent, the race of the defendant.

According to the Baldus study, defendants charged with killing white persons in Georgia received the death penalty in 11 percent of the cases, but defendants charged with killing blacks received the death penalty in only 1 percent of the cases. Cases were also divided according to the combination of the race of the defendant and the race of the victim. The study found that the death penalty was assessed in 22 percent of the cases involving black defendants and white victims; 8 percent of the cases involving white defendants and white victims; 1 percent of the cases involving black defendants and black victims; and 3 percent of the cases involving white defendants and black victims. Prosecutors sought the death penalty in 70 percent of the cases involving black defendants and white victims; 32 percent of the cases involving white defendants and white victims; 15 percent of the cases involving black defendants and black victims; and 19 percent of the cases involving white defendants and black victims.

The Baldus study also took into account 230 variables that could have explained these disparities on non-racial grounds. Even after taking account of these variables, the study concluded that defendants charged with killing white victims were 4.3 times as likely to receive a death sentence as defendants charged with killing blacks. Furthermore, black defendants were 1.1 times as likely to receive a death sentence as other defendants. The Baldus study concluded that black defendants such as McCleskey, who kill white victims, have the greatest likelihood of receiving the death penalty.

---

14   481 U.S. 279, 321 (1987).
15   *Id.*

The findings and conclusions of the Baldus study have been confirmed by other studies; these disparities exist even though African Americans constitute a majority of homicide victims. Although the Supreme Court accepted the validity of the Baldus study, it rejected McCleskey's claim that he had been sentenced to death based on his race. The Court refused to accept his statistics as evidence of race discrimination in violation of the Constitution. According to the Court, "at most, the Baldus study indicates a discrepancy that appears to correlate with race."[16] Rather, the Court held that in order to prove a claim of racial discrimination that violated the equal protection clause of the Constitution, McCleskey had to prove that the decisionmakers in *his* case acted with discriminatory purpose. Thus, in order to prevail on a claim that race was a factor in the decision to sentence him to death, an inmate must obtain evidence indicating that either the trial judge, the prosecutor, or the jury in *his* case took race into account. Alternatively, McCleskey could prevail if he could "prove that the Georgia Legislature enacted or maintained the death penalty statute *because of* an anticipated racially discriminatory effect."[17]

The Court held that the prosecutor need not even respond to a claim of racial discrimination based on statistics. The Court acknowledged that it "had accepted statistics as proof of intent to discriminate in certain limited contexts,"[18] such as jury selection and employment discrimination cases. It distinguished, however, capital sentencing decisions on a number of grounds, including the fact that the decision to impose the death penalty "rest[s] on consideration of innumerable factors that vary according to the characteristics of the individual defendant and the facts of the particular capital offense;"[19] and that, unlike jury selection and employment discrimination cases, the state has "no practical opportunity to rebut"[20] the statistics, given the prohibitions against questioning jurors on the motives and influences that led to their verdict. The Court did not explain, however, why the defendant should have the burden of proving that the jury decision was biased, given the fact that he faces the same limitation.

The Court was accurate in stating that McCleskey's claim went to the heart of the criminal justice system. First, had McCleskey prevailed, the effect would have been to abolish capital punishment since it is highly unlikely that any state would have been able to create a system that did not produce racial disparities. Second, as the Court stated, "the Eighth Amendment is not limited in application to capital punishment, but applies to all penalties. Thus, if we accepted McCleskey's claim that racial bias has impermissibly tainted the capital sentencing decision, we could soon be faced with similar claims as to other types of penalty."[21] The Court was obviously concerned that had it ruled in favor of McCleskey, black defendants

---

16   *Id.* at 312.
17   *Id.* at 298.
18   *Id.* at 293.
19   *Id.* at 294.
20   *Id.* at 296.
21   *Id.* at 315.

charged with crimes such as rape would have been able to produce statistical evidence that they received harsher sentences than whites and it would have been difficult for the Court to find a rationale to reject their claims. Justice Brennan, in his dissent, characterized this concern as "a fear of too much justice."[22] Finally, the Court was concerned with the effect that a decision favoring McCleskey would have had on the ability of prosecutors and juries to continue to exercise discretion, which the Court believes is fundamental to the criminal justice system. As a result of these concerns, the Court has created an impossible burden of proof for defendants and, as Justice Stevens has recognized, "the Court has allowed [racial discrimination] to continue to play an unacceptable role in capital cases."[23]

After he retired from the Court, Justice Powell, who wrote the decision in *McCleskey* and provided the crucial fifth vote, indicated that he regretted his vote and opinion in *McCleskey*. Upon reflection he probably came to two realizations. First, that Justice Brennan was correct when he wrote in his dissent that the outcome in *McCleskey* "reflects a devaluation of the lives of black persons."[24] Second, and most important, that the decision created a burden of proof that is for all practical purposes insurmountable. The next section will demonstrate the impossible hurdle the court created for any defendant claiming that race more likely than not played a role in his capital sentencing decision.

The Lower Courts' Response to *McCleskey*

The *McCleskey* decision held that in order to prevail on a claim of racial discrimination, a defendant sentenced to death must demonstrate that either the prosecutor, jury, or judge specifically discriminated against him or that the statute authorizing his death sentence was enacted for racial reasons. This standard is onerous for several reasons. The defendant is extremely limited in his ability to obtain information from the decisionmakers in his case. The Supreme Court has refused to allow discovery from prosecutors, even when racial disparities are shown to result from certain practices. Thus, the defendant has virtually no mechanism for obtaining information from the prosecutor regarding his decisionmaking. In addition, juries are not required to justify their decisions and are under no obligation to speak with the defense after their verdict has been rendered. Although judges must justify their decisions on the record, the defendant has no further opportunities to probe the judge as to whether any of her decisions may have been motivated by racial animus. Finally, it is highly doubtful that a state legislature would adopt and a governor would sign a death penalty statute for overt racial reasons. Therefore, a defendant is unlikely to prevail on a claim that

---

22　*Id.* at 339.
23　*Baze v. Rees*, 128 S. Ct. 1520, 1551 (2008).
24　*McCleskey v. Kemp*, 481 U.S. 279, 336 (1987).

his death sentence was imposed as a result of race absent an admission from one of the decisionmakers in his case.

Not surprisingly, no death row inmate has been able to prevail on a claim of race discrimination since the *McCleskey* decision in 1987 despite the fact that studies confirm that race continues to be a major factor in who is sentenced to death in the United States. For instance, Professor David Baldus replicated his Georgia study in Pennsylvania and New Jersey and the results were similar: that defendants who kill whites are significantly more likely to be sentenced to death than defendants who kill non-whites.[25] A few cases will be discussed to help illustrate the difficulty defendants have faced as a result of *McCleskey*. In *Dobbs v. Zant*,[26] the defendant was able to prove that the judge, the jurors, and even his defense attorney harbored racial animus towards him and that the prosecutor might have also; yet he still was not able to prevail under the *McCleskey* standard. Wilburn Dobbs was an African American tried for the murder of a white man in Walker County, Georgia. Walker County is a primarily rural area of Northwest Georgia where approximately 4 percent of the population is black. Walker County has a long history of segregation. In fact, desegregation efforts did not occur there until they were compelled by the federal government in the 1960s. Dobbs was tried only two weeks after being indicted by a jury composed of 11 whites and one African American. Most of the white jurors had been raised in segregated schools and social environments. All the jurors expressed reservations about interracial dating and marriage. Several of the jurors referred to blacks as "colored" and two jurors admitted using the word "nigger" on occasion.[27] Two of the jurors indicated that they were fearful of blacks.

The trial transcript revealed that the judge and defense attorney referred to Dobbs as "colored" and "colored boy" during the trial and that the prosecutor called Dobbs by his first name on one occasion. At one point, the trial judge said, "let's call them blacks." [28] The trial judge had been raised in a segregated environment and had voted as a state legislator for laws that encouraged segregation. Furthermore, the defense attorney was outspoken about his racial views:

> He said that many blacks were uneducated and would not make good teachers, but do make good basketball players. He opined that blacks are less educated

---

25   See David C. Baldus et al., *Racial Discrimination and the Death Penalty in the Post-Furman Era: An Empirical and Legal Overview, With Recent Findings from Philadelphia*, 83 Cornell L. Rev. 1838 (1998). See also, William J. Bowers et al., *Death Sentencing in Black and White: Empirical Analysis of the Role of Juror's Race and Jury Racial Composition*, 3 U. Pa. J. Const. L. 171 (2001) (finding that the chances of a death sentence for a black defendant whose victim is white are dramatically affected by the race and gender of his jurors).

26   963 F.2d 1403 (11th Cir. 1992).

27   *Id.* at 1408.

28   *Dobbs v. Zant*, 720 F. Supp. 1566, 1577 (N.D. Ga. 1989).

and less intelligent than whites either because of their nature or because "my granddaddy had slaves." He said that integration has led to deteriorating neighborhoods and schools and referred to the black community in Chattanooga as "black boy jungle." He strongly implied that blacks have inferior morals by relating a story about sex in a classroom. He also said that when he was young, a maid was hired with the understanding that she would steal some items. He said that blacks in Chattanooga are more troublesome than blacks in Walker County.[29]

On appeal, the court acknowledged "that Walker County's history of racial segregation appears to have had some influence on the views of the players in Dobbs's case."[30] The Court also found that "the references at trial to Dobbs as 'colored' may have had an influence on the jury's view of Dobbs as an individual."[31] Dobbs, however, was not able to prevail on a *McCleskey* claim despite the racial climate that existed at his trial. The Court held that the personal racial views of the judge and the defense attorney had never been communicated to the jurors and therefore did not influence the sentencing decision. As for the jurors, the Court held that although some of the jurors were racially prejudiced, Dobbs was unable to prove that any of the jurors' prejudice would make them favor the death penalty for a black person who murdered a white person.

In *Cornwell v. Bradshaw*,[32] Sidney Cornwell was charged with killing a three-year-old during a shoot-out between the rival gangs "Crips" and the "Bloods." When one of the state's witnesses balked at making his testimony fit with the government's theory of the case, the prosecutor asked him: "Do you give a f*** if we fry your n**** or not?"[33] Cornwell contended that the question "evinces obvious racial animus that tainted all of the proceedings against Cornwell," in violation of his constitutional rights.[34] The appellate court agreed that Cornwell demonstrated that the prosecutor acted with discriminatory purpose as required by *McCleskey*. The court, however, held that this was not sufficient. The court held that Cornwell was required to also show that he was prosecuted while similarly situated individuals of a different race were not, and his claim was rejected because he failed to make such a showing. The court failed to indicate how Cornwell could make such a showing without an opportunity for discovery from the prosecutor.

The lower courts, like the Supreme Court, have rejected studies indicating that the death penalty is being meted out in a particular jurisdiction in a discriminatory manner. Willie Lee Richmond claimed that Arizona's administration of the death

---

29   *Id.* at 1577.
30   *Id.* at 1578.
31   *Id.*
32   559 F.3d 398 (6th Cir. 2009).
33   *Id.* at 411.
34   *Id.*

penalty was racially, sexually, and socio-economically discriminatory. In support of his claim, he submitted the following:

> The proffer included that, although 15% of the victims of homicides in Arizona since 1973 have been black, every person under death sentence was convicted of killing a white victim; that [although] approximately 10% of the persons convicted of homicide in Arizona since 1973 have been women, no women are on death row. All three experts who had examined the Arizona death sentencing process from 1973 to the present [March 1987] found significant discrepancies based on the victim's race; two found evidence of discrimination based on the defendant's race, and one demonstrated significant disparities based on sex and economic status as well.[35]

William Henry Bell, an African American, based his *McCleskey* claim on a study that examined the county prosecutor's patterns of seeking the death penalty where "the defendant [was] black and the victim was white versus cases where both the defendant and the victim were black."[36] Specifically, the researchers examined 11 cases in which the prosecutors sought the death penalty from 1979 to 1989, the time period during which Bell was prosecuted. The death penalty was sought in four of the six cases in which African American defendants had been charged with killing white victims (66.7 percent). Death was only sought in 8 percent of the murder cases involving other racial combinations. The court held that Bell had not presented the "exceptionally clear proof of discrimination demanded by *McCleskey*"[37] and accepted the prosecutor's explanation for the disparities, and Bell's claim was therefore rejected.

Girvies Davis was African American and the victim of the crime was white. He claimed that the victim's race made it more likely that he would receive a death sentence. In support of his claim, he submitted a statistical study that demonstrated that a suspect accused of killing a white victim in Illinois was four times more likely to receive the death penalty than is a suspect accused of killing a black victim, even after pertinent non-racial factors have been taken into account. The Illinois Supreme Court rejected his claim based on *McCleskey*.[38]

Finally in *Keene v. Mitchell*,[39] a death row inmate presented the court with statistics indicating that African Americans constituted 17 percent of the county's population in which he was sentenced to death but 64 percent of the county's capital indictments. He even presented evidence that the death penalty was not sought in cases similar to his involving white defendants. For instance, the prosecutor did not seek death in the cases involving either his white co-defendant

---

35 *Richmond v. Lewis*, 921 F.2d 933, 949 (9th Cir. 1990).
36 *Bell v. Ozmint*, 332 F.3d 229, 237 (4th Cir. 2003).
37 *Id.* at 239.
38 *People v. Davis*, 518 N.E.2d 78 (Ill. 1987).
39 525 F. 3d 461, 463 (6th Cir. 2008).

or three white males who committed factually similar aggravated murders. This case demonstrates the difficulty defendants face in making a race discrimination claim. Because no two cases are ever identical, the prosecutor was able to justify the decision to seek death in the defendant's case and to distinguish the defendant's case from those of the white defendants he pointed to, despite the fact that the white defendants had also committed multiple murders and would appear to be candidates for the death penalty.

Death row inmates have presented courts with statistical studies indicating that African American defendants are more likely to be sentenced to death. They have presented studies indicating that those who kill whites are much more likely to be sentenced to death and executed than those whose victims are not white. They have also drawn comparisons to other cases involving similarly situated defendants of other races who have not been sentenced to death. These efforts to prove discrimination, which have been successful in employment, voting, education, and other cases, have been totally unsuccessful in cases involving life and death.[40] It is clear that, as a result of the *McCleskey* decision, a defendant has no chance of proving racial discrimination absent an admission by one of the decisionmakers in his case. That, of course, is an extremely unlikely occurrence.

Other Remedies for Racial Discrimination

The steps taken legislatively to address the problem of racial discrimination in the administration of capital punishment have been extremely minimal. In addition to the 35 states that employ the death penalty, the death penalty has been enacted by Congress and applies throughout the U.S. and its territories. Congress has provided for the death penalty in numerous situations, most of which, however, occur infrequently. For instance, anyone who assassinates the President or Vice President of the United States, or who commits treason, espionage, or genocide can be sentenced to death in federal court. The most important federal death penalty provision makes a murder committed by person involved in certain drug-trafficking activity punishable by death. The decision whether to seek death in a particular case is made by the U.S. Department of Justice.

In federal death penalty cases, the jury is instructed prior to its deliberations that race is not to be considered. Once the jurors have completed their deliberations, the jury must certify that race was not a factor in its decision. Despite these requirements, however, a majority of federal death row inmates are racial minorities. Moreover, there is a thorough review process prior to a decision by the Department of Justice to seek death. This review process is designed in part to ensure that race is not a factor in the decision to seek death. President Clinton

---

40   See S.L. Simpson, *Everyone Else is Doing It, Why Can't We? A New Look at the Use of Statistical Data in Death Penalty Cases*, 12 Gender, Race & Just. 509, 523–33 (2009).

was disturbed by the large number of minorities on the federal death row and as a result ordered the Department of Justice to conduct a study.[41] The study disclosed some troubling facts regarding the administration of the federal death penalty. First, the study found that from 1995 to 2000, the vast majority of cases in which death was sought involved minority defendants. Furthermore, U.S. Attorneys were almost twice as likely to recommend seeking the death penalty for an African American defendant when his victim was not African American. The study also uncovered the fact that in cases where federal prosecutors were seeking the death penalty, they were much more likely to offer plea deals to white defendants than to minority defendants.

Defendants are also allowed to question jurors regarding their racial attitudes. The Supreme Court has held that defendants have the right to question prospective jurors regarding their racial attitudes during voir dire.[42] This decision, however, is not as crucial today as it might have been in the past, given the fact that racist attitudes are not openly expressed anywhere near to the degree that they once were and that it is difficult to uncover subtle, unconscious biases jurors may harbor.

Congress failed to enact a measure that could have had a significant impact in determining whether death sentences are being meted out on the basis of race. The Racial Justice Act passed the House of Representatives but was never acted upon by the United States Senate. Two states, Kentucky and North Carolina, enacted their own Racial Justice Acts. Both the proposed federal version and the versions enacted in Kentucky and North Carolina would allow defendants who had been sentenced to death to use statistical evidence to demonstrate a prima facie case of racial bias. The burden would then shift to the prosecution to prove that the defendant's death sentence was not the result of racial bias. The court would ultimately decide if race was a factor in the defendant receiving a death sentence. The argument for the Racial Justice Act is as follows:

> It is not unreasonable to require publicly elected prosecutors to justify racial disparities in capital prosecutions. If there is an underrepresentation of black citizens in a jury pool, jury commissioners are required to explain the disparity. A prosecutor who strikes a disproportionate number of black citizens in selecting a jury is required to rebut the inference of discrimination by showing race neutral reasons for his or her strikes. If there are valid, race neutral explanations for the disparities in capital prosecutions, they should be presented to the public. Prosecutors, like other public officials, should be accountable for their actions. The bases for critical decisions about whether to seek the death penalty and whether to agree to a sentence less than death in exchange for a guilty plea

---

41 See *The Federal Death Penalty System: A Statistical Survey 1988–2000*, available at http://www.usdoj.gov/dag/pubdoc/_dp_survey_final.pdf.

42 See *Turner v. Murray*, 476 U.S. 28 (1996).

should not be shrouded in secrecy, but should be openly set out, defended, and evaluated.[43]

It would be much easier to determine how big a role race plays in these cases if defendants were allowed to obtain information from prosecutors regarding their charging decisions. In *United States v. Bass*,[44] a black defendant alleging racial discrimination in the government's decision to seek death in his case sought information relating to the federal government's capital charging practices. The lower courts held that he was entitled to this information since he produced "nationwide statistics demonstrating that the United States charged blacks with a death-eligible offense more than twice as often as it charges whites."[45] The Supreme Court held that in order to obtain this information, the defendant must make a credible showing that death was not sought in cases involving similarly situated individuals of a different race and that Bass did not make such a showing despite these statistics. According to the Court, "raw statistics regarding overall charges say nothing about charges brought against similarly situated defendants."[46] The Court also reiterated that this showing cannot be made with statistical evidence. This decision effectively shields the prosecutor's decisionmaking process from the defendant since it is obviously difficult for a defendant to make the required showing without the evidence that he is seeking from the government.

Racial Discrimination in Jury Selection

A majority of the U.S. general public continues to support capital punishment despite its many flaws. As one commentator has observed, this could be due to the fact that "the overwhelming majority of those accused of crimes are poor" and as a result:

> Because the criminal justice system deals almost exclusively with poor people, it is out of sight and out of mind for most Americans. They do not know what happens in criminal courts. They may assume that it is operating justly and fairly, or they may not even think about it.[47]

African Americans, however, are the only racial group in the United States that do not support the death penalty. Polls have consistently shown that a majority

---

43 S. Bright, *Discrimination, Death and Denial: The Tolerance of Racial Discrimination in Infliction of the Death Penalty*, 35 Santa Clara L. Rev. 433, 465–6 (1995).

44 536 U.S. 862 (2002).

45 *Id.* at 863.

46 *Id.* at 864.

47 S. Bright, *The Failure to Achieve Fairness: Race and Poverty Continue to Influence Who Dies*, 11 U. Pa. J. Const. L. 23 (2008).

of African Americans oppose capital punishment while a majority of every other racial group supports it. A majority of African Americans oppose capital punishment even though they constitute a disproportionate number of homicide victims. This is partly due to the historical use of the death penalty against African Americans, as outlined earlier. African Americans are also much more skeptical of the criminal justice system. The criminal justice system is not out of sight and out of mind for most African Americans. It is likely that most African Americans have either personally had an unpleasant experience with the criminal justice system or someone close to them has. They are often the victims of abusive police practices and racial profiling. As President Obama has said, "there is a long history in this country of African Americans and Latinos being stopped by law enforcement disproportionately."[48] Furthermore, racial minorities must continue to deal with a criminal justice system in which most of the actors are still largely white:

> [T]he criminal justice system is the part of American society that has been least affected by the Civil Rights Movement. Many courthouses throughout the country look about the same today as they did in the 1940s and 1950s. The judges are white, the prosecutors are white, and the court-appointed lawyers are white. Even in communities with fairly substantial African American populations, all of the jurors at a trial may be white.[49]

The fact that a majority of African Americans oppose capital punishment actually results in more African American defendants being sentenced to death. That is because of the manner in which the Supreme Court has allowed juries to be selected in death penalty cases. In *Witherspoon v. Illinois*, the Court held that a trial court could not automatically exclude jurors who oppose capital punishment and who would have conscientious scruples against inflicting it. The Court held that jurors could be excluded only if they made it unmistakably clear that they would automatically vote against the imposition of the death penalty without regard to the evidence. As long as a juror had an open mind and was at least willing to consider imposing death in a particular case, he could not automatically be excluded. This decision, however, was substantially modified in *Wainwright v. Witt*,[50] which held that a juror could be excused if his views about capital punishment prevent or substantially impair his duties as a juror. As a result, a juror who expresses a reluctance to impose capital punishment is almost certain to be struck by the prosecution. As Justice Stevens has pointed out, "millions of Americans oppose the death penalty" and "a cross section of virtually every

---

48   *News Conference by the President*, July 22, 2009, available at http://www. whitehouse.gov/the_press_office/News-Conference-by-the-President_July-22-2009.
49   *Id.* at 27.
50   469 U.S. 412 (1985).

community in the country includes citizens who firmly believe the death penalty is unjust but who nevertheless are qualified to serve as jurors in capital cases."[51]

As a result of these decisions, in order to serve on the jury in a death penalty case a juror must be "death qualified." A "death qualified" juror is someone who is willing to impose the death penalty. Prosecutors are usually able to remove any juror who has any qualms about imposing a death sentence. Studies of jurors who are able to survive the "death qualification" process indicate that they are not only more likely to vote for a death sentence than those who are excluded, but also are more likely to find capital defendants guilty.[52] These studies have also found that death qualified jurors are more skeptical of defenses involving mental illness [including the insanity defense], more receptive to eyewitness identification, that they tend to weigh aggravating circumstances [arguments for death] more heavily than mitigating circumstances [arguments for life] and are more likely to evaluate ambiguous scientific testimony in favor of the prosecution.[53] This study also found that "death-qualified jurors are more likely to be racist, sexist, and homophobic."[54]

The presence of African Americans on a capital jury can literally mean the difference between life and death for the defendant. The Capital Jury Project found that there is a "white male effect" in capital sentencing in cases involving black defendants and white victims. The project found that the presence of five or more white males on the jury dramatically increased the likelihood of a death sentence.[55] By contrast, the presence of black male jurors in the same cases substantially reduced the likelihood of a death sentence.[56] Furthermore, according to the study, white male jurors are more likely to believe that a black defendant is dangerous and not remorseful, and are the least likely to be able to identify with the defendant in a black defendant/white victim case.[57] There are several explanations for the disparity between white and black jurors. As discussed earlier, African Americans are much more skeptical of the criminal justice system and the death penalty. Furthermore, jurors bring their life experiences and socializations into the jury box. Many whites have racial stereotypes that associate blacks, especially black males, with crime and the prosecution can exploit these stereotypes. For instance, in deciding whether to sentence a defendant to death, jurors must wrestle with whether the defendant is likely to continue to be dangerous and a threat to society. Because of even unconscious stereotypes, many white jurors are likely

---

51   *Uttecht v. Brown*, 551 U.S. 1, 35 (2007).

52   See Dr. Butler's Research, available at http://psychology.usf.edu/faculty/data/bbutler.aspx.

53   Id.

54   Id.

55   W. Bowers, B. Steiner, and M. Sandys, *Death Sentencing in Black and White: An Empirical Analysis of the Role of Juror's Race and Jury Racial Composition*, 3 U. Pa. J. Const. L. 171, 192 (2001).

56   *Id.* at 193.

57   *Id.* at 212–22.

to view a black defendant as a continuing threat. In addition, blacks and other racial minorities may view and evaluate evidence differently because of their life experiences:

> Whites are more apt to make pro-prosecution interpretations of evidence, especially when defendants are black and particularly on highly determinative issues such as eyewitness identification, probable cause, and resistance to arrest. Blacks may be more critical in their interpretation of factual questions presented at trial, particularly when police testimony is involved. And in capital cases, blacks may be more sympathetic than white jurors to mitigating evidence presented by a black defendant with whom they may be better able to identify and empathize, and whose background and experiences they may feel they understand better than do their white counterparts.[58]

Studies have confirmed that the presence of African Americans in the jury box has an effect on deliberations and makes it much less likely that a death sentence will be meted out. This is especially so in cases involving black defendants and white victims. As a result, African Americans are often targeted by the prosecution and not allowed to serve as jurors in capital cases. Sometimes this is done explicitly – as in Philadelphia, Pennsylvania. In 1997, a senior assistant district attorney was caught on videotape instructing new lawyers in the district attorney's office how to strike African Americans from the jury.[59] The Dallas County District Attorney's Office adopted a formal policy of systematically excluding African Americans and other racial minorities from juries.[60] Most prosecutors, however, are much more subtle in excluding racial minorities. For instance, they will ask questions knowing that most minorities are likely to answer differently than most whites and use the responses as the basis for removing the minority jurors. To illustrate, in a Texas case, the prosecutor asked the prospective jurors whether they agreed with the verdict in the O.J. Simpson case. The Simpson case was racially charged, with most African Americans supporting the not guilty verdict and most whites opposing the verdict, a fact the prosecutor was obviously well aware of. Not surprisingly, most African Americans in the panel indicated that they supported the verdict, while most whites indicated that they did not. The prosecutor justified striking the African Americans based on their responses to that question.[61]

In addition to the death qualification process, prosecutors use peremptory challenges to eliminate African Americans and other racial minorities from the jury panel. If either party can demonstrate that a juror is biased and would not be the fair and impartial juror that the Constitution requires, that juror must be

---

58   *Id.* at 181.

59   L. Ditzen et al., *To Win, Limit Black Jurors, McMahon Said,* Philadelphia Inquirer, April 1, 1997.

60   *Miller-El v. Cockrell,* 537 U.S. 332, 334–5 (2003).

61   *Shelling v. State,* 52 S.W.3d 213, 217–20, 224 (Tex. 2001).

removed for cause. Frequently, however, the parties are not able to demonstrate that a juror is biased but intuitively they believe that to be the case. Therefore, both sides are allowed to strike a certain number of jurors whom they cannot remove for cause. These strikes can be exercised for almost any reason. There had been a long history of prosecutors exercising peremptory challenges to prevent African Americans from serving on juries. It was hoped that the Supreme Court's 1986 decision in *Batson v. Kentucky*[62] would put an end to this practice. In *Batson*, the Court held that the exclusion of potential jurors on account of their race violates the Equal Protection Clause. There is a three-step process for determining whether *Batson* has been violated: 1) the defense challenges the prosecutor's use of a peremptory challenge; 2) the prosecutor must provide an explanation for striking the juror or jurors in question; and 3) the trial court examines the prosecutor's explanation and determines whether the exercise of the peremptory challenge was based on race. If so, the juror cannot be removed. In the event that the defendant is convicted and the appellate courts later determine that a *Batson* violation occurred, the defendant is entitled to a new trial and does not have to prove that he was harmed by the exclusion of this juror.

Despite *Batson*, juries remain overwhelmingly white – even in communities with large minority populations – because courts routinely accept the prosecutor's reasons for removing minority jurors. In *Shelling v. State*,[63] an African American defendant objected to the prosecutor's strikes against three African Americans because they agreed with the verdict in the O.J. Simpson case. The defense argued that this was an attempt to remove African Americans from the jury since it was common knowledge that opinion regarding O.J. Simpson's acquittal was polarized along racial lines. The prosecutor justified the strike of the fourth African American on the grounds that she was employed by Goodwill, a social service organization. The courts accepted the prosecutor's explanation for these strikes. In *Hernandez v. New York*,[64] the prosecutor struck all Spanish-speaking jurors in a case involving a Latino defendant. The prosecutor's reason for rejecting these jurors was concern that they would not be able to "listen and follow the interpreter."[65] The prosecution's explanation was accepted. In *Purkett v. Elem*,[66] the prosecutor justified the striking of one African American potential juror because "he had long curly hair" and "also, he had a mustache and a goatee type beard."[67] The other African American in the jury pool was also struck because he had facial hair. According to the prosecutor, they were struck because their "mustaches and the beards look suspicious to me."[68] The Supreme Court held that

62   476 U.S. 79 (1986).
63   52 S.W.3d 213 (Tex. App. 2001).
64   500 U.S. 352 (1991).
65   *Id.* at 356.
66   514 U.S. 765 (1995).
67   *Id.* at 766.
68   *Id.*

although prosecutors must provide a legitimate reason for striking minority jurors, a legitimate reason "is not a reason that makes sense, but a reason that does not deny equal protection."[69]

How then does a defendant prove a *Batson* violation? Defendants who have prevailed were able to demonstrate that there were similarities between excluded minority jurors and accepted white jurors. In *Miller-El v. Dretke*,[70] 10 of 11 African Americans were removed by the prosecution. Miller-El prevailed because he was able to show similarities in the responses of black jurors who were removed and whites with similar views who were not. For instance, the prosecutor stated that he objected to a black juror, although this juror strongly favored capital punishment, because he believed that the death penalty was appropriate in the event that the defendant could not be rehabilitated. The prosecutor, however, did not strike two white jurors who expressed similar views. The prosecutor asserted that another black juror was objectionable because this juror indicated that life imprisonment may be a more severe punishment than death. The prosecution did not attempt to remove other non-black jurors who expressed similar sentiments. *Miller-El* also provided evidence that the Dallas County District Attorney's Office had a formal policy of removing black jurors at the time of Miller-El's trial.

In *Snyder v. Louisiana*,[71] all five of the prospective black jurors were eliminated by the prosecution through the use of peremptory strikes. After the defense challenged the prosecution's removal of a black college senior, the prosecution offered two reasons for the strike: 1) that the potential juror looked nervous; and 2) that his service on the jury might interfere with his duties as a student-teacher and that, in order to minimize the student-teacher hours missed, he might be inclined to find the defendant guilty of a lesser included offense in order to obviate the need for a penalty phase hearing. The Supreme Court found the prosecution's concern that the potential juror's service might interfere with his other obligations implausible in light of "the prosecutor's acceptance of white jurors who disclosed conflicting obligations that appear to have been at least as serious."

In *Devose v. Norris*,[72] an Arkansas defendant was charged with delivery of a controlled substance. Four of the five prospective jurors indicated that they had served on previous juries. The state exercised its only peremptory strikes on three prospective African American jurors. After the defense objected, the prosecution responded that these individuals were struck because "they were burned out." However, whites who had previously served as jurors were viewed as desirable jurors by the prosecution because it gave them a clearer understanding of certain issues. The prosecution's "juror burnout" rationale for striking the black jurors was found to be pretextual. The court also rejected the prosecution's argument that no *Batson* violation occurred because it accepted one black juror and one

69 *Id.* at 769.
70 545 U.S. 231 (2005).
71 552 U.S. 472 (2008).
72 53 F.3d 201 (8th Cir. 1995).

black alternate. Finally, in *Turner v. Marshall*,[73] the prosecution removed all of the African American men from the jury pool. The prosecution claimed to strike one of these men because of his hesitancy to look at gruesome photographs. The prosecution, however, did not strike a white juror who expressed a reluctance to view gruesome crime scene photographs. The appellate court concluded that there were racial reasons for the prosecutor's dismissal of the African American jurors.

Defendants, however, do not always prevail even if they can present a comparative analysis showing that the prosecutor treated black and white potential jurors differently. In *Howard v. Moore*,[74] although the prosecutor did not strike white jurors who gave similar answers to the black jurors that the prosecutor struck, the court rejected the defendant's *Batson* claim on the basis that the challenges could have been justified by differences in the jurors' demeanors, facial expressions, etc. The problem with the court's conclusion is that it was not based on the record – the prosecutor never asserted that he dismissed the black jurors as a result of their demeanor.

Conclusion

Race continues to be a major factor in determining whether a defendant will be sentenced to death. African Americans constitute just 13 percent of the population of the United States but make up almost half the death row population. Furthermore, those defendants who kill whites are much more likely to end up on death row than those who kill African Americans and other minorities, even though African Americans are almost half of the homicide victims in the United States. In addition, because over 90 percent of prosecutors and judges are white, the decision whether to seek death is being made by whites. The United States Supreme Court has completely ignored these racial disparity arguments. In cases challenging these racial disparities, the Court has indicated that it will only provide a remedy for obvious racial discrimination. The Court has been unwilling to address more subtle racial discrimination. In *McCleskey v. Kemp,* the Court refused to deal with the fact that juries and prosecutors devalue black lives by sentencing to death those who kill whites. The Court upheld McCleskey's death sentence despite the "strong probability that [the defendant's] sentencing jury was influenced by the fact that [he was] black and his victim was white."[75] Rather, the Court indicated that it will only address racial discrimination in the sentencing process if the defendant produces evidence of overt discrimination by the decisionmakers in his case.

---

73   121 F.3d 1248 (9th Cir. 1997).

74   131 F.3d 399 (4th Cir. 1997).

75   *McCleskey v. Kemp*, 481 U.S. 279, 366 (1987).

Lower courts have followed the lead of the Supreme Court and have likewise ignored evidence that racial bias infects the sentencing process.[76]

Those who make the decision to seek death – prosecutors and judges – are overwhelmingly white. The one area in which African Americans are supposed to be better represented is in the jury deliberations. Studies indicate that when African Americans participate in jury deliberations, the likelihood of a death sentence being imposed diminishes substantially. However, through the use of peremptory challenges, prosecutors have been able to limit African American participation in the jury deliberation process. Most African Americans continue to be sentenced to death by either all-white or disproportionately white juries. Again, while the Court has outlawed overt racial discrimination, it has refused to deal with the subtle tactics that prosecutors use to prevent blacks from serving on juries. As a result, prosecutors have figured out how to easily circumvent the law. The Supreme Court has laid out a roadmap for prosecutors to avoid a *Batson* violation, and they have for the most part followed it well. As long as the prosecution can articulate a race neutral reason for striking minority jurors, even a reason that is preposterous, and as long as no similarly situated whites are seated, the courts will not find a *Batson* violation. As a result, studies and anecdotal reports indicate that the discriminatory use of peremptory challenges remains a problem. For instance, a study of 317 capital trials in Philadelphia between 1981 and 1997 revealed that prosecutors struck 51 percent of black jurors and 26 percent of non-black jurors; defense counsel removed 26 percent of black jurors and 54 percent of white jurors.[77] This same study found that race-based uses of prosecutorial peremptories declined by only 2 percent after *Batson*. Another study found that in one North Carolina county, 71 percent of excused black jurors were removed by the prosecution, while 81 percent of excused white jurors were removed by the defense.[78] In a Washington D.C. murder case that spanned four trials, prosecutors excused 41 blacks or other minorities and six whites; defense counsel struck 29 white and 13 black venire members.[79] Although race-based stereotypes continue to influence jury selection, very few *Batson* challenges succeed.[80]

---

76 *Evans v. State*, 914 A.2d 25, 64 (2006) (court affirmed a death sentence despite the existence of a study showing that "the death penalty is statistically more likely to be pursued against a black person who murders a white victim than against a defendant in any other racial combination").

77 David C. Baldus et al., *The Use of Peremptory Challenges in Capital Murder Trials: A Legal and Empirical Analysis*, 3 U. Pa. J. Const. L. 3, 52–3, 73, n. 197 (2001).

78 M.R. Rose, *The Peremptory Challenge Accused of Race or Gender Discrimination? Some Data from One County*, 23 Law and Human Behavior 695, 698–9 (1999).

79 N. Tucker, *In Moore's Trials, Excluded Jurors Fit Racial Pattern*, Washington Post, Apr. 2, 2001, A1.

80 Equal Justice Initiative, *Illegal Racial Discrimination in Jury Selection: A Continuing Legacy*, 14 (June 2010), available at http://eji.org/eji/files/Race%20and%20jury%20selection%20Report.pdf; J.S. Brand, *The Supreme Court, Equal Protection and Jury Selection: Denying That Race Still Matters*, 1994 Wis. L. Rev. 511, 583–9.

Justice Thurgood Marshall predicted that the *Batson* decision would not achieve the Court's goal of eliminating racial discrimination in jury selection. He turned out to be prophetic. What can be done to alleviate the problem? Justice Marshall suggested that the only way to "end the racial discrimination that peremptories inject into the jury-selection process" was to "eliminat[e] peremptory challenges entirely."[81] Although Justice Breyer has adopted Justice Marshall's suggestion,[82] there is no indication that the Court is heading in this direction. The primary objection to eliminating peremptory challenges altogether is the belief by some that criminal defendants would be hampered in their ability to remove jurors they believe to be hostile. Another possibility is to discipline attorneys who use their peremptories to eliminate jurors based on race. The basis of such discipline would be the rule that prohibits a lawyer from engaging "in conduct that is prejudicial to the administration of justice."[83] It would be difficult to discipline attorneys for violating this rule for two reasons. The first would be that courts rarely find that *Batson* has been violated; and, second, even if there is such a finding, the attorneys would have to be reported to the Bar Association, which both the judge and opposing counsel have been reluctant to do. Racial discrimination in jury selection will cease only when the Supreme Court sends a clear message that it will not be tolerated. The Court needs to make it clear that many of the asinine justifications that attorneys put forth to justify their strikes will not be acceptable.

The harm caused by racial discrimination in jury selection is widespread. When attorneys remove jurors based on race, both the defendant and the juror who was removed are harmed. The defendant is harmed because the prosecution is more likely to win a conviction and death sentence even if such a result is not warranted by the evidence. The juror's psyche is harmed when he is removed because of his race. Faith in the criminal system is also undermined by racial discrimination in jury selection. It is difficult for anyone to have confidence in the criminal justice system when parties are allowed to eliminate individuals from serving on a jury because of race, especially in light of America's racial history.

Race will continue to play an important role in determining who is sentenced to death in the United States as long as the Supreme Court continues to abdicate its responsibility under the Constitution and challenge the institutional racism that produces these disparities.

---

81 *Batson v. Kentucky*, 476 U.S. 79, 102–3 (1986) (Marshall, J., concurring).
82 *Miller-El v. Dretke*, 545 U.S. 231, 266 (2005) (Breyer, J., concurring).
83 Model Rules of Professional Conduct R. 8.4.

Chapter 4
Innocence

The Growing Problem of Innocence in Capital Cases

The Case of Cameron Todd Willingham

Opponents of capital punishment have long believed that, given the death penalty's flaws, innocent individuals have been put to death. However, they have never been able to provide definitive proof. The failure to provide definitive proof has been used by death penalty proponents as evidence that the system ultimately does work. For instance, Justice Scalia has written that:

> It is a certainty that the opinion of a near majority of the United States Supreme Court to the effect that our system condemns many innocent defendants to death will be trumpeted abroad as vindication of these criticisms. For that reason, I take the trouble to point out that the dissenting opinion has nothing substantial to support it. It should be noted at the outset that the dissent does not discuss a single case – not one – in which it is clear that a person was executed for a crime he did not commit. If such an event had occurred in recent years, we would not have to hunt for it; the innocent's name would be shouted from the rooftops by the abolition lobby.[1]

Since Justice Scalia wrote this, substantial proof has emerged that an innocent person was put to death. *The New Yorker* magazine has provided such proof. In *"Trial by Fire, Did Texas Execute an Innocent Man?"*[2] the magazine provides details regarding the case of Cameron Todd Willingham. On December 23, 1991, Willingham's Cameron, Texas home caught fire, killing his three daughters – two-year-old Amber and one-year-old twins Karmon and Kameron. Several witnesses who saw Willingham immediately after the fire portrayed him as being devastated by the fire. He was seen wearing only a pair of jeans, his chest blackened with soot, his hair and eyelids singed, and was heard screaming, "My babies are burning up!" Shortly thereafter, the state's "expert" determined that the cause of the fire was arson and Willingham became the prime suspect since he was the only person, besides the victims, known to have been in the home at the time. Some witnesses also indicated later that Willingham did not seem

---

1   *Kansas v. Marsh*, 548 U.S. 163, 188 (2006) (Scalia, J., concurring).
2   Available at http://www.newyorker.com/reporting/2009/09/07/090007fa_fact_grann.

distraught by the fire, for instance, that he was more concerned with moving his car so that it would not catch fire than with saving his daughters.

The state's case against Willingham at trial consisted of its expert's conclusion that the fire was arson and the witnesses who testified regarding Willingham's lack of concern at the time of the fire. The state also presented the testimony of a jailhouse snitch who claimed that Willingham confessed to him while they were in jail together. The state's theory, however, regarding Willingham's motive was weak. The District Attorney argued that Willingham killed the children because they "were interfering with his beer drinking and dart throwing."[3] Furthermore, although the children had life insurance policies, they amounted to only $15,000, and their grandfather, who paid for them, was listed as the primary beneficiary. Before taking the case to trial, the prosecution offered Willingham a life sentence in exchange for a guilty plea. Willingham's attorneys advised him to accept the offer but he refused. He told them that "I ain't gonna plead to something I didn't do, especially killing my own kids."[4]

Willingham could not afford to hire counsel so he had to rely on lawyers appointed by the state, one of whom was a former state trooper and the other a local defense attorney, considered a Jack-of-all-trades because his practice was not confined to one area of the law. The only evidence his attorneys presented was the testimony of one witness during the guilt phase of the trial. The Willinghams' babysitter testified that she could not believe that Willingham could have killed his children. The defense retained one fire expert to counter the prosecution's expert but their expert agreed with the prosecution's expert that the cause of the fire was arson. The jury needed only one hour to convict Willingham.

Several years later, evidence began to emerge indicating that Willingham might not have caused the fire that killed his children. According to Willingham's wife, nothing unusual had happened in the days prior to the fire. Although Willingham had battered her in the past, he had never abused their children and they had not fought in the days prior to the fire and were preparing for the holidays. His wife also indicated that she remembered turning the space heater down but not off in the children's bedroom.[5] None of this information was ever presented to the jury during Willingham's trial. The jailhouse snitch who testified against Willingham at trial sent a "Motion to Recant Testimony" to the prosecutor, declaring "Mr Willingham

---

3   *Id.* at p. 4.

4   *Id.* at p. 5.

5   Although Willingham's ex-wife initially believed that he did not murder their children and she even wrote to then Governor Ann Richards in support of his release, indicating that "I know him in ways that no one else does when it comes to our children. Therefore, I believe that there is no way he could have possibly committed this crime," she has since stated that she believes Willingham is guilty. *Id.* See also, *Stacy Kuykendall's statement about the 1991 fire,* Star Telegram, October 25, 2009, available at http://www.star-telegram.com/texas/v-print/story/1709042.html.

is innocent of all charges."[6] Willingham's lawyers were never informed of this development and the witness subsequently recanted his recantation. This witness was also diagnosed with bipolar disorder and had memory problems. Furthermore, although the prosecutor denied that the witness was provided a deal in exchange for his testimony, the prosecutor urged the Texas Board of Pardons and Paroles to grant him parole, which was in fact granted.

The most significant evidence to emerge after Willingham's conviction was a report by Dr Gerald Hurst, an acclaimed scientist and fire investigator. He was asked to evaluate the conclusion of the state's expert that the fire was caused by arson. Without having visited the fire scene, Hurst was unable to determine the exact cause of the fire. Based on the evidence, however, he had little doubt that it was an accidental fire, likely caused by the space heater or faulty electrical wiring. He concluded that the state expert's determination that the fire was caused by arson was based on "junk science." Shortly before Willingham's scheduled February 2004 execution, Hurst's report was forwarded to the Texas Board of Pardons and Paroles along with his request for clemency. The Board rejected Willingham's request for clemency without even meeting to discuss his case. Willingham had one final opportunity to stop his scheduled execution. In Texas, the Governor needs a recommendation from the Board in order to grant clemency. However, the Governor is empowered to grant a 30-day reprieve, which could have been done in this case and would have allowed the Governor's office to further investigate Hurst's conclusion that the fire was accidental and not caused by Willingham. Hurst's report was received by the Governor's office 88 minutes prior to Willingham's scheduled execution. According to the *Houston Chronicle*, "it is unclear from the records whether [the Governor] read [the report] that day. [The Governor's office] has declined to release any of his staff's comments or analysis of the reprieve request."[7] Willingham was executed after declaring, "I am an innocent man, convicted of a crime I did not commit."[8]

The investigation into whether Willingham was wrongfully convicted and executed has continued. Other fire investigators have reviewed the case and determined that the methods used by the state's expert in making its determination that the fire was arson were flawed, and have also concluded that the fire was not caused by arson. The Texas Forensic Science Commission, created by the Texas legislature to explore and fix forensic flaws, retained an expert who concluded that the investigators in the Willingham case had no scientific basis for claiming that the fire was arson and that their investigation violated "not only the standards of today but even of the time period."[9]

---

6   Supra, note 2 at 8.
7   L. Olsen *Perry's Office Quiet on Expert's Arson Report*, Houston Chronicle, October 11, 2009.
8   Supra, note 2 at 17.
9   *Id.*

Two days before the Commission was planning to review the report, the Governor replaced three members of the Commission – including the chairman – and the meeting was canceled amid speculation that the Commission was likely to conclude that Willingham had been wrongly executed, the first such conclusion by any government official.[10]

The Problem of Wrongful Convictions

Although Cameron Todd Willingham was never exonerated while he was alive, inmates are being exonerated at an alarming rate across the country. The Innocence Project has identified more than 200 inmates who have been exonerated after their convictions, based on DNA alone. This problem is especially acute in capital cases for obvious reasons. According to the Death Penalty Information Center, since 1973, more than 130 inmates have been released from death row after evidence of their innocence emerged.[11] Justice Souter summarizes some of the other numbers regarding exonerations of death row inmates:

> When the Governor of Illinois imposed a moratorium on executions in 2000, 13 prisoners under death sentences had been released since 1977 after a number of them were shown to be innocent, as described in a report which used their examples to illustrate a theme common to all 13, of "relatively little solid evidence connecting the charged defendants to the crimes" ... During the same period, 12 condemned convicts had been executed. Subsequently the Governor determined that 4 more death row inmates were innocent ... Illinois had thus wrongly convicted and condemned even more capital defendants than it had executed, but it may well not have been otherwise unique; one recent study reports that between 1989 and 2003, 74 American prisoners condemned to death were exonerated ... many of them cleared by DNA evidence. Another report states that "more than 110" death row prisoners have been released since 1973 upon findings that they were innocent of the crimes charged, and "[h]undreds of additional wrongful convictions in potentially capital cases have been documented over the past century."[12]

Many commentators and legislators believe that the advent of DNA testing will make wrongful convictions fade away. While DNA certainly has helped in identifying the real perpetrators of crimes, individuals will continue to be

---

10   Governor Rick Perry was facing a tough reelection campaign and many believe that the Commission members were replaced to prevent any embarrassment to the Governor.

11   The Death Penalty Information Center keeps a running count of death row inmates who have been exonerated. This information is available at http://www.deathpenaltyinfo. org/innocence-and-death-penalty.

12   *Kansas v. Marsh*, 548 U.S. 163, 208–10 (2006) (Souter, J., dissenting).

wrongfully convicted in death penalty cases for several reasons. First, only 5–10 percent of all criminal cases involve biological evidence that could be subject to DNA testing. Second, there will continue to be wrongful convictions in capital cases because "homicide cases suffer an unusually high incidence of false conviction, probably owing to the combined difficulty of investigating without help from the victim, intense pressure to get convictions in homicide cases, and the corresponding incentive for the guilty to frame the innocent."[13] There are other factors that contribute to wrongful convictions. As Justice Souter has observed, "most of these wrongful convictions and sentences resulted from eyewitness misidentification, false confession and (most frequently) perjury."[14] Questionable scientific testimony and jailhouse snitch testimony have also contributed to wrongful convictions.

Eyewitness Testimony

Eyewitness misidentification and perjury may have caused Ruben Cantu to be convicted and subsequently executed. After two construction workers were robbed and shot, one fatally, 17-year-old Cantu was charged with the murder. "No physical evidence – not even a fingerprint or a bullet – tied Cantu to the crime."[15] Cantu was convicted and sentenced to death based solely on the eyewitness testimony of the lone surviving victim. This individual, an illegal immigrant at the time of the shooting who had been in the United States less than a year, identified Cantu only after police officers showed him Cantu's photograph on three separate occasions. Days after he was convicted and sentenced to death, Cantu wrote a letter to the residents of San Antonio declaring, "My name is Ruben M. Cantu and I am only 18 years old. I got to the 9th grade and I have been framed in a capital murder case."[16] The lone eyewitness in the case later recanted, saying that he felt pressured by the police to identify Cantu. Furthermore, the 15-year-old co-defendant in the case stated under oath that Cantu was not with him on the night of the shooting and was not otherwise involved in the crime. The former San Antonio District Attorney who prosecuted Cantu subsequently regretted his decision to seek the death penalty in the case, and the current District Attorney likewise agreed that the death penalty should not have been sought in the Cantu case. None of these later statements helped Cantu, as he was executed before these individuals came forward with their regrets.

An extended discussion of eyewitness testimony is warranted given the crucial role it plays in criminal cases. Erroneous eyewitness testimony has been described as "the single greatest cause of wrongful convictions in the U.S. criminal justice

13 *Id.* at 210.
14 *Id.* at 210.
15 L. Olsen, *The Cantu Case: Death and Doubt*, Houston Chronicle, July 24, 2006.
16 *Id.*

system."[17] Eyewitness testimony is often the most powerful evidence that a prosecutor presents in a criminal case. The Center on Wrongful Convictions identified and analyzed the cases of 86 defendants who had been sentenced to death but were later exonerated. The Center found that: 1) eyewitness testimony played a role in the convictions of more than half; 2) eyewitness testimony was the only evidence against 38 percent of the defendants; 3) only one eyewitness testified in 70 percent of the cases; 4) the eyewitnesses were strangers to 41 percent of the defendants and non-accomplice acquaintances in 20 percent; 5) the average time between the arrest of the defendant and exoneration was almost 12 years.[18]

Several complex factors contribute to erroneous eyewitness identifications. First, the stress of the event may affect the witnesses' perception. Second, identifications have proven to be less accurate when witnesses are identifying perpetrators of a different race. Third, factors like the lighting where the crime took place or the distance from which the witness saw the perpetrator are important. Fourth, the procedure used by the police may cause the witness to make an erroneous identification. For instance, the type of lineup used, the inclusion of fillers or members of a lineup or photo array who are not the actual suspect, whether the lineup is administered by an officer involved in the investigation and who is familiar with the suspect, and any police communication with the witness before and after the identification procedure that may suggest who the officer believes to be the suspect all can have an influence on witness identification. The Supreme Court has failed to develop effective standards to minimize misidentifications. The Court has not even outlawed unnecessarily suggestive identification procedures.[19]

False Confessions and Police Misconduct

The Supreme Court has tried to make it more difficult for the police to intimidate a suspect into falsely confessing to a crime. The Court has held that confessions that are not voluntary cannot be used at trial against a suspect. The Court's voluntariness standard examines the "totality of all the ... circumstances" surrounding the confession to assess whether the confession was coerced. If the confession is not "the product of an essentially free and unconstrained choice by its maker"[20] the use of the confession violates due process and must be suppressed. The Court has also applied the exclusionary rule to confessions that violate its famous Miranda decision. In *Miranda v. Arizona*,[21] the Court held that the police must provide a suspect with specific warnings prior to questioning him. A suspect must be warned

---

17   R. Warden, *How Mistaken Perjured Eyewitness Identification Testimony Put 46 Innocent Americans on Death Row*, available at http://www.deathpenaltyinfo.org/studycwc2001.pdf.

18   *Id.*

19   *Neil v. Biggers*, 409 U.S. 188 (1972).

20   *Culombe v. Connecticut*, 367 U.S. 568, 602 (1961).

21   384 U.S. 436 (1966).

that he has a right to remain silent and the right to have an attorney present during questioning. He must also be told that if he cannot afford to hire an attorney that one will be provided for him at the government's expense. *Miranda*, and subsequent decisions, however, provide the police with opportunities to question even a reluctant suspect and provides them with license to use questionable techniques during an interrogation. First, the police are only required to warn suspects who are in custody. Thus, the police can continuously question a suspect who is not in custody. Second, even if a suspect invokes his right to remain silent, the police are permitted to question the suspect after a period of time has elapsed.[22] Third, a suspect must unambiguously invoke his right to remain silent and his right to counsel.[23] Unless the suspect makes a clear statement indicating that he does not wish to speak to the police, the police are allowed to continue to interrogate him. For instance, the Court held that when a suspect stated to the police "[m]aybe I should talk to a lawyer," the statement was ambiguous and that the police were not required to stop questioning the suspect.[24] Fourth, the police are allowed to deceive a suspect during an interrogation.[25] For instance, the police might falsely inform a suspect of a co-defendant's confession implicating the suspect; or the police might use a "false-evidence ploy," during which the suspect is falsely told of evidence that implicated the suspect in the crime. Finally, the police have an incentive to obtain a *Miranda*-defective confession since the Court has held that these statements can be used for purposes such as obtaining additional evidence[26] or impeaching the defendant at trial.[27] Given the loopholes the Court has created for the police, it is not surprising that defendants continue to confess to crimes that they did not commit. A study by Professor Brandon Garrett found that at least 40 suspects since 1976 have confessed to crimes which DNA evidence later proved they did not commit.[28] In addition, some suspects – such as those who are mentally impaired, the young, and those easily led – are more prone to provide false confessions.

I had a first-hand opportunity to learn of tactics that police use in getting a suspect to say what they want to hear. In 1997 I was appointed to represent Howard Guidry in his habeas corpus proceedings. Guidry had earlier been convicted of murdering the wife of a police officer for remuneration and was sentenced to death. The state obtained a conviction and death sentence based upon three crucial pieces of evidence: 1) Guidry's confession to the police; 2) the testimony of the girlfriend of the individual accused of hiring Guidry; and 3) the testimony of two neighbors of the victim who identified a black male as the individual they saw leave the

---

22   *Michigan v. Mosley*, 423 U.S. 96 (1975).
23   *Davis v. United States*, 512 U.S. 452 (1994).
24   *Id.*
25   *Frazier v. Cupp*, 394 U.S. 731, 739 (1969).
26   *Michigan v. Tucker*, 417 U.S. 433 (1974).
27   *Harris v. New York*, 401 U.S. 222 (1971).
28   B.L. Garrett, *The Substance of False Confessions*, 62 Stan. L. Rev. 1051 (2010).

victim's home right after she was killed. Given the apparent strength of the state's case, the chance of obtaining relief appeared to be remote. About four months had passed after the victim had been killed without a suspect being arrested. The police were under a lot of pressure to make an arrest since the case had received a significant amount of attention in the local media. The police got the break they were hoping for when Guidry was arrested on an unrelated bank robbery charge. The police received a tip after Guidry's arrest of his possible involvement in the murder. The police questioned Guidry and during this interrogation he gave a statement confessing to the murder. Guidry had been appointed an attorney for the bank robbery charge and he maintained that he had requested to speak to this attorney prior to confessing. Guidry further claimed that the two interrogating detectives left the room for a period of time and, upon returning, told Guidry that they had spoken to Guidry's attorney and that this attorney had given permission for Guidry to speak with the officers. Guidry's trial counsel moved to suppress the confession.

Although the law is clear that once a custodial suspect requests to speak with his attorney the police must discontinue the interrogation,[29] these motions are rarely granted under these circumstances because typically the only evidence that such a request was made comes from the suspect and courts almost uniformly resolve credibility disputes in favor of law enforcement officers. Guidry, however, had evidence to corroborate that he had requested to speak with his attorney prior to confessing. First, after Guidry had been charged with murder and counsel had been appointed, his attorneys had a chance encounter with the officers who had interrogated Guidry and obtained his confession. This encounter occurred while the attorneys and officers were attending court on an unrelated matter. Guidry's attorneys decided to approach the officers and confront them about interrogating a suspect whom they knew was represented by counsel. One officer replied, "I talked to his lawyer and his lawyer said it was okay to talk to him,"[30] confirming Guidry's account that he had requested to speak with his lawyer during the interrogation. Another attorney present at the time who had no connection to the case whatsoever overheard this conversation between trial counsel and the officer.

At the suppression hearing, Guidry's two trial attorneys who were parties to this conversation and thus became witnesses testified to the details of their conversation with the officers. The third attorney, who had no connection to the case, confirmed that the officer had admitted to interrogating Guidry despite the fact that Guidry had invoked his right to counsel. The attorney appointed to represent Guidry on the bank robbery charge, whom the officers claimed had given them permission to speak with Guidry, testified that he instructed Guidry not to speak with any officers. Furthermore, he denied having any conversation with the officers and testified that he did not give anyone permission to speak with Guidry. Most remarkably, the officers denied having any conversation with the attorneys –

29 *Edwards v. Arizona*, 451 U.S. 477 (1981).
30 *Guidry v. Dretke*, 2003 U.S. Dist. LEXIS 26199 at 11 (S.D. Tex. 2003).

in effect, accusing three members of the bar of committing perjury. The trial judge summarily denied the motion to suppress, failing to resolve the credibility dispute between the attorneys and the officers and providing no explanation for why four members of the bar would risk their livelihood for Guidry. As a result of the trial judge's total failure to resolve the conflicting testimony as to whether Guidry requested to speak with his bank robbery attorney during the interrogation, the federal district court conducted an evidentiary hearing At this hearing, the officer who conducted the interrogation contradicted his earlier testimony and stated that he recalled having a conversation with Guidry's trial attorneys but that he did not recall the substance of the conversation. The federal district judge found that Guidry had presented clear and convincing evidence that he had invoked his right to counsel and that the police had ignored his request. Specifically, the district court found that Guidry's account of the interrogation was credible but that the officers' was not, and that they had tricked Guidry into confessing and as a result his constitutional rights had been violated. The U.S. Court of Appeals for the Fifth Circuit, a court that would never be accused by anyone of being lenient to defendants in death penalty cases, also agreed that Guidry's confession had been obtained in violation of his rights.[31]

Prosecutorial Misconduct

The prosecutor has a unique role in the American criminal justice system: "the prosecutor is an administrator of justice, and advocate, and and officer of the court … The duty of the prosecutor is to seek justice, not merely to convict."[32] As the Supreme Court explained in *Brady v. Maryland*:

> Society wins not only when the guilty are convicted but when criminal trials are fair; our system of the administration of justice suffers when any accused is treated unfairly. An inscription on the walls of the Department of Justice states the proposition candidly for the federal domain: "The United States wins its point whenever justice is done its citizens in the courts."[33]

As a result, the Supreme Court has imposed certain disclosure duties on prosecutors. In *Brady*, the Court held that the prosecution violates a criminal defendant's constitutional rights by failing to disclose, either intentionally or inadvertently, exculpatory evidence in its possession. Exculpatory evidence is any evidence that is favorable to the defendant, including that which could be used to

---

31 *Guidry v. Dretke*, 397 F.3d 306 (5th Cir. 2005), rehearing denied, 429 F.3d 154 (5th Cir. 2005).

32 American Bar Association Standards Relating to the Administration of Criminal Justice, Prosecution Standard § 3.12(b)–(c).

33 373 U.S. 83, 87 (1963).

impeach government witnesses. The Court has also held that prosecutors have an affirmative obligation to turn over exculpatory evidence, even in the absence of a specific request from the defendant, if it clearly supports a claim of innocence. The Court has reiterated this duty as follows:

> The State here nevertheless urges, in effect, that "the prosecution can lie and conceal and the prisoner still has the burden to ... discover the evidence." ... A rule thus declaring "prosecutor may hide, defendant must seek," is not tenable in a system constitutionally bound to accord defendants due process.[34]

Unfortunately, despite these very clear commands, prosecutorial misconduct is not uncommon. Clarence Brandley, for instance, spent almost 10 years on death row in Texas before being exonerated because of the prosecutors' failure to disclose evidence that placed other suspects at the scene of the crime.[35] In North Carolina alone, in less than a 10-year period, courts of appeals have reversed nine death sentences because of the prosecution's failure to disclose exculpatory evidence to the accused. The case of Alan Gell provides an excellent illustration.[36] In 1998, Gell, a high-school dropout, was convicted and sentenced to death for the murder of a retired truck driver. The state had no physical evidence connecting Gell to the murder, but its star witness testified that she saw Gell shoot the victim with a shotgun. The prosecution, however, failed to turn over the tape of a telephone conversation in which this witness said that she "had to make up a story" about the victim's death. The prosecution also contended that Gell killed the victim on April 3, 1995, despite possessing a statement from several witnesses indicating that they saw the victim alive after that date. These statements were crucial because Gell had an alibi after April 3: he was either in jail for car theft or out of state from April 4 until April 14, when the victim's body was discovered. Again, the prosecution failed to turn these statements over to the defense; Gell's conviction was overturned because of the prosecution's failure to disclose these key pieces of evidence.

Another convicted murderer, Charles Munsey, was released from death row because the prosecutor in his case withheld evidence that the state's main witness, a jailhouse informant, was never an inmate in the prison when he claimed Munsey confessed to him.[37] Death row inmate Glenn Edward Chapman had his conviction overturned because the prosecution failed to provide the defense with the statement

---

34 *Banks v. Dretke*, 540 U.S. 668, 696 (2004).

35 Information regarding Brandley's case is available at http://www.deathpenaltyinfo. org/innocence-cases-1984-1993.

36 The facts regarding the Gell case were reported in C. Headrick and J. Neff, *Death Row Inmate Granted New Trial*, News & Observer (Raleigh, N.C.), Dec. 10, 2002, at A1.

37 The facts of the Munsey case are detailed in Neff, *N.C. Prosecutors Stifled Evidence*, News & Observer (Raleigh, N.C.), Dec. 19, 2004, at A1.

of a jail inmate who confessed to the crime and the statement of the witness who said he saw another man with the victim on the night of the murder.[38]

There is every reason to believe that these cases are just the tip of the iceberg. The *Chicago Tribune* conducted a nationwide study of prosecutorial misconduct and found that:

> With impunity, prosecutors have violated their oaths and the law, committing the worst kinds of deception in the most serious of cases. They have prosecuted black men, hiding evidence that the real killers were white. They have prosecuted a wife, hiding evidence her husband committed suicide. They have prosecuted parents, hiding evidence their daughter was killed by wild dogs.[39]

The *Tribune* found that at least 381 defendants nationwide have had their homicide convictions thrown out because the prosecutors either concealed evidence suggesting innocence or presented evidence that they knew to be false. Of these 381 defendants, 67 had been sentenced to death. The newspaper concluded that these numbers "represent only a fraction of how often cheating occurs." Other studies have confirmed the *Tribune*'s conclusions. For instance, the *Pittsburgh Post-Gazette* conducted a two-year investigation and found that prosecutors "lied, hid evidence, distorted facts, engaged in cover-ups, paid for perjury and set up innocent people in a relentless effort to win indictments, guilty pleas and convictions."[40]

The Center for Public Integrity, a non-partisan organization that conducts investigative research on public-policy issues, analyzed 11,452 cases in which appellate court judges had reviewed charges of prosecutorial misconduct.[41] The Center found that in 2,012 of these cases individual judges and appellate court panels cited prosecutorial misconduct as a factor when dismissing charges at trial, reversing convictions, or reducing sentences. In 513 additional cases, an appellate judge, in either a concurring or dissenting opinion, contended that prosecutorial misconduct had occurred. The study also found that "in thousands more cases, judges labeled prosecutorial behavior inappropriate but allowed the trial to continue or upheld convictions using a doctrine called 'harmless error.'"[42] The Center further reported that some prosecutors had convicted innocent defendants in more than one case over the course of their careers, and that some of these prosecutors were cited multiple times for misconduct in other cases as well. It

---

38 *Id.*

39 K. Armstrong and M. Possley, *Verdict: Dishonor*, Chi. Trib., Jan. 10, 1999 at 1.

40 B. Moushey, *Win at All Costs*, Pittsburgh Post-Gazette, available at .http://www.post-gazette.com/win.

41 S. Weinberg, Center for Public Integrity, *Breaking the Rules: Who Suffers When a Prosecutor is Cited for Misconduct?* (2003), available at http://www.publicintegrity.org/pm/default.aspx?act=main.

42 *Id.*

noted that "misconduct often occurs out of sight, especially in cases that never go to trial. Those cases by definition do not generate appellate opinions."[43] Furthermore, a study of capital cases nationwide between 1973 and 1995 found that state or federal courts overturned 68 percent of death sentences due to "serious error."[44] The American Bar Association (ABA) has also studied the death penalty systems of eight states. One of its key findings was that "most states have [capital] cases in which courts have found serious misconduct by prosecutors ... yet the prosecutors are not disciplined by the State disciplinary organization or by the prosecutor's office."[45]

Why then is prosecutorial misconduct so prevalent? First, defendants rarely prevail on claims of prosecutorial misconduct. In order to prevail in court on a claim of prosecutorial misconduct, a defendant must prove that the prosecutor possessed materially exculpatory evidence and that he was prejudiced by the non-disclosure. That is, he must demonstrate that disclosure was reasonably likely to have produced a different outcome in his case. This is a high burden. The Center for Public Integrity found that the courts have rejected the vast majority of prosecutorial misconduct claims on harmless-error grounds, holding that the alleged misconduct did not affect the outcome of the case.[46] Thus, prosecutors know that even if they engage in misconduct in a case and are caught, there is only a minimal likelihood that the conviction will be reversed on such grounds. Second, even though the professional consequences of prosecutorial misconduct are theoretically very serious, prosecutors are very unlikely to face discipline for withholding evidence in order to win. Finally, prosecutors engage in misconduct in order to win. In most jurisdictions, prosecutors are elected and they know that voters are not likely to reward them with reelection because of their exoneration record; but rather their chances of being reelected are greatest in the event of a high conviction rate.

Ineffective Representation

Only a very small minority of those who commit murder are sentenced to death. Justice White wrote in 1972 that "there is no meaningful basis for distinguishing

---

43   *Id.*

44   J.S. Liebman et al., *Capital Attrition: Error Rates in Capital Cases 1973–1995*, Tex. L. Rev. 1839, 1850 (2000).

45   ABA Death Penalty Moratorium Implementation Project, State Death Penalty Assessments: Key Findings at 2 (Oct. 29, 2007), available at http://www.abanet.org/moratorium/assessmentproject/keyfindings.doc. The eight states studied were Alabama, Arizona, Florida, Georgia, Indiana, Ohio, Pennsylvania, and Tennessee.

46   S. Weinberg, Center for Public Integrity, *Breaking the Rules: Who Suffers When a Prosecutor is Cited for Misconduct?* (2003), available at http://www.publicintegrity.org/pm/default.aspx?act=main.

the few cases in which it is imposed from the many cases in which it is not."[47] We now know, however, that there is a basis for distinguishing these cases. As detailed in Chapter 2, there is a serious problem with the representation that most death row inmates receive. Those defendants who end up with death sentences are usually those who were poorly represented. The quality of defense counsel is the most important factor in determining which defendants end up on death row. As Justice Ginsburg has observed, "people who are well represented at trial do not get the death penalty."[48]

A defendant needs a competent attorney in order to establish his innocence at trial. He needs an attorney to investigate and one who knows the law. He needs an attorney who is skeptical and who will vigorously cross-examine the government's forensic experts regarding their findings. In addition, as former Attorney General Janet Reno has stated:

> A competent lawyer will skillfully cross-examine a witness and identify and disclose a lie or mistake. A competent lawyer will pursue weaknesses in the prosecutor's case, both to test the basis for the prosecution and to challenge the prosecutor's ability to meet the standard of proof beyond a reasonable doubt. A competent lawyer will force a prosecutor to take a hard look at the gaps in the evidence … A competent lawyer will know how to conduct the necessary investigation so that an innocent defendant is not convicted … In the end, a good lawyer is the best defense against wrongful conviction.[49]

Unfortunately the overwhelming majority of those on death row were not represented by competent attorneys. Cameron Todd Willingham, for instance, might have been acquitted had his attorney challenged the government's forensic evidence. Instead he ended up on death row and was executed for a crime that he may not have committed. Cameron Todd Willingham and many others on death row did not have competent counsel because they could not afford it.

The overwhelming majority of those who are charged with a capital crime are indigent and do not have the resources necessary to employ counsel or to obtain the expert and investigative support they will need to mount an effective defense. Therefore, they must rely on the indigent defense system. In most death penalty jurisdictions, defendants charged with capital murder are represented by either public defenders or appointed counsel. While some public defenders and appointed counsel perform admirably, many provide substandard representation to their clients. More than 40 years ago, the Supreme Court established the right to counsel for those accused of serious crimes.[50] The American Bar Association,

---

47 *Furman v. Georgia*, 408 U.S. 238, 313 (1972) (White, J., concurring).

48 Supreme Court Justice Ruth Bader Ginsburg, April 9, 2001.

49 *Remarks of U.S. Attorney General Janet Reno at the 2000 National Symposium on Indigent Defense*, available at http://www.sado.org/fees/reno_competent.pdf.

50 *Gideon v. Wainwright*, 372 U.S. 335 (1963).

however, has studied indigent defense systems in the United States and found that "forty years after *Gideon v. Wainwright*, indigent defense in the United States remains in a state of crisis."[51] The ABA study found that lawyers who provide representation in indigent defense systems are frequently unable to furnish competent representation because they lack the necessary training, funding, time, and other resources.

In 1956, Justice Hugo Black stated in *Griffin v. Illinois*, "There can be no equal justice where the kind of [justice] a [person] gets depends on the amount of money he has."[52] Unfortunately more than 50 years later, as one commentator has remarked, "today, it is better to be rich and guilty than poor and innocent."[53]

Questionable Scientific Testimony

Forensic science is a vital component of the criminal justice system. Thousands of guilty defendants have been convicted with the help of forensic evidence.[54] DNA testing has been especially helpful in identifying criminals and exonerating the innocent. The success of DNA, however, has caused the courts to overlook other questionable science. In theory, questionable science should not be admitted into evidence. In order to be admitted, scientific expert testimony must meet certain standards of reliability. Most states and the federal courts admit scientific expert testimony under either a standard adopted by the Supreme Court in *Daubert v. Merrill Dow Pharmaceuticals*[55] or by a standard adopted by an appellate court in *Frye v. United States*.[56] Under the *Daubert* standard, a judge acts as a "gatekeeper" and may admit scientific evidence as long as it is both relevant and reliable. Under the *Frye* standard, in order to be admitted, scientific evidence "must be sufficiently established to have gained general acceptance in the particular field in which it belongs."[57] Courts have, however, routinely admitted forensic scientific evidence even though many forensic testing methods have been applied with little

---

51   American Bar Association Standing Committee on Legal Aid and Indigent Defendants, *Gideon's Broken Promise: America's Continuing Quest for Equal Justice* at V, available at http://www.abanet.org/legalservices/sclaid/defender/brokenpromise/fullreport.pdf.

52   351 U.S. 12, 19 (1956).

53   S. Bright, *The Failure to Achieve Fairness: Race and Poverty Continue to Influence Who Dies*, 11 U. Pa. J. Const. L. 23, 37 (2008).

54   J. Pickrell, *Instant Expert: Forensic Science*, New Scientist.com, November 10, 2006, available at http://technology.newscientist.com/channel/tech/forensic-science/dn10501.

55   509 U.S. 579, 597 (1993).

56   *Frye v. United States*, 293 F. 1013, 1014 (D.C. Cir. 1923); see also *People v. Geier*, 161 P.3d 104, 142 (Cal. 2007).

57   *Frye* at 1014.

or no scientific validation and with inadequate assessments of their reliability.[58] The admission of fingerprint and microscopic hair examinations illustrates how courts have frequently admitted forensic scientific testimony to convict defendants despite the fact that this evidence has not been subject to the rigors of scientific research.

The admissibility of fingerprint examination evidence has long been a given since it has been venerated for so long. Fingerprint examination involves a comparison of questioned friction skin ridge impressions from fingers (or palms) left at a crime scene to known fingerprints. If an examiner determines that there are enough common points between the two prints, the conclusion is that the questioned print definitely belongs to the suspect.[59] The authority of fingerprint evidence rests on the assumption that no two fingerprints are alike and that multiple people will not have a certain number of ridge characteristics in common. This assumption, however, has been contested:

> Although conventional wisdom since the nineteenth century has accepted the doctrine that no two fingerprints are alike, no one has really proven the proposition's validity. But if the question of the uniqueness of fingerprints seems pediatric, consider a more practical concern: How reliable is fingerprint evidence anyway? Can forensic technicians really match a fragmentary or smudged print taken from a crime scene to one and only one human fingertip, to the exclusion of all others in the world?[60]

Microscopic hair examination has been employed since the nineteenth century. It consists of comparing the microscopic characteristics of hairs recovered at a crime scene with a suspect's hairs. Analysts seek to associate color, texture, pigment, and other identifiers. A match between hairs is not based on any scientific test or experiment. Rather, a match is the product of "eyeballing." The biggest flaw with microscopic hair examination is that hair from the same person may vary greatly, whereas hair from two unrelated individuals may be similar.[61] One study found hair comparison to be one of the clearest examples of "junk science:"

> In the early 1970s, the U.S. Law Enforcement Assistance Administration (LEAA) sponsored a proficiency testing program for 240 laboratories that

---

58   See, e.g., *Johnson v. Commonwealth*, 12 S.W.3d 258, 263–4 (Ky. 1999).

59   D. Ashbaugh, *Ridgeology: Modern Evaluative Friction Ridge Identification*, 33–4, available at http://onin.com/fp/ridgeology.pdf.

60   S. Cole, *The Myth of Fingerprints: A Forensic Science Stands Trial*, Lingua Franca, v. 10, n. 8 (November 2000).

61   J. Thornton and J. Peterson, *The General Assumptions and Rationale of Forensic Identification*, in Modern Scientific Evidence: The Law and Science of Expert Testimony, § 29:48 (David L. Faigman et al., eds, Eagan, Minn.: Thomson/West, 2007–08).

provided evidence in criminal cases. The labs botched many kinds of tests: paint, glass, rubber, fibers. But by far, the worst results came from hair analysis.

Out of ninety responses for the hair survey, the proportion of labs submitting "unacceptable" responses on a given sample – either by failing to make a match, or making a false match – ranged from 27.6 to 67.8 percent.

On five different samples, the error rates were 50.0 percent, 27.6 percent, 54.4 percent, 67.8 percent and 55.6 percent. In short, there was little difference between flipping a coin and getting a hair analyst to provide reliable results. The hallmark of the scientific process is that results are reproducible; given the same tests, with the same procedures, two labs should come up with identical results. LEAA found that not even the mistakes were consistent. Perhaps most revealing is that these were open tests. That meant the lab directors knew ahead of time that they were being tested, like the chef in the restaurant who knows that an influential food critic has reservations for that evening. A far more rigorous gauge would have replicated real-life conditions by having the samples submitted blindly, slipped into the laboratory as if they were just evidence from another case.[62]

Given these findings, it is not surprising that hair analysis has produced wrongful convictions. Forty-three of the first 200 prisoners exonerated by DNA evidence had been convicted largely on the strength of hair follicles found at the crime scene.[63] A related problem has been termed "white coat fraud."[64] This involves testimony from experts fabricating either their credentials[65] or findings.[66]

Jailhouse Snitches

The government often uses testimony from individuals who were incarcerated with the defendant claiming that the defendant confessed to them or at least made incriminating statements. These witnesses are, in the vernacular, "snitches." While the government's use of snitches has not been outlawed by the Supreme Court,[67] snitch testimony is highly suspect. These witnesses are often promised leniency in exchange for their testimony, or they may be killers with incentives to cast suspicion

---

62   B. Scheck, P. Neufeld, and J. Dwyer, *Actual Innocence: Five Days to Execution and Other Dispatches from the Wrongfully Convicted*, 158–71 (New York: Doubleday, 2000).

63   B.L. Garrett, *Judging Innocence*, 108 Colum. L. Rev. 55, 81 (2008).

64   Scheck et al., *Actual Innocence*, 107–25.

65   See, e.g., *Maddox v. Lord*, 818 F.2d 1058 (2nd Cir. 1987); *Doepel v. United States*, 434 A.2d 449 (D.C. App. 1981.); *Commonwealth v. Mount*, 257 A.2d 578 (1969).

66   See, e.g., *In re Investigation of the West Virginia State Police Crime Laboratory, Serology Division*, 438 S.E.2d 501 (W. Va. 1993).

67   *Illinois v. Perkins*, 496 U.S. 292 (1990); *Kuhlmann v. Wilson*, 477 U.S. 436 (1977).

away from themselves. According to the Center on Wrongful Convictions, snitches are "the leading cause of wrongful convictions in U.S. capital cases."[68]

As a result of the growing number of exonerations in both capital and non-capital cases and cases such as *Willingham* and *Cantu*, the public has become much more skeptical about capital punishment. While a majority of Americans continue to support capital punishment, support for the death penalty has declined in recent years. This decline in public support is due at least in part to the public's realization that the criminal justice system is fallible. In fact, given the option of life without parole, juries are increasingly exercising that option as they are sentencing fewer defendants to death. While the public's skepticism is healthy, innocent individuals continue to be sentenced to death, due largely to the fact that the causes of wrongful conviction previously discussed have not been adequately addressed and due to the difficulties that inmates face in obtaining evidence and in proving their innocence in court.

Obstacles to Proving Innocence

Obstacles to Proving Innocence at Trial

Defendants claiming innocence at trial typically attempt to do so either through an alibi defense or through evidence of third-party guilt. The evidence needed to prove an alibi defense would usually be available to the defendant as long as counsel has conducted a thorough investigation. Most often, evidence needed to prove third-party guilt, such as forensic evidence and witness statements, is possessed by the government. However, the defendant may not be able to obtain the information he needs because of prosecutorial misconduct or because his lawyers never requests the evidence, and because of severe limitations that have been placed on the defendant's access to DNA and other evidence. The problems of prosecutorial misconduct and incompetent representation have been previously discussed. Therefore, this section will be devoted to a discussion of DNA and the defendant's access to DNA and other physical evidence.

While DNA evidence has become crucial in establishing guilt and exonerating the innocent, its impact can be overstated because it is limited to a small number of cases. DNA is most relevant only in cases involving sexual assault or in cases in which the defendant left bodily fluids such as saliva. For that reason, only a small number of the more than 100 death row exonerations have occurred because of DNA. Furthermore, even in those cases in which DNA might play a role in exonerating the defendant, he must overcome many procedural obstacles before obtaining DNA evidence.

---

68 *How Snitch Testimony Sent Rany Steidl and Other Innocent Americans to Death Row*, p. 3, available at http://www.law.northwestern.edu/wrongfulconvictions/issues/causesandremedies/snitches/SnitchSystemBooklet.pdf.

The government has a strong incentive to pursue DNA evidence of guilt; but the same incentive does not exist to pursue DNA evidence of innocence. Therefore, the defendant usually has to pursue DNA evidence to prove his innocence. A criminal defendant, however, has no constitutional entitlement to any evidence in the possession of the state other than exculpatory evidence. Any physical evidence that has not yet been tested is not exculpatory and *Brady* does not require its disclosure. Whether physical evidence or any other evidence that is not immediately exculpatory but which might be helpful to the defendant has to be disclosed by the prosecution varies widely depending on state law.

Florida and Texas provide great examples of the variations in state practice with respect to discovery. Florida law entitles the defendant to the names and addresses of any witnesses who may have information relevant to the case.[69] The defense may freely depose eyewitnesses, alibi witnesses, witnesses present during the making of defendants' statements, investigating officers, witnesses known to the prosecution to have evidence negating the guilt of the defendant, and under certain circumstances, expert witnesses.[70] In addition, the prosecution must disclose any physical evidence in its possession and make it available to the defendant for testing.[71] Texas, on the other hand, provides defendants with very limited discovery opportunities. In Texas, defendants are able to obtain physical evidence, documents, photographs, and written statements only upon a showing of "good cause."[72] In order to take a witness's deposition, the defendant must demonstrate that there is a "good reason" for taking the witness's deposition.[73] As Texas law illustrates, although DNA evidence is now admissible in all states, there is a good chance the defendant may not have access to this or other evidence that may be helpful to proving his innocence at trial.

Post-Conviction Obstacles to Proving Innocence

Most jurisdictions allow defendants to move for a new trial based on newly discovered evidence. However, these jurisdictions impose strict time limits for such motions, ranging from three years in federal court[74] to a month or less in 15 states.[75] In four states, the motion can be made at any time subject to the court's discretion. In addition, many jurisdictions will not consider new evidence if it was discoverable by reasonable diligence prior to trial.[76] This requirement has the

---

69   Fla. R. Crim. P. 3.220(b)(1)(A).

70   Fla. R. Crim. P. 3.220(h)(1)

71   Fla. R. Crim. P. 3.220(b)(1)(k).

72   Tex. Cr. Code Ann. § 39.14.

73   Tex. Cr. Code Ann. § 39.02.

74   Fed. R. Crim. P. 33(b)(1).

75   See, e.g., Ark. R. Crim. Proc. 33.3(b); Fla. R. Crim. Proc. 3.590(a); Ind. R. Crim. Proc. 16(A); Mo. R. Crim. Proc. 29.11; Tex. R. App. Proc. 21.4(a); Va. Sup. Ct. R. 3A:15(b).

76   See, e.g., Cal. Penal Code 81181(8); Ohio R. Crim. Proc. 33(A)(6).

effect of penalizing the defendant again for having had incompetent trial counsel. Finally, defendants moving for a new trial based on newly discovered evidence are often required to demonstrate that the evidence would have changed the outcome had it been presented at trial.[77]

Post-conviction review – state and federal habeas corpus actions – is available in every jurisdiction that has the death penalty. The purpose of post-conviction review is to provide defendants with a final chance to prove that they were wrongfully convicted and/or sentenced to death. A death row inmate faces numerous hurdles in obtaining post-conviction relief based on a claim of actual innocence in both state and federal court. In state court, a claim of actual innocence may not even be cognizable in a post-conviction proceeding. In those states that recognize such a claim, the standards a prisoner must satisfy are often onerous. The inmate typically must establish that the newly discovered evidence was previously unavailable. In addition, the inmate has the burden of proving his innocence in the post-conviction proceeding and that burden is extremely high. For instance, in California, the newly discovered evidence must "point unerringly to innocence"[78] to warrant habeas relief. In Illinois, the new evidence must "establish a substantial basis to believe that the defendant is actually innocent"[79] in order to obtain post-conviction relief. In Texas, in order to obtain relief, an inmate must prove that "no rational trier of fact could find proof of guilt beyond a reasonable doubt."[80]

The most significant hurdle, however, may be the fact that once convicted, death row inmates have no constitutional right to a lawyer to seek post-conviction review of their conviction and sentence.[81] While most states do provide defendants who have been sentenced to death with an attorney to represent them in their post-conviction proceedings, a few, most notably Alabama and Georgia, do not. In those states that do provide attorneys for the post-conviction phase, the representation is frequently mediocre. Texas, for instance, does appoint attorneys to represent death row inmates in their state habeas corpus proceedings. The *Austin American-Statesman* newspaper examined the legal work of many of the attorneys who had been appointed to represent Texas death row inmates in their post-conviction proceedings.[82] The newspaper's "review of the state writ system found a pattern of feeble death penalty appeals, demonstrating little or none of the investigation or thoughtful effort required to do the job right." The newspaper further found

---

77 See, e.g., LA Code Crim. Proc. Ann. art 851(3) (2007); Miss. Unif. Cir. & County Ct. Proc. 10.05.3.

78 *In Re Weber*, 523 P.2d 229, 243 (Cal. 1974).

79 725 Ill. Comp. Stat. § 5/122-I (2008).

80 *Ex parte Elizondo*, 947 S.W.2d 202 (Tex. Crim. App. 1994).

81 *Pennsylvania v. Finley*, 481 U.S. 551 (1987).

82 C. Lindell, *Lawyer's Writs Come Up Short*, Austin American Statesman, October 30, 2006 at A11; C. Lindell, *New Appeals, Old Arguments*, Austin American Statesman, October 30, 2006 at A11; C. Lindell, *When $25,000 is the Limit on a Life*, Austin American Statesman, October 30, 2006 at A1.

that "some lawyers copied from their previous appeals or from other attorneys, whether the facts applied to their current cases or not. Others recycled claims that have been denied time and again, ignoring obvious avenues of investigation."

Although death row inmates seeking post-conviction relief in federal court are entitled to counsel in the event that they are indigent, those inmates claiming actual innocence also face numerous obstacles when they seek post-conviction relief in federal court. Because of the Supreme Court's concern for finality and comity, the Court has created a number of hurdles for death row inmates seeking to prove their innocence, the most significant being the Court's refusal to allow free-standing actual innocence claims. The case of Troy Davis provides an illustration of just how difficult it is to even get a court to consider a claim of actual innocence once the defendant has been convicted.

On August 19, 1989, a police officer was murdered in a parking lot in Savannah, Georgia.[83] A homeless man had been verbally harassed and chased into a parking lot. The police officer had been working there as an off-duty security guard. Troy Davis and another individual heard the commotion and silently followed the scuffle. In the parking lot, Redd Coles threatened the retreating homeless man with a gun. Davis approached and tried to break up the fight but the homeless man was injured and in severe pain and yelled for help. The police officer responded and was shot dead with a .38 caliber revolver. After a highly visible police canvass of Coles' neighborhood, Coles approached the police with his attorney and implicated Troy Davis in the shooting. Within an hour of Coles' visit to the police station, a warrant for the arrest of Davis was obtained. The police held a press conference announcing that Davis was the prime suspect in the police officer's shooting, and Davis' name and picture was released to the press. A photo array was assembled that included Davis' picture but no picture of Coles. The photo array was not shown to any eyewitness until at least five days after the shooting. In the interim, Davis' picture – the same picture used in the photo array – appeared on television and on wanted posters near where the eyewitnesses lived and worked.

Five days after making a public commitment to the theory that Troy Davis was the shooter, the police learned that Coles was carrying a .38 caliber gun on the night of the shooting. Coles' gun was never subject to ballistics testing; nor did the police ever search Coles' house or car, and they never included Coles' picture in witness photo spreads. The police did search Davis' home but they never found any weapons or ammunition. The murder weapon was never recovered. All the police energy was directed at building a case against Davis. They failed to investigate even the possibility that Coles was the actual murderer. At Troy Davis' trial, the state presented the testimony of nine witnesses, including Coles. Davis never confessed to the murder. No murder weapon was ever recovered. In addition, no fingerprint evidence was presented. In short, the state's case consisted solely of the testimony of these nine witnesses. After Davis was convicted and sentenced to death, seven of the nine witnesses recanted their testimony. The two remaining

---

83   The facts are taken from *In re: Troy Anthony Davis*, 565 F.3d 810 (11th Cir. 2009).

non-recanting witnesses were Coles and another witness who identified Davis at trial two years after the incident, despite admitting to police immediately following the shooting that he would not be able to recognize the shooter. Furthermore, three witnesses now state that Coles confessed to the killing, and one of the state's trial witnesses says that Coles essentially confessed to him but that he had said nothing sooner because he and Coles are related. "Thus, no one at this time contends that Davis has ever confessed to the shooting; conversely, multiple witnesses maintain that Coles has confessed."[84]

Why is it that an inmate can present such a strong case of innocence – seven of nine trial witnesses have recanted their testimony against him and the motives of the two who have not recanted are highly suspect – and still be executed? Let us review the obstacles that Troy Davis and any convicted inmate faces in asserting a claim of actual innocence.

The Supreme Court's Refusal to Recognize Actual Innocence Claims

It is often stated that the United States has the best criminal justice system in the world. One could point to the number of appeals that defendants sentenced to death are allowed before they are executed to support this contention. A death row inmate can bring a myriad of claims after his conviction in attempting to overturn his conviction and/or sentence. Allegations that either his trial or appellate counsel was ineffective, that the prosecutor withheld exculpatory evidence, that the jury was selected in a racially discriminatory manner, that any statements he may have given were obtained illegally, that he was not allowed to present mitigating evidence and that it was not properly considered are just a few of the claims available to a death row inmate after he has been convicted and sentenced to die. Curiously, one claim that has not been available to him is a claim that he is factually innocent. How can it be that although we are now fully aware of the fact that the criminal justice system in the United States is fallible, the Supreme Court has refused to allow an inmate to assert his innocence in federal court even if he has new evidence to support his claim?

In *Herrera v. Collins*,[85] the Supreme Court confronted the question whether an inmate who had been convicted and sentenced to death could pursue a freestanding claim of actual innocence during his federal post-conviction proceedings. Herrera had produced affidavits indicating that another individual had confessed to the crime that Herrera had been convicted of committing. The Court assumed "for the sake of argument …, that in a capital case a truly persuasive demonstration of 'actual innocence' made after trial would render the execution of a defendant unconstitutional, and warrant federal habeas relief if there were no state avenue

---

84   *Id.* at 828.
85   506 U.S. 390 (1993).

open to process such a claim."[86] In a concurring opinion, Justice O'Connor, joined by Justice Kennedy, stated that, regardless of whether one used the "verbal formula" from the Eighth Amendment or Fourteenth Amendment, "the execution of a legally and factually innocent person would be a constitutionally intolerable event."[87] Justice Blackmun, joined by Justices Stevens and Souter, declared that "the Constitution forbids the execution of a person who has been validly convicted and sentenced but who, nonetheless, can prove his innocence with newly discovered evidence."[88] He explained that the execution of an actually innocent person violated the Constitution's ban on cruel and unusual punishment and its guarantee of substantive due process.[89] Between Justice O'Connor's concurrence and Justice Blackmun's dissent, five justices agreed that the execution of an actually innocent person would violate the Eighth Amendment.

Despite these pronouncements, the Court has never held that an inmate can seek to have his conviction vacated in a federal habeas proceeding based on a claim of actual innocence, even if he, like Troy Davis, can produce compelling new evidence of his innocence. Instead, the Court stated in *Herrera* that "the trial is the paramount event for determining the guilt or innocence of the defendant."[90]

The Antiterrorism and Effective Death Penalty Act

An additional hurdle death row inmates face in proving their innocence is the Antiterrorism and Effective Death Penalty Act of 1996 (AEDPA). The AEDPA was enacted in response to the bombing of the federal building in Oklahoma City. It contains many provisions that affect death row inmates and their ability to obtain relief in federal court. Most of these provisions will be discussed in a subsequent chapter on appeals. Several provisions impact claims of innocence and present a challenge in getting the merits of those claims considered in federal court.

Although inmates are precluded from making freestanding innocence claims, they sometimes make claims that they were unable to prove their innocence at trial based on the fact that their constitutional rights were violated. For instance, an inmate may present to the court statements from witnesses implicating another individual in the commission of the crime and claim that his attorney was ineffective for failing to interview these witnesses prior to trial. In order to have such a claim considered in federal court, the AEDPA requires that an inmate first present the claim to the state courts. Failure to present the claim to the state courts generally precludes it from being considered later in federal court, with one exception that will be discussed in a later section. Amazingly, attorneys representing death row

---

86   *Id.* at 417.
87   *Id.* at 419–21. (O'Connor, J., concurring).
88   *Id.* at 431. (Blackmun, J., dissenting).
89   *Id.* at 431–7. (Blackmun, J., dissenting).
90   Id. at 416.

inmates frequently do not present these claims in state court and thus they are waived as a result. Federal courts can conduct evidentiary hearings or otherwise consider any claim that was not presented to the state courts.

Evidence of a death row inmate's innocence is often revealed after he has spent many years on death row. According to the Death Penalty Information Center, those inmates who have been exonerated spent an average of 10 years on death row.[91] Therefore, an inmate may exhaust his state and federal appeals before this additional evidence has been revealed. The AEDPA only allows the inmate to file a new appeal based on this evidence if this evidence was not previously available to him and if he can prove by "clear and convincing evidence" that he would not have been convicted had this evidence been considered by the jury.[92] This provision of the AEDPA is so onerous that even someone who presents a compelling case of innocence, like Troy Davis, cannot satisfy it. After his initial appeals were exhausted, Davis sought to file a second appeal claiming for the first time that he was actually innocent of the crime. The U.S. Court of Appeals for the Eleventh Circuit would not allow Davis to pursue a second appeal. A divided panel of the Eleventh Circuit held that Davis did not meet the requirements of the AEDPA for filing a second appeal. First, the Eleventh Circuit held that most of the evidence that he based his freestanding innocence claim on was available at the time he filed his initial appeal. Second, the Eleventh Circuit held that although some of the evidence was not previously available to him, "Davis had not even come close to making a prima facie showing that his *Herrera* claim … would 'establish by clear and convincing evidence'" that he would not have been convicted.[93] In an unusual move, the Supreme Court ordered a hearing into Davis's innocence claim, although it still has not held that such a claim could be the basis of habeas relief. After the federal district court conducted the hearing, it held that Davis failed to establish by clear and convincing evidence that no reasonable juror would have convicted him in light of the new evidence. On September 21, 2011, Troy Davis was executed despite the serious questions that have been raised about his guilt. As the Davis case illustrates, if the Supreme Court adopts the same burden of proof, a capital defendant would have to prove that not a single juror would vote to convict him in light of his new evidence – a standard almost no defendant would be able to satisfy.

Claims of Innocence as a Gateway to Federal Habeas Review

As mentioned earlier, an inmate who fails to raise a claim in state court is usually barred from having the claim considered in federal court. Occasionally, however, an inmate obtains evidence that was never considered by the jury which may have

---

91 http://www.deathpenaltyinfo.org/innocence-list-those-freed-death-row.
92 28 U.S.C. § 2244(b)(2).
93 *In Re: Troy Anthony Davis*, 565 F.3d 810, 824 (11th Cir. 2009).

resulted in his acquittal had it been presented. If the failure to present the evidence was the result of ineffective assistance of counsel, prosecutorial misconduct, or some other constitutional violation, the Supreme Court has held that these claims can be considered in federal court, even though they were not presented to the state courts initially, if the inmate can establish that he is actually innocent of the crime.[94] Thus, the inmate cannot make a freestanding claim that he is innocent but he can use his innocence to have other claims considered that would ordinarily be barred because of the failure to present them in state court.

To establish the requisite probability that he was actually innocent, the petitioner must provide "new, reliable evidence – whether it be exculpatory scientific evidence, trustworthy eyewitness accounts, or critical physical evidence – that was not presented at trial."[95] This new evidence must prove that it is "more likely than not that no reasonable juror would have convicted him in light of the new evidence."[96] At the same time, the Court has said that this standard does not require absolute certainty about the petitioner's guilt or innocence.[97] The only death row inmate able to satisfy this stringent standard and to ultimately be exonerated is Paul House. After Carolyn Muncey was found murdered in the woods near her East Tennessee home in the summer of 1985, the police focused on two suspects: her husband, who had a history of serious domestic abuse, and House. House became the prime suspect after a witness claimed to have seen House emerge the day after the murder from the woods near where Muncey's body was found. House was charged with the murder after his girlfriend failed to corroborate his claim that on the night of the murder he was with her, and especially after testing indicated that semen on the victim's clothes and blood on her nightgown matched House's blood type. In addition, bloodstains on House's jeans matched the victim's. DNA testing was not in use at the time and would not be in use for several more years.

After House was convicted and sentenced to death, he filed a writ of habeas corpus in state and federal court. He failed to raise a claim of ineffective assistance of counsel in state court but pursued this claim in federal court. In federal court, he presented new evidence of his innocence, which included: 1) testimony from the state's medical examiner that the blood on House's jeans likely came from the sample taken from the victim after her body was discovered. The medical examiner testified that half of a vial of the victim's blood sample was unaccounted for and that law enforcement agents must have spilled it onto House's pants, either accidentally or intentionally; 2) two witnesses who had known the victim's husband for years and who said he had confessed to them that he murdered his wife; 3) several witnesses who said the husband had physically assaulted his wife; 4) two witnesses who contradicted the husband's alibi; and, most importantly, 5) newly conducted DNA testing that demonstrated "in direct contradiction of

---

94   *Schlup v. Delo*, 513 U.S. 298 (1995); *House v. Bell*, 547 U.S. 518 (2006).
95   *House v. Bell*, 547 U.S. 518, 537 (2006).
96   *Id.* at 538.
97   *Id.*

evidence presented at trial ... that semen on Mrs. Muncey's [clothing] ... came from her husband, ... not House."[98] Amazingly, both the federal district court and the Sixth Circuit Court of Appeals denied relief despite this compelling new evidence.

A divided Supreme Court did overturn House's conviction. The Court held that the DNA evidence, along with the forensic tampering with the blood evidence and the testimony of witnesses implicating the victim's husband, cast considerable doubt on House's guilt. The Court's holding did not mean that House was immediately exonerated. Rather, it meant that the federal district court could then consider House's ineffective assistance of counsel claim. More than 20 years after his trial, the district court granted relief on the ineffective assistance claim and ordered the state to retry House or release him.[99] The prosecutor subsequently dropped the charges against House.

The likelihood of a death sentenced inmate meeting this standard is minimal. According to Professor Myrna Raeder:

> in the 10 years after *Schlup* was decided, less than 10 percent of decisions citing that case resulted in consideration of otherwise barred claims, and of those 31 cases only 20 were resolved in favor of the petitioner. Thus, [11] individuals with enough evidence to suggest their probable innocence were denied relief.[100]

Access to Post-Conviction DNA Evidence

Paul House was fortunate that he was able to submit the semen from the crime scene for DNA testing after he had been convicted. Many death row prisoners are not so fortunate. The Supreme Court has refused to recognize a constitutional right to post-conviction DNA testing. The Court confronted this issue in *District Attorney's Office for the Third Judicial District v. Osborne.*[101] The state performed testing on sperm found in a condom at the crime scene. After Osborne was convicted of sexual assault, he sought to perform a more advanced DNA test than was available at the time of his trial. The Court of Appeals for the Ninth Circuit agreed with Osborne that he had a constitutional right to perform DNA testing, based on the prosecutorial duty to disclose exculpatory evidence. Although it acknowledged that "modern DNA testing can provide powerful new evidence unlike anything known before," the Supreme Court reversed. The Court held that the availability of post-conviction DNA testing is a task that "belongs primarily to the legislature."[102] Thus, the majority prefers to leave to the states the decision

---

98   *Id.* at 540.
99   *House v. Bell*, 2007 U.S. Dist. LEXIS 94176 (E.D. Tenn. 2007).
100   M. Raeder, *PostConviction Claims of Innocence*, 24 Crim. J. 14, 22 (Fall 2009).
101   129 S. Ct. 2308 (2009).
102   *Id.* at 2316.

whether to make DNA available to inmates once they have been convicted. The four dissenters pointed out that "the DNA test Osborne seeks is a simple one, its cost modest, and its results uniquely precise. Yet for reasons the State has been unable or unwilling to articulate, it refuses to allow Osborne to test the evidence."[103]

Crucial to the Court's decision refusing to recognize a constitutional right to post-conviction DNA testing is the fact that most states have enacted legislation dealing with the subject. The Court overlooked the fact that four states, including three active death penalty states (Alabama, Mississippi, and South Carolina) have no statutes addressing an inmate's access to post-conviction DNA testing.[104] In these states, DNA testing is only available when law enforcement officials consent to testing or when a court grants it. Most importantly, although it is true that 44 states have enacted legislation providing access to post-conviction DNA, the Court ignored the fact that most post-conviction DNA statutes create procedural hurdles an inmate must overcome before DNA testing can be done. The vast majority of jurisdictions require that the inmate demonstrate by a preponderance of evidence that DNA testing could prove his innocence. In some states, the burden is even more onerous. A few states require clear and convincing evidence that the DNA test will prove innocence. The problem with imposing a standard to obtain DNA testing is that it is often the case that the inmate can only prove his innocence through the DNA evidence. One scholar who has studied this issue found that "few convicts eventually exonerated by post-conviction DNA testing had any evidence of innocence to present to the courts prior to obtaining DNA testing."[105]

The Texas statute is illustrative of the burden that inmates face in obtaining post-conviction DNA testing.[106] In Texas, a convicted inmate can request DNA testing of any biological material from the crime scene. However, several limitations are placed on his ability to test this evidence. First, he must demonstrate by a preponderance of the evidence that he would not have been convicted if exculpatory results had been obtained through DNA testing. Second, he can only request testing of evidence not previously tested unless newer testing techniques are available. Third, he cannot test evidence that was available at the time of trial. He is therefore precluded from testing evidence that trial counsel failed to have tested.

Henry Skinner was convicted of bludgeoning to death his live-in girlfriend and sentenced to death.[107] On the night of her murder, the victim attended a party during which her uncle, who had previously raped her, was "hitting on" her, which caused her to leave the party. Skinner was represented by an attorney who had previously

---

103   *Id.* at 2331.

104   Information regarding the availability of post conviction DNA evidence was obtained from B.L. Garrett, *Claiming Innocence*, 92 Minn. L. Rev. 1629 (2008).

105   *Id.* at 1697.

106   Tex. Cr. Code Ann. § 64.

107   Details regarding the case are available at http://www.medillinnocenceproject.org/skinner.

prosecuted him. Skinner's attorney did not request that certain important items from the crime scene be tested: the uncle's windbreaker covered with human hairs and sweat which was found directly next to the victim's body, a bloodstained knife, skin found underneath the victim's fingernails, and hairs removed from the victim's hands. After his conviction, Skinner sought to have these items tested. Because these items were available at Skinner's trial, the courts have turned down his request to have them tested.

Claims of Insufficient Evidence

The Supreme Court has created an opportunity for an inmate convicted based on insufficient evidence to have the conviction overturned on appeal. In *Jackson v. Virginia*,[108] the defendant's conviction will be overturned if, viewed in the light most favorable to the prosecution, the evidence was so insufficient that no reasonable juror could vote to convict. Thus if an inmate can demonstrate that there is not sufficient evidence to support each and every element of the crime, he is entitled to have his conviction reversed. This requires a showing that there was no evidence on a crucial element to support the conviction, not simply a showing that the evidence was weak. The Court also emphasized in *Jackson* that "the standard ... does not permit a court to make its own subjective determination of guilt or innocence."[109] Therefore, claims of insufficient evidence almost never succeed because there is almost always at least minimal evidence from which a jury could infer guilt.

Clemency

The Court has refused to allow freestanding innocence claims partly because the death row inmate has an opportunity to correct any miscarriage of justice by requesting executive clemency. In fact, the Court discussed the Texas clemency procedure available to Herrera in great detail. However, a review of the Texas clemency process illustrates exactly why inmates cannot rely on it to prove their innocence. While it is true that the Governor of Texas may pardon a defendant, commute a conviction, or commute a sentence, he may do so only after receiving a favorable recommendation from a majority of the Board of Pardons and Paroles. This Board is not required to meet as a body to determine clemency matters; as a result, inmates are not able to testify before the Board. Board members cast their votes by fax, a process that has become known as "death by fax." The Board is not required to give any reasons for its decisions and it is not bound by any specific criteria. Board members may, but need not, review documents and letters

108   443 U.S. 307 (1979).
109   *Id.* at 319, n. 13.

in support of clemency petitions prior to voting on a clemency application. The Board need not hold hearings and investigate or verify the clemency application. A federal judge concluded that "it is abundantly clear the Texas clemency procedure is extremely poor and certainly minimal ... [and that] administratively, the goal is more to protect the secrecy and autonomy of the system rather than carrying out an efficient, legally sound system."[110] It is not surprising, therefore, that between 1976 and 2004 the State of Texas approved only one application for clemency from a prisoner on death row.

The Texas Board of Pardons and Paroles has been presented with some compelling clemency requests, but it has rejected them nonetheless. Gary Graham had the misfortune of being represented by an attorney who had been publicly reprimanded by the state bar, suspended three times for misconduct, and criticized for his poor handling of capital murder cases. In Graham's case, his attorney failed to: 1) conduct an investigation; 2) interview two eyewitnesses who told the police that Graham was not the killer; 3) present an alibi defense;(4) introduce ballistics evidence to show that the gun taken from Graham when he was arrested was not the murder weapon; and 5) inform the jury that although the state's theory was that Graham killed the victim in order to rob him, the victim had $6,000 in cash in his back pocket when the police searched his pants. The Texas Board of Pardons and Paroles turned down Graham's clemency request and he was subsequently executed. Texas is certainly not alone in rejecting compelling clemency requests. Other states have also rejected compelling clemency requests, most notably the Georgia Board of Pardons and Paroles, which has rejected Troy Davis's compelling clemency petition containing recantations by seven of the nine eyewitnesses who testified against him at his trial.

There are 51 different systems of clemency in the United States. Typically, few rules govern the clemency process. It is not surprising, therefore, that the clemency process is fraught with arbitrariness and capriciousness. Governors have granted clemency based on gender; some, like Governor Richardson of New Mexico, have granted clemency because they lack confidence in the system; while others have granted clemency because they were personally opposed to capital punishment. Governor George W. Bush would only grant clemency: 1) if the inmate did not have access to the courts (whether the access was meaningful was irrelevant); and 2) if the inmate was innocent. Governor Bush refused to even consider clemency under any other circumstance, including the case of Karla Faye Tucker. She was convicted of a committing a gruesome double murder with a pickax. There was no question concerning her guilt. By all accounts she was reformed during her incarceration – becoming a born-again Christian, she admitted her guilt and asked for forgiveness. Most of the evangelical Christian community, a group that ordinarily supports capital punishment, urged Governor Bush to grant clemency. So did prominent Bush supporters like Reverends Pat Robertson and

---

110   *Faulder v. Tex. Bd. of Pardons & Paroles*, No. A98 801, SS at 9 (W.D. Tex. Dec. 28, 1998).

Jerry Falwell. Their pleas were to no avail. Bush refused to grant clemency and Tucker was executed.

The Supreme Court has made it clear that it will not police the clemency process. In *Ohio Parole Authority v. Woodard*,[111] an Ohio death row inmate challenged the Ohio clemency process on due process grounds. In Ohio, the Parole Authority must conduct a clemency hearing at least 45 days prior to a scheduled execution. Prior to the hearing, an inmate may request an interview with one or more parole board members. An inmate has no right to have counsel attend and participate in either the interview or the hearing. The inmate in *Woodard* filed suit alleging that Ohio's clemency process violated his due process rights. In particular, he objected to the short notice of the parole interview (seven days before the interview was scheduled) and the Board's prohibition of legal assistance at the interview. The Court held that "pardon and commutation decisions have not traditionally been the business of courts; as such, they are rarely, if ever, appropriate subjects for judicial review."[112] Justice Stevens criticized the majority's reasoning due to the fact that "even procedures infected by bribery, personal or political animosity or the deliberate fabrication of false evidence would be constitutionally acceptable."[113] In fact, the Texas federal judge who was so critical of the clemency process in Texas felt compelled by the Supreme Court's decision in *Woodard* to conclude that the Texas clemency procedure did not violate due process.

Clemency is a poor substitute for freestanding actual innocence claims. At one time clemency was an important part of the death penalty process. For instance, Florida commuted nearly a quarter of its death sentences between 1924 and 1966; North Carolina commuted nearly a third of its death sentences between 1909 and 1954.[114] In the modern era of capital punishment, clemency has become a freak occurrence. The popularity of the death penalty has made it political suicide for Governors to grant clemency on all but the rarest occasions. Governors now see it as the courts' responsibility to correct any injustices:

> Where the sentence had been affirmed as constitutional at all stages of judicial review, however, the assumption within governors' offices tended to be that the sentence ought not to be disturbed, an assumption very different from the one that had prevailed for the preceding several centuries, when the executive branch was supposed to exercise its independent judgment as to the propriety of an execution. When the courts moved in, the governors moved out.[115]

---

111 523 U.S. 272 (1998).

112 *Id.* at 276.

113 *Id.* at 290 (Stevens, J., concurring).

114 S. Banner, *The Death Penalty: An American History*, 291 (Cambridge, Mass.: Harvard University Press, 2002).

115 *Id.* at 292.

Possible Solutions

The best way to avoid wrongful convictions is to make sure that defendants have competent legal representation and that prosecutors perform their constitutional duty to disclose exculpatory evidence. Of course this will not always happen, and inmates will continue to be wrongly convicted. Therefore there has to be some mechanism for reviewing claims of wrongful conviction. The most obvious thing that can be done to prevent wrongful convictions and executions is to allow freestanding claims of actual innocence during state and federal habeas proceedings. An inmate should be able to present such a claim based on evidence that was not presented at trial and to have their new evidence reviewed by a federal court without any procedural constraints. There are compelling reasons for allowing freestanding actual innocence claims. First and foremost, it is often the case that evidence of an inmate's innocence does not emerge until well after he has been convicted and sentenced to death. The evidence indicating that the fire that killed Cameron Todd Willingham's children was not arson did not emerge until the eve of his execution. In Illinois, Anthony Porter spent 16 years on death row and came within two days of execution before evidence of his innocence emerged. A Northwestern University journalism professor and his students learned the identity of the real killer from a witness to the killing and eventually obtained a confession.

Another reason for allowing freestanding claims of innocence is that evidence of a death row inmate's innocence often does not emerge earlier due to the fact that he was poorly represented at trial. Consider the case of Earl Washington, a Virginia death row inmate convicted of raping and murdering Rebecca L. Williams. His conviction was based on a confession consisting of "yes" answers to a series of leading questions. In addition, during the confession, Washington "offered erroneous details [about the murder], such as misidentifying the crime scene, confessing at first to stabbing the victim twice when her body bore 38 wounds, and identifying the victim as black," despite the fact that she was white.[116] Washington had an I.Q. of 69. Despite the obvious problems with his confession, it was offered into evidence by the prosecution and was not challenged by Washington's attorneys. His lawyers also failed to present to the jury "serology evidence that no trace of the defendant was found on a blanket used in the rape and homicide."[117] On October 2, 2000 – 16 years after his conviction and death sentence was imposed – Washington was finally exonerated after tests confirmed that Washington's DNA was not on any of the evidence discovered at the crime scene.

The Supreme Court has been reluctant to allow freestanding claims of actual innocence. In *Herrera v. Collins,* the Court expressed its concern that "[f]ew rulings would be more disruptive of our federal system than to provide habeas

---

116   F. Clines, *New DNA Tests Seen As Key to Virginia Case,* New York Times, Sept. 7, 2000, at A18.

117   *Id.*

review of freestanding claims of actual innocence."[118] This concern, however, is misplaced. First, some states permit inmates to raise freestanding claims of actual innocence during their state habeas proceedings. A death row inmate in Texas, for instance, can raise a freestanding actual innocence claim based on new evidence.[119] The ability to present freestanding actual innocence claims has certainly not overburdened the Texas courts and prevented the state from carrying out more executions than any other state in the nation. Second, many death row inmates have confessed their guilt, which would usually preclude an actual innocence claim. Given the fact that most inmates will not be able to produce new evidence, and have confessed, it is unlikely that many freestanding actual innocence claims will in fact be made.

Allowing freestanding innocence claims raises other concerns. First is the concern for finality. Critics argue that once a jury has convicted and sentenced an inmate to death, the jury's decision is entitled to respect and should be overturned only in extraordinary circumstances. The possible execution of a factually innocent individual is certainly an extraordinary circumstance warranting federal court review. Moreover, in death penalty cases, the goal of accuracy should trump finality. A second objection is the likelihood that frivolous claims of innocence will be made by inmates desperate to stop their executions. Federal courts are confronted daily with all sorts of claims, some of which are frivolous, and are able to resolve those claims expeditiously. There is no reason to be concerned that federal courts will not be able to likewise resolve frivolous claims of innocence. In addition, these claims would have to be based on new evidence. Unless the inmate produced new evidence, there would be no review.

A further concern would be that some attorneys would not present evidence of their client's innocence until the last possible moment. It is hard to fathom that there are attorneys who would risk their client's life and commit professional malpractice in this manner. Another objection to allowing claims of actual innocence would be the concern for federalism. Proponents of federalism believe that claims of actual innocence can be presented in most state courts and should be presented there. Even though state court review is possible, it is important to have a further layer of review especially for actual innocence claims. Federal courts review other claims presented first to the state courts and there is no reason why they should not be able to also consider actual innocence claims which are based on new evidence. Finally, in *Herrera*, some of the justices believed that there is no need for a claim of actual innocence given the availability of executive clemency in every state. As discussed earlier, the clemency process is highly political and not an effective and reliable assurance against wrongful executions. The Texas

---

118   *Herrera v. Collins*, 506 U.S. 390, 401 (1993).

119   In *State ex rel. Holmes v. Court of Appeals*, 885 S.W.2d 389, 397 (Tex. Crim. App. 1994), the Texas Court of Criminal Appeals announced that it would entertain post-conviction applications for writ of habeas corpus alleging actual innocence as an independent ground for relief.

Board of Pardons and Paroles was presented with new evidence indicating that the Willingham children were not murdered yet the Board did nothing to prevent Cameron Todd Willingham's execution.

In order to be meaningful, should the Court allow freestanding actual innocence claims, it should not make the burden of proof so onerous that no defendant would ever be able to obtain relief. For instance, if the Court were to adopt the standard of proof adopted by the federal district court in Troy Davis's case – which required clear and convincing evidence that no reasonable juror would have convicted him in light of the new evidence – it is difficult to conceive of a defendant other than one who produces definitive DNA evidence or a confession who could satisfy this standard. It is doubtful that even Cameron Todd Willingham would have been able to convince a court that not one juror would have voted to convict him in light of the new evidence from the arson experts. At least one juror might have concluded that Willingham was guilty given the fact that he was in the home when the fire occurred and given what some believe was a lack of remorse immediately after the fire.

It is also possible that wrongful executions may be prevented by creating an independent innocence commission, as North Carolina has done.[120] The North Carolina Innocence Inquiry Commission was created in response to the Duke Lacrosse Rape Case, in which three members of the Duke University lacrosse team were accused of rape and it was later revealed that the prosecutor withheld evidence of their innocence. There were also several high-profile exonerations in death penalty cases that contributed to the Commission's creation. The Commission is empowered to consider claims of factual innocence by any living person convicted of a felony in North Carolina. In order for the claim to be considered, the convicted felons must assert that they are completely innocent of any criminal responsibility for the crime, including any lesser included offenses. The claim must be based on credible, verifiable evidence that has not previously been presented at trial or in a post-conviction hearing. The Commission is composed of eight members that include a superior court judge, a prosecuting attorney and a criminal defense lawyer, a victim's advocate, a member of the general public, a sheriff, and two members appointed by the Chief Justice of the North Carolina Supreme Court. The other members are chosen by both the Chief Justice and the Chief Judge of the North Carolina Court of Appeals. The Commission is assisted by a Director who also has a staff. After a preliminary investigation, the Commission has discretion whether to conduct a formal inquiry. A formal inquiry is a factfinding investigation and is not adversarial. In the event it conducts a formal inquiry, the Commission has the authority to compel the testimony of witnesses and conduct discovery. In order for the claim to go forward, five Commission members must vote yes, unless the convicted person confessed – which then requires the concurrence of each member. In the event that the Commission determines that there is sufficient evidence of factual innocence, an evidentiary hearing is conducted before a

---

120   See N.C. Gen. Stat. § 15-A-1463(a).

three-judge panel. This hearing is adversarial in nature. Both the prosecutor and the defense attorney are allowed to present evidence. The standard of review is "whether the convicted person has proved by clear and convincing evidence that [he or she] is innocent of the charges."[121] The conviction is vacated only if all three judges are in agreement that the convicted person satisfies the standard. No appeal of the decision is permitted.

One may wonder why there is a need for an independent commission given the availability of executive clemency. The Commission is preferable in several respects. First, there are standards governing the Commission and its decisional process. There are no standards governing the clemency process. Second, the Commission is isolated from partisan politics. Conversely, in most states, the decision to grant pardons or commutations is either made by the Governor or a board appointed by the Governor. A Governor wanting to appear tough on crime may be reluctant to grant relief even in justifiable cases. Third, the Commission consists primarily of individuals with law enforcement backgrounds and is balanced between individuals aligned with the prosecution and defense. On the other hand, clemency decisions are often made by individuals with no law enforcement backgrounds. Although they are imperfect, especially in the inability to appeal decisions of the Commission, these independent commissions appear to be a step in the right direction.

Wrongful convictions can also be minimized by addressing some of the factors that cause these convictions. Eyewitness identifications have always been important and should continue to be used. However, there are certain reforms that could be made to ensure greater reliability. For instance, Illinois does not allow a defendant to be sentenced to death based solely on the testimony of an eyewitness.[122] North Carolina enacted a statute that should be a model for other states: individuals or photographs must be presented to the witnesses sequentially to prevent the witnesses from comparing the individuals in the lineup and choosing the one who most resembles the suspect; witnesses are informed that the suspect may not be in the lineup; witnesses are also informed that they are not required to make an identification; fillers – individuals who are not suspects but who physically resemble the suspect – must be in the lineup; and the lineup must be conducted by an independent administrator who is unaware of the identity of the suspect to ensure that subtle hints are not given to the witness.[123] To combat the problem of false confessions, North Carolina requires that in homicide cases the entire interrogation be electronically recorded.[124]

Prosecutors commit misconduct in order to win. Thus, if appellate courts reverse more convictions based on prosecutorial misconduct, that is likely to have a significant impact on prosecutors' behavior. To that end, the Supreme Court could

---

121   N.C. Gen. Stat. § 15A-1469(h).

122   720 Ill. Comp. Stat. 5/9-1 (h-5) (2007).

123   N.C. Gen. Stat. § 15A-284-52.

124   N.C. Gen. Stat. § 15A-211.

make it easier to prove prosecutorial misconduct by eliminating the requirement that the inmate prove prejudice. In addition, judges could deter prosecutors from engaging in misconduct by referring those found to have done so to the state bar for discipline. Judges could prevent the misuse of scientific evidence by denying admission to scientific testimony that has not undergone the rigors of scientific evaluation. Courts could refuse to admit jailhouse snitch testimony on the grounds that its probative value is outweighed by its prejudicial effect unless it is corroborated by other evidence.

Costs

It would be logical to conclude that having a death penalty would be cheaper than housing an inmate in prison for life. However, the exact opposite is the case. The death penalty is much more expensive. Because "death is different" the costs of a death penalty case is much greater: more mental health and forensic experts will be required; jury selection will be longer; two trials are required, one to determine guilt and the other punishment; and the appeals are longer and more complex. Furthermore, the accused is entitled to two trial attorneys and to legal representation during his appeals. In addition, the prosecutor and courts must devote more resources and time to capital cases. To demonstrate in numbers the cost difference, the California Commission on the Fair Administration of Justice found that the state of California spent $137 million per year on death penalty cases, whereas these cases would have cost $11.5 million had the offenders been given life without parole.[125]

Most of the reforms proposed in this book would increase the cost of the death penalty. Massachusetts considered reinstating the death penalty but wanted to ensure that if it did, no innocent person or any person who is guilty but legally ineligible for the death penalty would ever be wrongly condemned to death. The Commission appointed by the Governor to study the issue proposed several reforms but acknowledged that "it is not possible to have a death penalty system that is both inexpensive and at the same time capable of being relied upon to produce accurate and fair results."[126]

Conclusion

Death penalty proponents would point to the number of exonerations as evidence that the system is working. Proponents might also argue that, given scientific

---

125   California Commission on the Fair Administration of Justice, available at http://www.ccfaj.org/documents/CCFAJFinalReport.pdf.

126   Report of Governor's Council on Capital Punishment at 5, available at http://www.lawlib.state.ma.us/docs/5-3-04Governorsreportcapitalpunishment.pdf.

advances, the chances of an innocent individual being executed has become small. Even in the event of a wrongful conviction and death sentence, given the long appellate process and DNA and other scientific methods for determining guilt, the wrongly convicted inmate is likely to be eventually exonerated. However, this argument presupposes that the criminal justice system works as it is supposed to: i.e., that the prosecutor disclosed all exculpatory evidence; that the defense attorney was competent and subjected the government's case to adversarial testing; and that the defendant was provided with the opportunity and resources to review and challenge the government's case. The reality is that the system often does not function as it should. The prosecutor does not always disclose evidence; the defense attorney is frequently incompetent and therefore fails to challenge the government's case; and the defendant faces many barriers to proving his innocence once he has been convicted, such as the onerous standard that a defendant must satisfy in order to test scientific evidence after he has been convicted.

Death penalty proponents have also always pointed to the fact that opponents have never been able to prove that an innocent individual has been executed as further proof that the system works. They have noted that death penalty opponents had been unable to prove definitively that an innocent person has been executed. This argument can no longer be made now that Cameron Todd Willingham was executed despite strong credible evidence that he did not commit the crime. Everyone acknowledges that the criminal justice system is fallible. Therefore the system has to be able to rectify mistakes when they are made. However, as this chapter illustrates, there are too many obstacles an inmate faces in order to prove his innocence.

Chapter 5

Mental Illness

The law has long prohibited the conviction of an individual who is so mentally ill that he is unable to distinguish right from wrong. Furthermore, when an indigent defendant's sanity is in question, the trial court must provide him with expert psychiatric assistance. Many death row inmates do not meet the legal definition of insanity yet they suffer from serious mental illness. This chapter will discuss and assess how the Supreme Court and lower courts have dealt with a number of issues related to a death-sentenced defendant's mental state: 1) an inmate who is mentally retarded; 2) an inmate who was sane when he committed the crime but has since become insane while on death row; 3) the ability of the state to medicate an inmate for the purpose of carrying out his execution; and 4) the circumstances under which an inmate sentenced to death is allowed to waive his appeals and "volunteer" to be executed.

Mental Retardation

The Diagnostic and Statistical Manual of Mental Disorders (DSM) is the standard reference book used by mental health professionals to diagnose patients. The DSM defines mental retardation as significantly subaverage general intellectual functioning in at least two of the following skill areas: communication, self-care, home living, social/interpersonal skills, use of community resources, self-direction, functional academic skills, work, leisure, health, and safety. According to the American Association of Mental Retardation (AAMR) – now the American Association on Intellectual and Developmental Disabilities (AAIDD) – an Intelligence Quotient (I.Q.) score of around 70 or as high as 75 indicates a limitation in intellectual functioning.[1] Mentally retarded individuals are held criminally responsible for the crimes that they commit. As Justice Stevens pointed out, "[t] hose mentally retarded persons who meet the law's requirements for criminal responsibility should be tried and punished when they commit crimes."[2] However, because of their limitation in intellectual functioning, many believe that mentally retarded individuals do not act with the same moral culpability as individuals who are not mentally retarded and therefore they should not be executed. The Supreme Court has twice addressed whether the Eighth Amendment prohibits the execution

---

1 www.aamr.org/content_100.cfm?navID=21.
2 *Atkins v. Virginia*, 536 U.S. 304 (2002).

of mentally retarded persons. The first case involved John Paul Penry.[3] Although Penry was an adult when he raped and murdered Pamela Carpenter, he had the reasoning capacity of a seven-year old and his ability to function in the world was that of a nine- or 10-year-old. He was born with organic brain damage caused by trauma to the brain at birth. His condition was aggravated by the abuse he suffered as a child. His mother struck Penry on the head, broke his arm several times, burned him with cigarette butts, and forced him to eat his own feces and drink urine. He dropped out of first grade and his aunt spent a year just trying to teach him to sign his name. He was unable to recite the alphabet and could not count. I.Q. testing over the years revealed Penry's I.Q. to be between 50 and 63, which indicates mild to moderate retardation.

Penry argued that because his reasoning capacity was that of a seven-year-old, his execution would be disproportionate to his moral culpability. Specifically, Penry argued that "because of his diminished ability to control his impulses, to think in long-range terms, and to learn from his mistakes, he 'is not capable of acting with the degree of culpability that can justify the ultimate penalty.'"[4] The Court refused to hold that the Constitution categorically prohibited the execution of all mentally retarded individuals. According to the Court, it could not conclude that all mentally retarded individuals "inevitably lack the cognitive, volitional, and moral capacity to act with the degree of culpability associated with the death penalty."[5] Also important to the Court was that at the time of its decision, Georgia was the only state that had categorically prohibited the execution of mentally retarded individuals and hence such executions were not unusual. The Court did hold that during the sentencing proceeding, a defendant had the right to present evidence of his mental retardation as a mitigating factor that diminished his moral culpability.

Thirteen years later, the Court confronted the issue again in *Atkins v. Virginia*.[6] Atkins was convicted of abduction, armed robbery, and capital murder and sentenced to death. During the sentencing phase of his case, Atkins presented expert testimony that he was mildly mentally retarded. This conclusion was based on the fact that Atkins had an I.Q. of 59, and also on the expert's interviews with people who knew Atkins and on his school and court records. The government's expert concluded that Atkins was of "average intelligence, at least" and diagnosed Atkins as having antisocial personality disorder.[7] According to the majority, the Court's previous decision in *Penry* had to be reexamined "in light of the dramatic shift in the state legislative landscape that has occurred in the past 13 years."[8] The Court cited the number of state legislatures that had enacted bans on executing

---

3   *Penry v. Lynaugh*, 492 U.S. 302 (1989).
4   *Id.* at 336.
5   *Id.* at 338.
6   536 U.S. 304 (2002).
7   *Id.* at 309.
8   *Id.* at 310.

mentally retarded offenders since the *Penry* decision and concluded that "[i]t is not so much the number of these States that is significant, but the consistency of the direction of change ... [that] provides powerful evidence that today our society views mentally retarded offenders as categorically less culpable than the average criminal."[9] The Court concluded that "the practice, therefore, [of executing mentally retarded individuals] has become truly unusual, and it is fair to say that a national consensus has developed against it."[10] The Court further concluded that the execution of mentally retarded defendants failed to contribute measurably to the goals of deterrence or retribution. Mentally retarded individuals are not as deterrable as others because they are less likely to be able to process the information regarding the possibility of execution and control their conduct based on that information. As for retribution, their mental impairment makes them less culpable and therefore less deserving of the death penalty. Finally, the Court believed that the risk would be too high that mentally retarded individuals would be executed even though they are not the most culpable offenders given the fact that many would be unable to give meaningful assistance to their attorneys, make poor witnesses, and that their demeanor may portray a lack of remorse for their crimes. The Court did not require any specific procedure for determining those offenders who are mentally retarded, but rather left that task to the states.

In Justice Scalia's dissenting view, "seldom has an opinion of this Court rested so obviously upon nothing but the personal views of its Members."[11] Justice Scalia challenged the majority's assertion that a national consensus had formed against executing the mentally retarded. He also expressed his concern that mental retardation can readily be feigned:

[o]ne need only read the definitions ... to realize that the symptoms of this condition can readily be feigned. And whereas the capital defendant who feigns insanity risks commitment to a mental institution until he can be cured (and then tried and executed), the capital defendant who feigns mental retardation risks nothing at all.[12]

This is obviously a serious concern. However, a viable claim of mental retardation cannot be made by a desperate inmate on the eve of his execution. A successful claim would require evidence of retardation from adolescence, such as school records and I.Q. tests. Moreover, mental health professionals are trained to detect whether an inmate is feigning his condition. Next I will review the procedures that the states adopted in order to implement *Atkins* and address Justice Scalia's concerns.

9   *Id.* at 315–16.
10   *Id.* at 316.
11   *Id.* at 338 (Scalia, J., dissenting).
12   *Id.* at 353.

The Court left to the states the task of actually implementing its decision. Specifically, the states are free to define mental retardation and to decide whether the determination of mental retardation will be made by a judge or jury, whether the determination is to be made before trial or during the sentencing phase, and the burden of proof. Some believe that by investing the states with these crucial decisions the Court leaves too much room for reluctant states to avoid its decision and as a result some defendants who are mentally retarded will be executed. The case of Milton Mathis is a good example of why some are concerned with vesting the states with the authority to make the determination. Mathis was sentenced to death in Texas. Prior to the *Atkins* decision, the Texas Department of Corrections administered an I.Q. test to Mathis. The test determined that he had an I.Q. in the 60s. In addition, Mathis failed the first, fifth, and eighth grades and dropped out of high school in the ninth grade. After the *Atkins* decision was announced, he made a claim that he could not be executed because of his mental retardation. The prosecutor challenged Mathis's assertion that he was retarded by claiming that he was "street smart." The courts rejected Mathis's mental retardation claim and he was executed.

State Procedures

In this section I will review the procedures that a few active death penalty states have adopted for determining whether an inmate is mentally retarded. The states have generally been in agreement in defining mental retardation by adopting the definition in the DSM, although a few states have adopted a more restrictive definition, for instance, by requiring an I.Q. of less than 70. However, the states have not been consistent in assigning the responsibility for determining whether the defendant is retarded. Some states invest this authority in the judge, while others place the responsibility on the jury. As will be seen, whether the factfinder is a judge or the jury is often outcome determinative. The states also disagree on the burden of proof the defendant must satisfy in order to prove that he is retarded. Some states place on the defendant the burden of proving that he is retarded by a preponderance of evidence; others require clear and convincing proof; while a few even require proof beyond a reasonable doubt. Obviously the burden of proof can be outcome determinative.

In Texas, the legislature did not enact any legislation in response to the Supreme Court's decision. Since there are so many death row inmates in Texas, the courts were left with the responsibility for determining the procedure for adjudicating mental retardation claims in Texas. The Texas Court of Criminal Appeals used a definition of mental retardation previously adopted by the legislature: "significant subaverage general intellectual functioning that is concurrent with deficits in adaptive behavior and originates during the developmental period."[13] The

---

13   *Ex parte Briseno*, 135 S.W.3d, 1, 6 (Tex. Cr. App. 2004).

Court held that the defendant has the burden of proving that he is retarded by a preponderance of the evidence and that this determination is to be made by the jury during the sentencing phase.[14] Arkansas, like most states, defines mental retardation the same as Texas.[15] In Arkansas, there is a rebuttable presumption that a defendant with an I.Q. of 65 or less is retarded. Otherwise, the defendant has the burden of proving mental retardation by a preponderance of the evidence. The defendant must claim that he is mentally retarded prior to trial and the determination is made by the judge before trial commences. If the judge determines that he is not mentally retarded, the defendant can raise the issue before the jury during the sentencing proceeding.

In Florida, the defendant must prove to a judge by clear and convincing evidence that he is retarded.[16] In Oklahoma, the defendant has to prove to a judge that he is retarded by clear and convincing evidence in an evidentiary hearing prior to trial.[17] A defendant with an I.Q. score of 76 or above cannot successfully claim to be mentally retarded. In North Carolina, the determination of whether a capital defendant is mentally retarded is made prior to trial before the judge.[18] The defendant must prove by clear and convincing evidence that he is retarded. In Alabama, the trial judge determines whether a preponderance of the evidence proves that the defendant is mentally retarded.[19] In Georgia, a defendant must prove to a jury that he is mentally retarded beyond a reasonable doubt.[20] In Virginia, the jury makes the determination during sentencing and the defendant must prove he is retarded by a preponderance of evidence.[21] In California, the state with the largest death row in the nation, the judge decides whether the defendant is mentally retarded by a preponderance of the evidence.[22] Finally in Ohio, the only state outside the south that carries out a significant number of executions, the judge decides prior to trial and the burden is on the defendant to prove he is retarded by a preponderance of the evidence.[23]

In most states in which the judge makes the initial determination, the defendant can submit the issue to a jury should the judge find that defendant is not retarded. Table 5.1 provides a summary of the procedures in the leading death penalty states.

---

14   *Neal v. State*, 256 S.W.3d 264, 272 (Tex. Cr. App. 2008).
15   Ark. Code Ann. § 5-4-618 (2007).
16   Fla. Stat. § 921.137(4) (2010).
17   Okla. Stat. Ann. tit. 21, § 701.10(b) (2007).
18   N.C. Gen. Stat. § 15A-2005(a)(1)(c) (2007).
19   *Ex parte Edward Perkins*, 851 So.2d 453 (Ala. 2002).
20   Ga. Code Ann. § 17-7-131(a)(3) (2007).
21   Va. Code Ann. § 19.2-264.3:1.1 (2007).
22   Cal. Pen. Code § 13.76(b)(1).
23   *State v. Lott*, 97 Ohio St.3d 303 (2002).

Table 5.1   State procedures to determine mental retardation

State	Factfinder	Burden of Proof
Alabama	Judge	Preponderance
Arkansas	Judge	Preponderance
California	Judge	Preponderance
Florida	Judge	Clear and convincing
Georgia	Jury	Beyond a reasonable doubt
North Carolina	Judge	Clear and convincing
Ohio	Judge	Preponderance
Oklahoma	Judge	Clear and convincing
Texas	Jury	Preponderance
Virginia	Jury	Preponderance

As the synopsis in Table 5.1 indicates, there is tremendous variation in the procedures adopted by the states. The procedures adopted are important since they can have an effect on the substantive right. Some of the procedures the states have adopted appear to be problematic. For instance, some states require the decision whether the defendant is retarded to be made by the same jury that sentences the defendant to death, whereas others allow the judge to make the determination prior to the trial commencing. There is a strong risk of prejudice when the jury makes the determination since they have been exposed to the circumstances of the offense or the consequences of the factual determination regarding mental retardation.

The burden of proof also varies tremendously. Some states require the defendant to prove by a preponderance of the evidence that he is retarded, while others have adopted a much higher burden of proof such as clear and convincing evidence or even proof beyond a reasonable doubt of retardation. The burden of proof a state adopts will obviously affect whether the inmate will be able to prove retardation, especially in borderline cases where there are multiple I.Q. tests. Moreover, every state requires that the defendant prove that he was mentally retarded before his 18th birthday. This may be difficult for poor inmates whose I.Q. was never tested during adolescence, or whose need for special education was never met, or who dropped out of school at an earlier age. A foreign national would also have difficulty establishing that he was mentally retarded during his adolescence. It is doubtful that an individual from a poor third world nation received special education or I.Q. tests while growing up. Moreover, many foreign nationals have not received any formal schooling. Despite these problems, the U.S. Supreme Court has not reviewed any state's procedures implementing the ban on executing mentally retarded individuals.

Given the procedural variations it is not surprising that the success rate for mental retardation claims varies widely from state to state. One study of the success rate of *Atkins* claims in North Carolina and Alabama found that defendants were considerably more successful in North Carolina.[24] The authors of the study compared the success rates in these two states between 2002 and 2008. Their data indicates that North Carolina courts adjudicated at least 21 *Atkins* claims and have determined that 17 of these defendants were mentally retarded, a success rate of about 80 percent. By contrast, Alabama courts adjudicated at least 26 *Atkins* claims during the same time period and found only three of these claims to be meritorious, a success rate of about 12 percent. Since the burden of proof is higher in North Carolina (clear and convincing) than in Alabama (preponderance of evidence), these findings are surprising and suggest that other factors are at least equally important. The authors of the study, for instance, attribute the disparity between the states to the greater availability of funding in North Carolina to adjudicate mental retardation claims. The authors attribute the disparities to additional factors:

> Moreover, Alabama, unlike North Carolina, defines mental retardation more restrictively than do either of the professional organizations cited by the Supreme Court; it applies a strict IQ cutoff and assesses adaptive functioning deficits by focusing on what the claimant can do rather than focusing, as those clinical definitions require, on the individual's limitations. This suggests that success rate may be related to the jurisdiction's general sensitivity to capital cases, the state courts' interpretation of the *Atkins* requirement that it "generally conform" to clinical definitions of mental retardation, or both.[25]

In order to fully understand the impact of the *Atkins* decision, I compiled data for some of the other leading death penalty states. The data represents every reported decision in which an appellate court decided a contested *Atkins* claim on the merits between 2002 and 2010. It is quite possible, however, that these numbers may not include every successful *Atkins* claim. For instance, it is likely that on occasion the defendant was able to prove to either a judge or jury that he was mentally retarded and the case proceeded without the possibility of a death sentence being imposed. Furthermore, it is possible that there might be a few instances in which the prosecution conceded that the defendant was mentally retarded. The findings below, however, are not likely to be skewed significantly by such cases given the infrequency in which either of these events is likely to have occurred. In addition, although the findings consist of only the success rate on appeal and not at trial, the appellate court applies the state standard for determining mental retardation that would be applied at trial. Therefore, these findings and the study discussed earlier are likely to be fairly representative of the success rate of *Atkins* claims in each state.

In Texas, there were 55 reported instances of death row inmates claiming to be mentally retarded. Twelve of these defendants were successful, resulting in a

24 J.H. Blume et al., *An Empirical Look at Atkins vs. Virginia and its Application in Capital Cases*, 76 Tenn. L. Rev. 625 (2009).
25 *Id.* at 629.

success rate of 22 percent. In Virginia, six inmates claimed to be mentally retarded but none were successful, including the defendant in *Atkins v. Virginia*.[26] Likewise, none of the three Georgia defendants who asserted that they were retarded were successful. In Oklahoma, seven of 14 inmates were successful in proving that they were mentally retarded, a success rate of 50 percent. In Ohio, five of 18 defendants were able to prove that they were retarded, a success rate of 28 percent. In Florida, only one of 14 inmates was successful in asserting an *Atkins* claim, a success rate of 7 percent. Finally, in Arkansas, one of two defendants was successful, a 50 percent success rate but a very small sample. The findings are summarized in Table 5.2.

Table 5.2   Percentage of successful retardation claims by state

State	Total Cases	Successful	Percentage
Alabama	26	3	12
Arkansas	2	1	50
Florida	14	1	7
Georgia	3	0	0
North Carolina	21	17	80
Ohio	18	5	28
Oklahoma	14	7	50
Texas	55	12	22
Virginia	6	0	0

In the four states with the highest success rates (North Carolina, Arkansas, Oklahoma and Ohio) the judge decides whether the inmate is retarded prior to trial. In two of the four states with the lowest rates of success (Virginia, Georgia) the jury makes the determination whether the defendant is mentally retarded after hearing the details of the crime and the aggravating evidence offered by the prosecution in favor of a death sentence. The data suggests that whether the determination is made by a judge or jury is the most significant factor – although other factors, such as whether the definition of mental retardation is restrictive or flexible and the funding provided for experts, is also crucial. The burden of proof does not appear to have as much impact on the outcome. For instance, the success rate in North Carolina is 80 percent and much higher than most states despite the fact that the defendant has the burden of proving that he is retarded by clear and convincing evidence. The success rate is also high in Oklahoma despite the fact that the defendant has to prove by clear and convincing evidence that he is retarded. The success rate in Virginia and Alabama is low even though the defendant's burden of proof is only preponderance of the evidence.

26   Atkins's death sentence was commuted to life on other grounds.

Scalia's Concerns

First, Justice Scalia was concerned that inmates would be able to easily feign claims of mental retardation in order to avoid their execution. The states have addressed this concern by requiring proof of mental retardation prior to the defendant's 18th birthday. Furthermore, the numbers do not bear this out as most defendants have been unsuccessful in claiming mental retardation. Second, Justice Scalia was concerned that the courts would be burdened with many frivolous claims. During the eight years following the decision, this has not been the case. Texas, for instance, has had more *Atkins* claims than any other state; but Texas also has a very large death row population, so that is to be expected. However, the number of inmates claiming to be mentally retarded in Texas represents less than 10 percent of its death row population. In other states, only a minuscule number of inmates have claimed to be mentally retarded. The numbers fail to substantiate the claim that inmates will be able to easily manipulate the definition of mental retardation or that the courts will be swamped with inmates making *Atkins* claims.

Insanity

It is not surprising that the conditions on death row often create or exacerbate inmates' mental problems. For example, death row inmates in Texas are housed alone in small cells measuring 6½ feet by 10 feet, containing a bed and a toilet, for 23 hours a day. They are allowed to leave their cells for one hour a day of recreation, which is also done alone. They have no access to television. Their access to other humans is extremely limited. They are allowed one non-attorney visitor a week for two hours. They are not allowed conjugal visits. They even meet with their attorneys through glass partitions. They receive meals in their cells. Death row inmates in Texas are not allowed to participate in work programs. They literally do not have any physical contact with another human being from the moment that they are incarcerated on death row until the day of their execution. Given these harsh conditions, the Court has had to decide whether there are any circumstances in which an inmate's mental illness becomes so severe that the state is precluded from carrying out his execution.

The American Bar Association (ABA) has recommended a two-prong test for determining whether a death row inmate suffering from mental illness should be executed:

> (a) Convicts who have been sentenced to death should not be executed if they are currently mentally incompetent. If it is determined that a condemned convict is currently mentally incompetent, execution should be stayed.

(b) A convict is incompetent to be executed if, as a result of mental illness or mental retardation, the convict cannot understand the nature of the pending proceedings, what he or she was tried for, the reasons for the punishment or the nature of the punishment. A convict is also incompetent if, as a result of mental illness or mental retardation, the convict lacks sufficient capacity to recognize or understand any fact which might exist which would make the punishment unjust or unlawful, or lacks the ability to convey such information to counsel or the court.[27]

The ABA Standard sets forth a two-prong test when inquiring into the competency of a defendant who has been sentenced to death. The first requires that the defendant be able to recognize the nature of the punishment and the reason for the punishment. The second requires that the defendant be able to assist counsel or the court in identifying exculpatory or mitigating information. In *Ford v. Wainwright*,[28] the Supreme Court adopted the first prong of the ABA Standard but rejected the second prong.

After Alvin Bernard Ford was convicted of murder and sentenced to death, he became increasingly delusional. He believed that he had become a target of a complex conspiracy involving the Ku Klux Klan designed to force him to commit suicide. He believed that his family members were being tortured and sexually abused as part of the conspiracy. He also believed that 135 of his family and friends had been taken hostage along with senators and many other leaders. He referred to himself as "Pope John Paul III" and reported having appointed nine new justices to the Florida Supreme Court. The U.S. Supreme Court was asked by Ford's lawyers to determine whether his insanity prevented the state from executing him. The Court gave three primary reasons for holding that the execution of the insane violates the prohibition on cruel and unusual punishment. First, the Court noted that the common law prohibited the execution of prisoners who had become insane. Second, the Court held that the execution of an insane individual does not serve one of the death penalty's critical justifications: retribution. The death penalty's retributive function is only served if the inmate is aware of his execution and the purpose of his execution. Third, the execution of insane individuals was cruel in that it deprived the inmate of an opportunity to prepare, mentally and spiritually, for his death. As with mental retardation, the Court gave the states discretion in defining insanity; but at a minimum, the definition must include individuals who fail to understand that they are being executed and the connection of their execution to the crime they committed. The Court also held that the determination of whether an inmate could be executed had to be made at a hearing in which the defendant was permitted to present evidence regarding his mental state.

---

27   ABA Criminal Justice Mental Health Standards § 7-5.6.
28   477 U.S. 399 (1986).

The Court's decision in *Ford v. Wainwright* has had little effect. One of the most notorious cases involved Arkansas death row inmate Ricky Ray Rector.[29] After shooting and killing a police officer, Rector unsuccessfully attempted suicide by shooting himself in the forehead. The trauma to his forehead resulted in the severance of about 3 inches of the frontal lobe, commonly referred to as a frontal lobotomy. As a result of the frontal lobotomy, Rector suffered from gross memory loss. When dealing with content and meaning he was severely impaired and would have a near-total inability to conceptualize beyond a response to immediate sensations or provocations. In fact, he seemed unable to grasp either the concept of past or future. Prior to his execution, mental health experts found that Rector would be unable to work in a collaborative, cooperative environment with his attorney, although they did find that he knew he was being executed. The court of appeals held that Rector was not insane because he knew that he was being executed for the crime that he committed. That holding was called into question by Rector's conduct prior to his execution. For instance, just hours before his execution, Rector and his attorney watched news broadcasts of his execution and Governor Bill Clinton's denial of his clemency request. He told his attorney "I'm gonna vote for him. Gonna vote for Clinton."[30] Rector ate all of his last meal except for his dessert, a large portion of pecan pie, which he put aside to be eaten later – after his execution. His execution became entangled in presidential politics as it was scheduled during the 1992 presidential campaign and received a lot of attention since Governor Bill Clinton of Arkansas was seeking the presidency. Clinton returned to Arkansas to oversee Rector's execution and refused to grant clemency despite Rector's obvious mental deficiencies. Pundits and political analysts have speculated that Clinton wanted to appear tough on crime and used Rector's execution to send that message to the voters.

There were other troubling cases in which the lower courts determined that an inmate was competent to be executed despite indications that the inmate was not completely in touch with reality. In *Garrett v. Collins*,[31] Garrett was found to be sane despite his belief that he would escape death through the supernatural intervention of his aunt. In *Patterson v. Dretke*,[32] the petitioner was mentally ill and expressed his delusional belief that he would be given amnesty. A mental health expert expressed doubt about his rational and factual understanding of his impending execution. The Court found that he was competent because of writings in which Patterson repeatedly sought a stay of execution. An Indiana court thought that it was irrelevant that the petitioner believed that "God will turn back the clock to before the killings" because of his good behavior in prison.[33] The petitioner had also been preoccupied with matters that would occur after he was executed. In

---

29   *Rector v. Clark*, 923 F.2d 570 (8th Cir. 1991).

30   M. Frady, *Death in Arkansas*, The New Yorker, Feb. 23, 1993 at 105, 111.

31   951 F.2d 57 (5th Cir. 1992).

32   370 F.3d 480 (5th Cir. 2004).

33   *Baird v. State*, 833 N.E.2d 28 (Ind. 2005).

Lowenfield v. Butler,[34] the petitioner was a paranoid schizophrenic and unable to understand the death penalty, but was found nonetheless to be competent.

Because the lower courts were focused solely on whether the inmate knew that he was being executed, the Court subsequently tried to convey to the lower courts that the meaning of insanity was broader than that. Scott Panetti[35] sought to represent himself at his capital murder trial. A court-ordered psychiatric examination revealed that he suffered from a fragmented personality, delusions, and hallucinations. He was prescribed medication that would be difficult for a person not suffering from extreme psychosis even to tolerate. At his trial, he engaged in behavior described as "bizarre," "scary," and "trance-like." His condition worsened after his trial. He continued to suffer from severe delusions. For instance, he believed that the state wanted to execute him in order to stop him from preaching. As is frequently the case, the state claimed that he was feigning his condition. According to the Supreme Court, an inmate is not sane simply because he is aware of the fact that he is going to be executed: "A prisoner's awareness of the State's rationale for an execution is not the same as a rationale understanding of it." The inmate must understand the "meaning and purpose of the punishment to which he has been sentenced" in order to be executed. Otherwise, according to the Court, the retributive justification for capital punishment is not achieved:

> it might be said that capital punishment is imposed because it has the potential to make the offender recognize at last the gravity of his crime and to allow the community as a whole including the surviving family and friends of the victim to affirm its own judgment that the culpability of the prisoner is so serious that the ultimate penalty must be sought and imposed. The potential for a prisoner's recognition of the severity of the offense and the objective of community vindication are called into question, however, if the prisoner's mental state is so distorted by a mental illness that his awareness of the crime and punishment has little or no relation to the understanding of those concepts shared by the community as a whole.[36]

Panetti makes it clear that an inmate is not mentally competent to be executed simply because he is aware of his execution. Defendants, however, who have exhibited delusional thinking regarding their impending execution have the greatest chance for success. As the Court articulated in *Panetti*, "[g]ross delusions stemming from a severe mental disorder may put an awareness of a link between a crime and its punishment in a context so far removed from reality that the punishment can serve no proper purpose."[37] Since *Panetti*, the lower courts have found merit to insanity claims where there is evidence that the inmate suffers from

---

34   485 U.S. 995 (1988) (Brennan, J., dissenting).

35   *Panetti v. Quarterman*, 551 U.S. 930 (2007).

36   *Id.* at 958–9.

37   *Id.* at 960.

a delusional thought process regarding his pending execution, even though he may in fact be aware of its occurrence.[38]

Medication of Inmates

The state is not permanently barred from executing an inmate who satisfies the Supreme Court's insanity standard. In the event that an inmate is determined to be mentally incompetent to be executed, the inmate's pending execution is stayed until such time that he becomes mentally competent. This raises the question whether the state can accelerate the inmate's competence by treating him with antipsychotic drugs against his will.

The United States Supreme Court has not directly addressed the issue of whether the states are allowed to medicate an inmate in order to execute him. The Court has, however, addressed whether it is appropriate for the state to medicate an inmate against his will in order to make the inmate competent to stand trial.[39] The Court has held that an inmate could not be medicated solely for the purpose of rendering him competent to stand trial. The Court did hold that an inmate could be involuntarily medicated in order to stand trial in certain circumstances. An inmate can be medicated if the treatment is medically appropriate, is substantially unlikely to have side effects that may undermine the fairness of the trial, and if there are no less intrusive alternatives. By analogy, he Court might allow an inmate scheduled to be executed to be involuntarily medicated if there was a medical necessity – for instance, if the inmate was actually worse off without the medication – and if there were no less intrusive alternatives. Only one lower federal court has had to confront this issue.[40] Eighteen years after Charles Singleton had been sentenced to death he was placed on an involuntary medication regime after it was determined that his psychosis made him a danger to himself and others. After the medication took effect his symptoms subsided. He claimed that he would be incompetent to be executed but for the medication that he was forcibly administered. He conceded that he was competent while medicated, but he argued that as soon as he discontinued

---

38 See e.g., *Billot v. Epps*, 671 F. Supp.2d 840, 881 (S.D. Miss. 2009) (finding that the defendant was insane and could not be executed even though he was aware of his imminent execution based on a delusion that he would be sent to mental hospital and then released); *Wood v. Quarterman*, 572 F. Supp. 2d 814, 818 (W.D. Texas 2008) ("petitioner's allegedly delusional statements to mental health expert near time of petitioner's trial and his subsequent statements to his state and federal habeas counsel, at least arguably suggest petitioner lacks a rational understanding of the causal link between his role in the criminal offense and the reason he has been sentenced to death"); *Thompson v. Bell*, 580 F.3d 423, 436 (6th Cir. 2009) (citing Thompson's "long documented history of delusions and psychosis" as one of the reasons Thompson was entitled to a hearing on his competency to be executed).

39 *Sell v. United States*, 539 U.S. 166 (2003).

40 *Singleton v. Norris*, 319 F.3d 1018 (8th Cir. 2003).

the medication he would be incompetent to be executed and that the state could not render him competent by forcibly medicating him. The Eighth Circuit found that the medication was medically necessary since it kept his symptoms under control. The Eighth Circuit also found that there were no less intrusive means of treating his psychosis short of medication. As a result, the Eighth Circuit upheld the forced medication of Singleton and he was subsequently executed.

Volunteers

The first scheduled execution after the death penalty was reinstated in 1976 involved Gary Gilmore. Gilmore attempted suicide six days after telling the Utah Supreme Court that he did not wish to pursue his appeals. Both the Utah Supreme Court and the United States Supreme Court allowed Gilmore to waive his appeals and he was executed.[41] More than 100 inmates have also waived their appeals and volunteered to be executed since 1976.[42] Whether an inmate sentenced to death ought to be allowed to waive his appeals is a controversial issue. Those who favor allowing inmates to waive their appeals are usually in favor of capital punishment. They argue that the decision whether to appeal a conviction is vested in the client in non-capital cases and should likewise be made by the client even in capital cases. They also argue that, by volunteering, the inmate is accepting his punishment – which he should have a right to do. Those who believe that death row inmates should not be allowed to waive their appeals make several arguments in opposition. First, they argue that allowing an inmate to waive his appeals amounts to nothing more than state-assisted suicide. Second, they argue that the decision by a death row inmate to waive his appeals is really coerced and not voluntary given the horrible conditions of death row. Third, the inmate ought not to be allowed to waive his appeals in order to ensure that death is the appropriate punishment. Justice Marshall argued that without appellate review "an unacceptably high percentage of criminal defendants would be wrongfully executed" either "because they were innocent of the crime, undeserving of the severest punishment relative to similarly situated offenders, or denied essential procedural protections by the State."[43] For instance, an individual may feel hopeless and waive his appeals despite the fact that he is innocent, or an egregious constitutional violation may never be remedied because of the lack of appellate review.

When a death row inmate wishes to waive his appeals he also creates a dilemma for his attorneys. Should the attorney accept the client's wishes or fight them? The attorney has several professional obligations to his client which may be in conflict with the client's desire to waive his appeals. An attorney is required to zealously

41 *Gilmore v. Utah*, 429 U.S. 1012 (1976).
42 Information on volunteers available at http://www.deathpenaltyinfo.org/information-defendants-who-were-executed-1976-and-designated-volunteers.
43 *Whitmore v. Arkansas*, 495 U.S. 149, 171 (1990) (Marshall, J., dissenting).

represent his client. Furthermore, as the ABA Guidelines for the Performance of Counsel in Death Penalty Cases provides:

> Some clients will initially insist that they want to be executed – as punishment or because they believe they would rather die than spend the rest of their lives in prison … It is ineffective assistance of counsel to simply acquiesce to such wishes, which usually reflect overwhelming feelings of guilt or despair rather than a rational decision.[44]

The ABA Guidelines also place on an attorney the duty of conducting a thorough investigation.[45] According to the Guidelines this investigation should be conducted irrespective of the wishes of the client.[46] The Guidelines also place on the attorney for a death row inmate the duty of litigating all potentially meritorious claims. The Supreme Court has applied a competency standard to death row inmates who seek to waive their appeals.[47] The first question the courts must resolve is whether the inmate has a rational and factual understanding of the consequences of his decision. The next question for the courts to resolve is whether the inmate's waiver is knowing, intelligent, and voluntary. This requires a showing that the inmate understands the rights that he is waiving and that he was not coerced into waiving these rights. One scholar who has studied the issue of volunteers rejects the Supreme Court's approach because in many cases it allows the state to assist an inmate in committing suicide.[48] Blume's study revealed that it is the desire of most volunteers to commit suicide.[49] Although the Supreme Court does not require courts to delve into the motivation of the inmate waiving his appeals, he argues that the courts should be required to do so. He proposes that the courts should base a decision on whether the inmate should be allowed to waive not just on the inmate's mental competency but also on whether the inmate is volunteering to accept his punishment or is trying to commit suicide:

> If, in a particular case, a desire to accept the justness of the imposed punishment motivates the individual, then the only barrier to waiver to further appeals should be incompetency. But if a desire to commit suicide motivates the particular death-row inmate, then that desire should not be accommodated.[50]

---

44 American Bar Association Guidelines for the Performance of Defense Counsel in Death Penalty Cases (2003) at 10.5 comm. p. 71.

45 *Id.* at 10.7.

46 *Id.*

47 *Gilmore v. Utah*, 429 U.S. 1012 (1976).

48 J.H. Blume, *Killing the Willing: "Volunteers," Suicide and Competency*, 103 Michigan Law Review 939 (2005).

49 *Id.* at 967.

50 *Id.* at 968.

One final issue that has arisen with regard to volunteers is whether an inmate ought to be allowed to commit suicide. Inmates whose executions are imminent are placed on suicide watch. Occasionally, however, an inmate is able to make an attempt to kill himself. An Ohio inmate tried to kill himself nine days before his scheduled execution by overdosing on pills he had stockpiled on death row. Ohio spent $6,000 on medical bills to successfully treat him. He was executed as scheduled. David Lee Herman slashed his throat and slit his wrist just 24 hours prior to his scheduled execution. He was flown from death row in Huntsville, Texas, to the prison hospital in Galveston, Texas, where he was successfully treated. He was then flown back to Huntsville for his execution, which proceeded as scheduled. The question arises as to why the state would revive someone who wants to die, and whom the state will soon execute. An obvious argument for allowing death row inmates to commit suicide is that since they are going to be executed anyway, suicide would save the state money and resources. Ohio and Texas spent a lot of money treating these inmates, only to execute them a short time later. There are two primary reasons the state provides medical treatment for death row inmates who attempt to take their own life. First, the state is constitutionally required to provide medical treatment to inmates.[51] Second, the retributive function of capital punishment would not be served by allowing an inmate to kill himself. The retributive function is only served if the state executes the individual and he is aware of the purpose of his execution. The inmate who kills himself "cheats" the state out of its right to execute him.

Conclusion

Because of their depraved upbringings and the conditions they face during their incarceration, many individuals on death row suffer from mental illness. The Supreme Court has set broad parameters – prohibiting the execution of the mentally retarded and those who become insane – while leaving important procedural details, such as the definition of mental retardation, the burden of proof, the identity of the factfinder, to the states. As this chapter illustrates, the flaw in this approach is the lack of uniformity, which heightens the risk of unjust executions.

---

51   *Estelle v. Gamble*, 429 U.S. 97, 103 (1976).

Chapter 6
Death Penalty Procedures and Appeals

The Process

The appeals process is an integral part of carrying out the death penalty. Death penalty cases proceed in three stages (Table 6.1). First, there is the trial and a direct appeal in the event that the defendant is convicted. Second, the defendant must ask the state courts to review his conviction for any constitutional errors by filing a writ of habeas corpus. Third, if unsuccessful in state court, the defendant can seek relief in federal court for any constitutional violations that occurred during trial or during the process of convicting him.

Table 6.1   Death penalty appeals process

Direct Appeal	State Habeas	Federal Habeas
Trial	Trial court	U.S. district court
State High Court	State High Court	U.S. Court of Appeals
U.S. Supreme Court	U.S. Supreme Court	U.S. Supreme Court

The process of convicting and sentencing an individual to death differs substantially from the ordinary criminal process. There are numerous and very complex rules and procedures that apply solely to capital cases. I will therefore review the process and the special rules that apply to each stage of the process.

Prosecutorial Discretion

Prosecutors are the most important actors in the criminal justice system. Their power is awesome. They decide whether to prosecute, whom to prosecute, which crimes to charge, and the number of charges to be brought. Although the grand jury is supposed to be a check on prosecutorial power and discretion, prosecutors tend to control the grand jury process: the fox is guarding the henhouse.[1] Prosecutors also decide whether to plea-bargain with a defendant, allowing them to have a tremendous influence over the sentences meted out. Indeed, in most states,

---

1   William J. Campbell, *Eliminate the Grand Jury*, J. Crim. L. & Criminology 174 (1973).

prosecutors alone have the power to request the death penalty in murder cases. Despite the fact that prosecutorial decisions are sometimes affected by political and other extralegal considerations, the Supreme Court's jurisprudence has rendered much of this decisionmaking virtually unreviewable.[2]

Once a crime has occurred and a suspect has been apprehended, the prosecutor has to decide whether to seek the death penalty. Absent proof of consciously intentional racial or similar discrimination,[3] prosecutors can do as they please. The only restraints the Supreme Court has placed on this decision are the limits it has placed on the crimes that are punishable by death. In *Coker v. Georgia*,[4] the Court had to decide whether the Eighth Amendment's ban on cruel and unusual punishment prohibited the execution of an individual convicted of a brutal rape who did not kill his victim. Coker had been incarcerated for raping three separate women, killing one, and attempting to kill another when he escaped from prison and brutally raped Elnita Carver. After he raped Mrs Carver, he told Mr Carver, who was present during the rape, that he would kill his wife if the police caught him because "[I] don't have nothing to lose – [I am in] prison for the rest of [my] life anyway." Mrs Carver was not physically harmed and Coker was subsequently apprehended.

Georgia law permitted the prosecutor to seek death for the rape and Coker was convicted and sentenced to death. The Supreme Court held that "a sentence of death is grossly disproportionate and excessive punishment for the crime of rape and is therefore forbidden by the Eighth Amendment as cruel and unusual punishment."[5] Crucial to the Court's decision is the fact that the rape victim does not die and therefore to kill the rapist would be excessive. In a controversial passage, the Court explained its rationale:

> Rape is without doubt deserving of serious punishment; but in terms of moral depravity and of the injury to the person and to the public, it does not compare with murder, which does involve the unjustified taking of human life. Although it may be accompanied by another crime, rape by definition does not include the death of or even the serious injury to another person. The murderer kills; the rapist, if no more than that, does not. Life is over for the victim of the murderer; for the rape victim, life may not be nearly so happy as it was, but it is not over and normally is not beyond repair. We have the abiding conviction that the death

2   *Ashe v. Swenson*, 397 U.S. 435, 452 (1970).

3   In *McCleskey v. Kemp*, 481 U.S. 279, 286–7 (1987), the Supreme Court held that a defendant needed "exceptionally clear proof" in order to sustain an allegation of an abuse of prosecutorial discretion based upon racial discrimination. In *United States v. Armstrong*, 517 U.S. 456, 458–61 (1996), the Court refused to permit discovery in a case alleging racial discrimination by the prosecutor in the charging and sentencing decision absent proof that similarly situated whites had not been prosecuted.

4   433 U.S. 584 (1977).

5   *Id.* at 592.

penalty, which is "unique in its severity and irrevocability," is an excessive penalty for the rapist who, as such, does not take human life.[6]

The Court was probably also concerned that allowing rape to be punishable by death would provide the perpetrator an incentive to kill the victim since he would be able to prevent the victim from testifying against him without facing any greater punishment for killing her. Because the Court used such sweeping language in striking down the death penalty for rape, the decision was interpreted as a prohibition on executing anyone for a crime other than murder. Although Justice Powell concurred in the decision not to execute Coker, he interpreted the Court's decision as prohibiting the death penalty for any crime that did not result in the death of the victim, and as a result he believed the Court had gone too far: "The plurality, however, does not limit its holding to the case before us or to similar cases. Rather, in an opinion that ranges well beyond what is necessary, it holds that capital punishment *always* – regardless of the circumstances – is a disproportionate penalty for the crime of rape."[7] Therefore, even though Congress has authorized the Department of Justice to seek the death penalty for several non-homicide offenses such as drug trafficking in large quantities, and a few states had authorized the death penalty for non-homicide crimes such as aggravated kidnapping, death was never imposed in these instances because *Coker* appeared to preclude it.

The law seemed settled until Louisiana enacted a statute authorizing the death penalty for the rape of a child under the age of 12. In Louisiana's view, the holding in *Coker* applied only to those who raped adult women. It did not apply to those who raped children. Patrick Kennedy was convicted of raping his eight-year-old stepdaughter and was sentenced to death pursuant to the Louisiana statute. The Court affirmed the holding in *Coker*:

> in determining whether the death penalty is excessive there is a distinction between intentional first-degree murder on the one hand and nonhomicide crimes against individual persons, even including child rape, on the other. The latter crime may be devastating in their harm, as here, but "in terms of moral depravity and of the injury to the person and to the public" they cannot be compared to murder in their "severity and irrevocability."[8]

The Court was also concerned with the effect that allowing the death penalty for rape would have on its efforts to narrow the death penalty to those "most deserving of death." Since child rape is much more prevalent than first degree murder, there would be many more death sentences; and the Court believed that a meaningful

---

6   *Id.* at 598.

7   *Id.* at 601 (Powell, J., concurring).

8   *Kennedy v. Louisiana*, 128 S. Ct. 2641, 2660 (2008) (quoting *Coker v. Georgia*, 433 U.S. 584, 598 (1977)).

distinction could not be made to limit the death penalty to certain child rapists and exclude others.

Prosecutors often seek to charge participants in a felony that results in death with felony murder. Felony murder is popular with prosecutors because it is a relatively easy crime to prove. If the prosecutor can prove that a dangerous felony such as rape, robbery, or kidnapping occurred, and that the defendant was a participant in the felony, then the defendant is guilty of felony murder. It is irrelevant whether the murder was intended or foreseen by the defendant. Given the popularity of felony murder, it is not surprising that the Supreme Court has twice had to deal with the issue of whether a person convicted of felony murder could be sentenced to death. In *Edmund v. Florida*,[9] the driver of the "getaway" car in an armed robbery of a dwelling was sentenced to death after the occupants of the house were killed by Edmund's accomplices. Because Edmund did not intend to kill, the Court held that he could not be sentenced to death. The Court, however, later modified this holding. In *Tison v. Arizona*,[10] the defendant assisted a convicted murderer in escaping from prison. During the escape, the inmate shot and killed a family while attempting to steal a car. The defendant participated in the theft of the car but was not present when the family was killed. The Court held that he could be sentenced to death even though he did not intend to kill since he was a major participant in the robbery of the family, and had acted with reckless indifference to human life by helping a convicted murderer escape from prison and arming him with a weapon.

The Court has not ruled out the possibility that the death penalty could be sought in cases of treason or espionage that do not result in death. The Court has otherwise been pretty clear in limiting the death penalty to crimes involving murder. Since there are many murderers, there has to be a procedure for determining the most culpable killers. Most states accomplish this goal by requiring the sentencer to balance aggravating and mitigating circumstances.

Trial and Sentencing

In *Gregg v. Georgia*,[11] the Court indicated that arbitrariness in the imposition of the death penalty could best be minimized by the use of bifurcated proceedings. Thus, death penalty cases occur in two phases. Phase one involves the trial itself and the determination of the defendant's responsibility for the crime. This phase is similar to most criminal trials, with two exceptions. First, indigent defendants facing the death penalty are assigned two defense attorneys. Second, more time is spent selecting the jury in capital cases than in non-capital cases.

---

9   549 U.S. 1132 (2007).

10   481 U.S. 137 (1987).

11   428 U.S. 153 (1976).

Death penalty cases diverge tremendously from non-capital cases during the sentencing phase. The Supreme Court has held that a defendant cannot be sentenced to death automatically upon conviction. This applies even to an individual who killed while serving a sentence of life without parole. Therefore, if the defendant is convicted, a sentencing hearing commences "at which the sentencing authority is apprised of the information relevant to the imposition of sentence and provided with standards to guide its use of the information."[12] In non-capital cases, a defendant's sentence is usually determined by a judge. Until recently, some states also empowered the judge to determine whether a defendant should receive a death sentence. In *Ring v. Arizona*,[13] the Supreme Court held that because of the defendant's constitutional right to a jury trial, the defendant can only be sentenced to death based on factors found by a jury. Thus, the trial judge can impose a death sentence but only on the basis of facts found by a jury. As a result of the Court's decision in *Ring*, the sentencing decision in capital cases is made by the jury in most states.

In order to sentence a defendant to death, the jury must find the existence of at least one aggravating factor in addition to the murder. According to the Court, the presence of at least one aggravating factor "serves the purpose of limiting the class of death-eligible defendants."[14] Aggravating factors differ from state to state. Some of the most common include: the killing of a law enforcement officer, murder for remuneration, the murder of a child, the killing of more than one person during the same criminal transaction, a premeditated murder, and an intentional killing during the commission or attempted commission of robbery, sexual assault, arson, burglary, or kidnapping.

Other evidence typically offered by the prosecution during the sentencing phase are: 1) the defendant's prior convictions; 2) the defendant's prior bad acts, even if these bad acts did not result in a conviction; and 3) victim impact statements. The admissibility of victim impact statements has been contentious and the subject of three separate, sharply divided decisions by the Supreme Court. As a result of the victims' rights movement, many states began to permit statements from family members of the deceased as to the impact that the loss of the deceased has had on their lives. In the first two cases challenging the admissibility of victim impact statements, a sharply divided Supreme Court held that victim impact testimony is not relevant to the sentencing phase because the victim is not on trial.[15] According to the majority, victim impact evidence does not even minimally assist the jury in determining the defendant's moral culpability and whether he should be executed. Furthermore, the Court held that such evidence is extremely prejudicial and appeals to the jury's emotions and therefore runs the risks that the sentencing

---

12 *Id.* at 153.
13 536 U.S. 584 (2002).
14 *Blystone v. Pennsylvania*, 494 U.S. 299, 306–7 (1990).
15 *Booth v. Maryland*, 482 U.S. 496 (1987).

decision will be based more on emotion than reason. Two years later, the Court reaffirmed this holding.[16]

Four years later, however, the Court overturned its two earlier decisions and held that victim impact testimony is admissible. The new majority's primary rationale for overturning the earlier decisions was that "the state has a legitimate interest in countering the mitigating evidence which the defendant is entitled to put in."[17] The majority also argued that victim impact testimony permits the jury to assess the specific harm resulting from the defendant's actions. Justice Marshall, however, did not believe that the majority had a principled reason for overturning the earlier decisions which had been reaffirmed just two years earlier. According to Justice Marshall, "power, not reason, is the new currency of this Court's decisionmaking" because "[n]either the law nor the facts supporting [the two earlier decisions] underwent any change in the last four years. Only the personnel of this Court did."[18]

In its holding that victim impact evidence did not violate the Eighth Amendment, the Court indicated that the prosecution did not have an unfettered right to present such testimony. The Court indicated that victim impact testimony would violate the defendant's rights "in the event that evidence is introduced that is so unduly prejudicial that it renders the trial fundamentally unfair."[19] For instance, family members are not allowed to give their opinions as to whether the defendant should be executed. However, victim impact evidence has been largely unregulated by the courts. Prosecutors have been allowed to present testimony from not only immediate family members but also from co-workers, friends, distant family members, and neighbors regarding the impact of the victim's death on them.

Victim impact evidence often creates a dilemma for defendants. After the prosecution presents a positive portrait of the victim, should the defendant counter with adverse evidence regarding the victim's character? For instance, suppose the prosecution presents the victim impact testimony of the victim's wife to the effect that the victim was a loving and devoted husband and father. The defense has evidence indicating that the husband committed adultery and was frequently absent from his children's lives. This evidence would directly contradict the prosecution's presentation, but defense counsel may alienate the jury by presenting adverse evidence regarding the murder victim. Another dilemma for the defense is whether and how much should the victim impact witness be cross-examined.

During the sentencing phase of a capital case, the defendant has a constitutional right to offer mitigation evidence. According to the Supreme Court, relevant mitigation evidence includes "any aspect of a defendant's character, or record and any of the circumstances of the offense that the defendant proffers as a basis

---

16   *South Carolina v. Gathers*, 409 U.S. 805 (1989).
17   *Payne v. Tennessee*, 501 U.S. 808, 825 (1991).
18   *Id.* at 844.
19   *Id.* at 825.

for a sentence less than death."[20] What is relevant mitigating evidence has been an enduring source of conflict. Defendants frequently proffer evidence of their horrendous upbringing, childhood abuse or neglect, evidence that they suffered from some mental illness short of insanity, or that they were beclouded by drugs or alcohol when they killed the victim. There is no question this evidence is mitigating and relevant and is therefore admissible. The Court has also held that the defendant's youthfulness is also relevant to the sentencing determination.[21] In *Penry v. Lynaugh*,[22] the fact that the defendant had a low I.Q. and suffered from organic brain damage was held to be admissible sentencing phase evidence. The Court has also held that a defendant's positive adjustment to prison is evidence the jury should consider in deciding whether to impose death.[23] In *Hitchcock v. Dugger*,[24] the Court held that the trial court's failure to permit consideration of evidence that the defendant was a "fond and affectionate uncle" was constitutional error.

Defendants will sometimes offer evidence regarding the circumstances of the crime for which they have been convicted. They will do so in order to inform the jury that they were minor participants in the crime or to diminish their general moral culpability, if for instance, they did not intend for the crime to be committed. In *Lockett v. Ohio*,[25] Sandra Lockett was the getaway driver in an armed robbery of a pawnshop. At her sentencing hearing, she attempted to offer as a mitigating circumstance the fact that she did not cause or intend the victim's death. Ohio law at the time did not allow the sentencer to consider such evidence in determining whether to sentence the defendant to death. The Court held, however, that evidence regarding the circumstances of the crime is mitigating evidence which a defendant facing death has a right to present.

Not all evidence a defendant offers during the sentencing phase is admissible. Courts do not permit the defendant to offer testimony from the family members of the victim to express their wish that the defendant not be sentenced to death. Lower courts have been divided over whether a defendant has the right to present "execution impact" evidence to the jury. Capital defendants are parents, spouses, brothers, sisters, and someone's child. Execution impact evidence is testimony from the defendant's family members regarding the impact that the defendant's execution will have on their lives. For instance, some family members may still rely on the defendant for emotional support even while he is incarcerated. The admissibility of execution impact evidence is the subject of significant disagreement among appellate courts. Some courts have admitted this evidence because "testimony by the relatives of a capital defendant may be informative

---

20 *Lockett v. Ohio*, 438 U.S. 586, 604 (1978).
21 *Eddings v. Oklahoma*, 455 U.S. 104 (1982).
22 492 U.S. 302 (1989).
23 *Skipper v. South Carolina*, 476 U.S. 1 (1986).
24 481 U.S. 393 (1987).
25 438 U.S. 586 (1976).

about certain aspects of the defendant's character."[26] These courts have found that although execution impact evidence is not direct evidence about the defendant's character or background, it does constitute valuable circumstantial evidence of his character by demonstrating that the defendant has the capacity to be of emotional value to others.[27] There is also the argument that the defendant should be allowed to present testimony about the impact that his execution will have on his family when the government presents victim impact testimony. As one judge commented:

> If the value of the victim's life is permitted to be brought before the jury, however, then I see no option under Supreme Court jurisprudence but to permit the defendant to counter this evidence with evidence of the value of his own life. The principles of relevance underlying F.R.E. [Federal Rules of Evidence] 403 as well as the fundamental guarantee of due process and fairness require the admission of defendant's countervailing evidence of a similar nature in order to prevent unfair prejudice to the defendant's case.[28]

Other courts have refused to admit execution impact evidence on the grounds that it simply is not relevant to the defendant's character, record, or the circumstances of the offense.[29]

Other evidence the defendant has no right to present includes: evidence about the likely general conditions the defendant would face as a life prisoner – including the certainty of confinement and lower-than-expected costs; testimony from social scientists on the questionable deterrent value of the death penalty; testimony from theologians about the dubious religious basis for retribution; and testimony from journalists on the physical agonies a person suffers in the electric chair. Finally, the Court has held that a defendant does not have the right to a jury instruction that the jury could consider as a mitigating factor at the penalty phase any residual or lingering doubt about the defendant's guilt that it carried over from the guilt phase.[30]

The jury then weighs the aggravating and mitigating circumstances. The jury can impose death if the aggravating factors outweigh the mitigating factors. In *Kansas v. Marsh*,[31] the Court held that the jury can impose a death sentence even if the aggravating and mitigating circumstances are equal. Therefore, the jury could impose death anytime it finds the aggravating factors outweigh or equal the mitigating circumstances. In reality, because the jury does not have to justify its decision, it can reject the death penalty even if it finds that there are no mitigating circumstances.

26   *State v. Stevens*, 879 P.2d 162, 167 (Or. 1994).
27   *Id.* at 168.
28   *Jackson v. Dretke*, 450 F.3d 614, 620 (5th Cir. 2006 (Dennis, J., dissenting).
29   *State v. Stenson*, 940 P.2d 1239, 1282 (Wash. 1997).
30   *Franklin v. Lynaugh*, 487 U.S. 164 (1988).
31   548 U.S. 163 (2006).

Every state requires a unanimous death verdict. Some states also require that a life verdict be unanimous – although in the event the jury deadlocks, the judge is required to hand down a default term of life without the possibility of parole.

Appeals

If convicted, the defendant's appeal proceeds in three stages. Stage I is the direct appeal. A defendant sentenced to death in federal court appeals his conviction in the federal system. A defendant convicted and sentenced to death in state court seeks a reversal in the state's highest court. If this appeal is rejected, he can seek review by the U.S. Supreme Court. In *Gregg v. Georgia*,[32] the Court opined that the direct appeal was an additional safeguard against arbitrariness and caprice. The defendant is entitled to counsel during the direct appeal phase. If his direct appeal is unsuccessful, the defendant can seek post-conviction relief by filing a writ of habeas corpus alleging that his conviction and/or sentence was obtained in violation of his constitutional rights. The defendant must first file his writ in state court. Unlike the direct appeal, the defendant does not have a constitutional right to counsel for the state habeas proceedings. Most states, however, provide counsel in order to expedite the proceedings. A few do not, most notably Alabama and Georgia. Inmates in these states must rely on pro bono assistance or their own pro se efforts. The lack of counsel is significant because an inmate's claims are usually waived unless first presented in state court, and an inmate proceeding pro se is likely to forfeit some valid claims. Furthermore, an inmate who is mentally retarded or mentally ill is especially in need of counsel.

Inmates are rarely successful during the state habeas proceedings. Their cases are often decided by elected judges. Therefore, they have a much greater chance of success in federal court. However, what they do – or better yet, what they fail to do – in state court significantly impacts on their federal litigation. In the next two sections, I will discuss the federal habeas process and the obstacles an inmate faces in seeking federal habeas relief.

The Writ of Habeas Corpus: Its History and Purpose

A significant number of death sentences have been reversed after the inmate has filed a writ of habeas corpus in federal court. The federal writ is therefore the most important stage in a death row inmate's appellate process. There are two primary reasons why death row inmates achieve greater success in federal court. First, relief is difficult to obtain in state court due to the fact that most state judges, especially in active death penalty states like Texas, are elected. Federal judges, by contrast, receive life tenure upon confirmation and therefore do not have to face the voters.

---

32   428 U.S. 153 (1976).

Second, almost without exception, a prerequisite for receiving a death sentence is the inability to retain counsel sufficiently motivated or talented. Somewhat ironically, once convicted and sentenced to death, inmates often receive better counsel in federal court. Some of the best advocates in the country – attorneys from organizations such as the National Association for the Advancement of Colored People (NAACP) Legal Defense and Education Fund, the American Civil Liberties Union, the Southern Poverty Law Center, law schools and professors, and large law firms – will often provide representation to death row inmates in federal court.

The writ of habeas corpus, as is the case with most American law, originated in England. In 1641, the Habeas Corpus Act was passed, providing that anyone imprisoned by a court, the king, his counsel, or his councils had the right to be brought upon demand to judges of the Court of King's Bench or to the Court of Common Pleas without delay. The colonies then introduced habeas corpus into the American legal scheme. At the time of the Constitutional Convention in 1787, all but one of the original member states had adopted either an express constitutional provision pertinent to habeas corpus or a practice allowing it. As a result, there was no debate about the habeas corpus provision in the U.S. Constitution. The Judiciary Act of 1789 empowered federal courts to issue writs of habeas corpus. The Habeas Corpus Act of 1867 made the federal writ applicable to state prisoners. The inclusion of habeas corpus in the federal Constitution resulted from the belief that the writ provided important protections for the individual against the sovereign. Although the Constitution includes a provision permitting the suspension of the writ, only during the Civil War was the writ suspended. Thus, throughout U.S. history the writ of habeas corpus has been available to defendants who claim deprivation of mandated procedural protections, whether convicted by either the federal government or the states.

The ability of federal courts to reverse state court convictions through the writ of habeas corpus has proven to be controversial. Opponents of federal review argue that state court judgments are entitled to respect and that states have legitimate interests in the finality of their criminal judgments. According to opponents, state courts are able to correct any errors that occurred at trial. Proponents have advanced several arguments in favor of federal review of state court convictions: 1) federal courts should have the primary responsibility for enforcing federal constitutional rights; 2) federal review is vital given the racial history of many state courts, especially those in the south; 3) federal habeas should be available to discourage state courts from neglecting federal constitutional principles; and 4) federal habeas should be available where prisoners have been denied a full and fair opportunity to air federal constitutional claims in state court. This debate has been reflected in the Supreme Court's decisions over the years.

The Warren Court greatly expanded the federal writ. For instance, the Warren Court allowed an inmate's federal writ to be considered on the merits even if he failed to have the claim considered in state court, as long as he did not deliberately bypass state court; held that an inmate was generally entitled to an evidentiary hearing on any unresolved factual issues; and allowed inmates to file second or successive petitions after the failure of their initial petitions. The Warren Court sent a clear message that it would monitor violations of federal constitutional rights and not allow procedural rules to present obstacles to consideration of meritorious claims. The subsequent Burger and Rehnquist courts significantly curtailed an inmate's ability to obtain federal habeas relief. For instance, the Burger Court reversed several decisions of the Warren Court and made it more difficult for federal courts to entertain claims that have not been litigated in state court. Justice Rehnquist had long been an opponent of federal review of state convictions and death sentences. His court did not hide its agenda, stating in one case that because of "'the profound societal costs that attend the exercise of habeas jurisdiction' we have found it necessary to impose significant limits on the discretion of federal courts to grant habeas relief."[33] In addition to making it extremely difficult for a claim that was not presented in state court to be considered on the merits in federal court, the Rehnquist Court also placed restrictions on the circumstances under which a federal court could even conduct an evidentiary hearing to resolve disputed factual issues.

Despite the retrenchment by the Burger and Rehnquist courts, inmates continued to achieve success in having their convictions and death sentences reversed in federal court. That provided a motivation for Congress to significantly limit the federal courts' habeas jurisdiction. Although Congress cannot eliminate the writ of habeas corpus, it can regulate it – which it has done on several occasions, and most importantly when it enacted the Antiterrorism and Effective Death Penalty Act of 1996 (AEDPA). After the Oklahoma City terrorist bombing, Congress wanted to "get tough on crime," so it enacted the most significant habeas reform since 1867. President Clinton, facing reelection and wanting to avoid charges that he was "soft" on crime, signed the bill into law over the objections of civil libertarians. The stated purpose of the AEDPA was to end prolonged habeas litigation in capital cases. An additional unstated but clear goal of the AEDPA was to restrain the federal courts' ability to review death sentences and to grant relief, since death row inmates had achieved a great deal of success in having their convictions and death sentences overturned in federal court prior to the enactment of the AEDPA. As a result of the AEDPA, as one scholar has observed, "federal habeas litigation is now overwhelmingly concerned with the procedural posture of an inmate's claim rather than the merits of those claims."[34] One study of the effect of the AEDPA on habeas litigation confirms this assertion. This study examined the disposition of habeas litigation both prior to and after the enactment of the AEDPA. The study found that:

> AEDPA is affecting the disposition of cases in lower federal courts ... the total percentage of cases in the federal courts that are disposed of on procedural grounds, as opposed to on the merits, has risen since 1997. In 1997, 2976 cases were

---

33   *Calderon v. Thompson*, 523 U.S. 538, 554–5 (1998).

34   J.M. Steiker, *Restructuring Post-Conviction Review of Federal Constitutional Claims Raised by Prisoners: Confronting the New Face of Excessive Proceduralism*, 1998 U. Chi. Legal F. 315, 317 (1998).

terminated on procedural grounds, and 1,094 cases were terminated on the merits. Thus, 73 percent of all habeas cases in 1997 were decided on procedural grounds. By 2004, 82 percent of all [habeas] cases were terminated on procedural grounds.[35]

Limits on Federal Habeas Relief

The AEDPA poses many obstacles, often insurmountable, for death row inmates seeking relief in federal court.

Exhaustion

The AEDPA codified the requirement that an inmate first seek relief in state court. In the event he fails to do so, the federal courts generally cannot consider the merits of his claims. Proponents of the exhaustion requirement believe that state courts should be given an opportunity to correct any errors before federal review commences. Closely related to exhaustion is the doctrine known as procedural default. The defendant cannot obtain relief in the event that his attorney fails to comply with a state procedural rule. For instance, if the attorney fails to properly object to the admission of certain evidence, the defendant generally cannot challenge the admission of this evidence.

The defendant's failure to exhaust or comply with state procedural rules is forgiven if the petitioner can demonstrate "cause" for failing to adhere to the state process and resulting "prejudice" from its enforcement. The Court has indicated that "the existence of cause must ordinarily turn on whether the prisoner can show that some objective factor external to the defense impeded [the defendant's] efforts to comply with the state procedural rules."[36] Examples of external factors constituting cause for failure to exhaust or comply with a procedural rule include a change in the law or interference by state officials. Cause does not exist simply because the defendant had inadequate counsel who failed to preserve the defendant's rights. Alternatively, as discussed in the chapter on innocence, the defendant's failure to comply with state exhaustion and procedural rules can be excused if he can establish a colorable claim of innocence. Because of the substandard representation that most death row inmates receive, unexhausted or procedurally defaulted claims are common, and federal courts spend much time and effort determining whether the inmates can justify their failure to preserve a legal claim in state court.

---

35   J. Blume, *AEDPA: The "Hype" and the "Bite,"* 91 Cornell L. Rev. 259, 286 (2006).

36   *Murray v. Carrier*, 477 U.S. 478, 488 (1986).

Deference to State Courts

Prior to the enactment of the AEDPA, federal courts could review de novo any state court decision. The AEDPA now provides that:

> An application for a writ of habeas corpus on behalf of a person in custody pursuant to the judgment of a State court shall not be granted with respect to any claim that was adjudicated on the merits in State court proceedings unless the adjudication of the claim ... resulted in a decision that was contrary to, or involved an unreasonable application of, clearly established federal law, as determined by the Supreme Court of the United States.[37]

Although President Clinton's signing statement paid lip service to meaningful federal court review of state court convictions, the AEDPA now requires federal courts to give deference to state court decisions. According to the Supreme Court, the federal courts cannot overturn a state court decision based on the fact that it was erroneous. In order for a federal court to overturn a state court decision, that decision must also be "unreasonable." A few examples of when a state court decision is unreasonable is when it relies on the wrong Supreme Court precedent, is based on facts not supported by the record, has rendered a decision clearly inconsistent with precedent, and when the state court has overlooked or ignored important facts.

This provision was enacted in order to ensure both comity for and the finality of state court criminal convictions. Proponents argue that although distrust of state courts might have been justified in an earlier era, state courts have changed significantly and should no longer be regarded as hostile to or incapable of enforcing federal law. In addition, proponents argue that federal habeas review should serve the purpose of remedying extraordinary injustices, and should not be used to correct ordinary and mundane constitutional errors that should be corrected on direct appeal. Several objections have been made to this deference provision. First, by requiring deference to state court decisions, even those that are erroneous, the new law inhibits the development of uniform constitutional law by the federal courts. For instance, state courts will be primarily responsible for the development of the law of ineffective assistance of counsel. One state court may hold that a sleeping lawyer was ineffective, while a state court in another jurisdiction may hold otherwise. Because there is debate over this issue, the decisions of both courts are not unreasonable. Thus, in one jurisdiction, a sleeping lawyer would be ineffective, yet in a different jurisdiction, he would not be.

A related objection is that federal courts should have the primary and ultimate responsibility for interpreting and developing federal law. It is difficult to recall any other area of the law in which federal courts are required to defer to state courts on their interpretation of federal law. As a matter of fact, the opposite is usually the case; that is, federal judges are believed to have greater expertise on

---

37   28 U.S.C. § 2254 (d)(1) (2000).

federal law and therefore have the primary responsibility for interpreting that law. Finally, the AEDPA's deference provision places a lot of reliance on the good faith of state courts. There is no evidence to suggest that state courts are accepting this new responsibility seriously and providing death row inmates with a thorough, meaningful review of their claims. No state better illustrates that this reliance is misplaced than Texas, where the state habeas process is merely perfunctory.

Texas is a perfect example because it has become the nation's laboratory for capital punishment. Before I explain the nuts and bolts of the Texas habeas process, it is important to understand the political context in which these cases are decided. The manner in which Texas selects its judges accounts for, to a large degree, the flaws in its habeas system. Texas is one of nine states selecting judges through partisan elections. As a result, judicial candidates often go to great lengths to demonstrate their support for capital punishment. A successful candidate for a seat on the state's highest court for criminal matters, the Texas Court of Criminal Appeals, campaigned on a platform promising "greater use of the death penalty, greater use of the harmless error doctrine, and sanctions for attorneys who file 'frivolous appeals especially in death penalty cases.'"[38]

In Texas, a death row inmate files his state writ of habeas corpus in the same court in which he was initially convicted. Thus, he must request the same judge who presided over his conviction to find that conviction was unconstitutional and never should have been rendered. The most egregious aspect of the Texas habeas process is the manner in which the petitions are resolved. Typically, legal disputes are resolved in an adversarial hearing, during which live witnesses testify and both sides test the accuracy of the witness testimony through cross-examination. Instead of resorting to the traditional method of resolving factual disputes by hearing live testimony, most trial judges in Texas utilize a procedure known as a "paper hearing." Paper hearings are hearings where the state court did not hear live testimony, but instead relied on affidavits. Rather than require each party to bring its witnesses to court and subject these witnesses to cross-examination, the trial judge conducts a "trial by affidavit." For instance, in *Perillo v. Johnson*,[39] a condemned woman alleged that her trial counsel provided ineffective assistance of counsel after learning that her attorney represented another participant in the crime who testified against her. She was given no opportunity to question the attorney regarding his relationship with the witness. The prosecution submitted an affidavit from the attorney and the Texas courts upheld her conviction and death sentence based solely on the affidavit.

After the papers are filed, both parties are required to submit proposed findings of fact and conclusions of law for the court to consider before it creates its own written findings of fact and conclusions of law. Texas judges, however, almost always adopt verbatim the prosecutor's proposed findings and conclusions. One study revealed "that the trial court's findings were identical or virtually identical

---

38   S. Bright, *Death in Texas*, The Champion 2, 8 (1999).

39   79 F.3d 441, 447 (5th Cir. 1996).

IN THE COURT OF CRIMINAL APPEALS OF TEXAS

WR-63,590-01

EX PARTE ROBERT GENE WILL, II

ON APPLICATION FOR WRIT OF HABEAS CORPUS

CAUSE NO. 862715 IN THE 185TH DISTRICT COURT

HARRIS COUNTY

Per Curiam.

O R D E R

This is an application for writ of habeas corpus filed pursuant to the provisions of Article 11.071, Tex. Code Crim. Proc.

On January 23, 2002, applicant was convicted of the offense of capital murder. The jury answered the special issues submitted pursuant to Article 37.071, Tex. Code Crim. Proc., and the trial court, accordingly, set punishment at death. This Court affirmed applicant's conviction and sentence on direct appeal. *Will v. State*, No. 74,306 (Tex. Crim. App. April 21, 2004).

Applicant presents three allegations in his application in which he challenges the validity of his conviction and resulting sentence. The trial court did not hold an evidentiary hearing. The trial court adopted the State's proposed findings of fact and conclusions of law recommending that the relief sought be denied.

This Court has reviewed the record with respect to the allegations made by Applicant. We adopt the trial judge's findings and conclusions. Based upon the trial court's findings and conclusions and our own review, we deny relief.

IT IS SO ORDERED THIS THE 29TH DAY OF MARCH, 2006.

Figure 6.1   Texas Court of Criminal Appeals Order

to those submitted by the prosecutor in 83.7% of the cases examined."[40] Once the trial court makes findings, the case is forwarded to the Texas Court of Criminal Appeals. The Court of Criminal Appeals usually makes a decision without oral

---

40 Texas Defender Service, *Lethal Indifference: The Fatal Combination of Incompetent Attorneys and Unaccountable Courts in Texas Death Penalty Appeals* at 54 (2002), available at www.texasdefender.org/publications.

argument; and the court fails, in most cases, to even write a detailed opinion explaining its decision. Typically, the court will issue a non-published per curiam order, as shown in Figure 6.1.

Any post-conviction process that fails to provide an inmate with competent counsel, that does not require an inmate to be mentally competent to assist counsel during his habeas proceedings, that fails to resolve factual disputes with evidentiary hearings, that allows assertions by prosecutors to go unchallenged, that permits the prosecutor to write the court's findings of fact and conclusions of law, and that allows its highest court to render decisions without oral arguments, written opinions or any meaningful substantive review of most of the petitions would seem to require federal oversight.

Statute of Limitations

The AEDPA imposes a one-year statute of limitations. A death row inmate has one year after his direct appeal has concluded to file a petition in federal court. This period is tolled while a petition is pending in state court. Prior to the AEDPA, there was no time limit. The limitations period reflected Congress's decision to expedite collateral attacks by placing stringent time restrictions on them. As one scholar has noted, the "AEDPA's statute of limitations has had a significant impact on habeas corpus litigation."[41] Some death-sentenced inmates have been denied federal review of their convictions as a result of the AEDPA's statute of limitations. The *Houston Chronicle* has reported that six inmates have been executed without their federal appeals even being considered because their attorneys failed to timely file their habeas petitions.[42] Some of these attorneys have subsequently been appointed to represent other death row inmates despite their obvious incompetence.

An example of the impact of the AEDPA's statute of limitations can be seen in *Rouse v. Lee*.[43] In this case, an African American defendant was convicted and sentenced to death by an all-white jury. After his conviction, Rouse filed a federal habeas petition alleging that one of the jurors expressed intense racial prejudice against African Americans – calling them "niggers" and opining that African Americans care less about life than white people do, and that African American men rape white women in order to brag to their friends. This juror deliberately concealed the fact that his mother had been the victim of a crime similar to the crime Rouse was on trial for so that he could serve on Rouse's jury. Because Rouse's federal habeas petition was filed one day late, the federal court refused to consider his strong evidence of this juror's racial prejudice.

---

41   Blume, *AEDPA: The "Hype" and the "Bite,"* 259.

42   L. Olsen, *Texas Death Row Lawyers' Late Filings Deadly to Inmates*, Houston Chronicle, March 22, 2009.

43   339 F.3d 238 (4th Cir. 2003).

Second Appeals

Sometimes evidence emerges after a death row inmate has exhausted his habeas proceedings in state and federal court. Prior to the AEDPA, the inmate had an opportunity to file a second federal habeas petition, known as a successor petition, based on this newly discovered evidence. The AEDPA precludes death row inmates from having successor petitions considered unless the inmate can prove that his evidence is new and that he can prove by clear and convincing evidence that he is innocent of the crime. To understand how the AEDPA restricts successor petitions, suppose that an attorney discovers a videotape indicating that his client's confession was obtained as a result of police misconduct. This videotape is not discovered until after his client's habeas petition has been rejected and his appeals are exhausted. The AEDPA would preclude a second habeas petition despite the egregious constitutional violation, unless the inmate could also prove his innocence by clear and convincing evidence.

Non-Retroactivity

Another major hurdle death row inmates face in obtaining habeas relief is the doctrine of non-retroactivity adopted by the Supreme Court in *Teague v. Lane*[44] and later codified in the AEDPA. In *Teague*, the defendant, who was African American, was convicted by an all-white jury of three counts of attempted murder, two counts of armed robbery, and one count of aggravated battery. During jury selection, the prosecutor used all 10 of his peremptory challenges to exclude African Americans from the jury. On appeal, the defendant argued that the prosecutor's use of peremptory challenges to strike blacks from the jury denied the defendant his right to a trial that is representative of the community. Both the Illinois Supreme Court and the U.S. Supreme Court rejected the defendant's claim on direct appeal. The defendant then filed a federal habeas petition. While his habeas petition was pending, the U.S. Supreme Court held that the Equal Protection Clause forbids the prosecution from using its peremptory challenges to exclude potential jurors because of their race. The Court had to decide whether Teague could take advantage of this new decision.

The Court held that it would apply any newly rendered decision to cases still on direct review. A decision, however, announcing a "new rule" of constitutional law would not apply to defendants whose convictions were affirmed on direct appeal and who had habeas petitions pending. Thus, Teague could not take advantage of the Court's decision outlawing discriminatory jury selection because his direct appeal had been rejected by the time of the Supreme Court's new decision. As a result of the Court's decision in *Teague*, death row inmates can only obtain habeas relief on claims that are based on settled law, such as *Miranda*. They are precluded

---

44   489 U.S. 288 (1989).

from obtaining relief if the law is not clear; they cannot prevail on novel legal arguments and cannot benefit from Supreme Court decisions holding that certain practices employed during their trial were unconstitutional.

Harmless Error

Even if a death row inmate is able to prove that his constitutional rights were violated, there is a strong likelihood that his conviction and sentence will not be reversed. That is because the courts apply the harmless error doctrine to most constitutional violations. A habeas petitioner alleging that his constitutional rights were violated has to prove not only that his rights had been violated but also that the constitutional violation "had substantial and injurious effect or influence in determining the jury's verdict."[45] Therefore, the courts will not grant relief if they believe that the defendant would have been convicted despite the constitutional violation. When determining whether constitutional error is harmless, the courts simply scrutinize the whole record for other evidence of guilt; if it exists, then the admitted error is deemed harmless because the court (not the jury) finds guilt beyond a reasonable doubt, regardless of the effect on the jury. One commentator argues that the harmless error doctrine "raises troubling questions for a nation committed to fair processes, meaningful review, and overriding constitutional norms."[46]

Conclusion

The AEDPA and other procedural rules reflect a compromise between advocates of federal supervision over state criminal processes and defenders of state autonomy. This compromise has required federal courts to engage in what one commentator describes as "excessive proceduralism."[47] Instead of considering the merits of an inmate's constitutional claims, federal courts now spend an extraordinary amount of time sorting through highly technical procedural doctrines.

---

45   *Brecht v. Abrahamson*, 507 U.S. 619 (1993).

46   Harry T. Edwards, *To Err is Human, But Not Always Harmless: When Should Legal Error Be Tolerated*, 70 N.Y.U. L. Rev. 1167, 1194 (1995).

47   Steiker, *supra* note 34.

Chapter 7
International Law
and the Death Penalty

This chapter will discuss the effect that international law has had on the death penalty both worldwide and within the United States. The chapter will begin with a review of the status of the death penalty under international law. Next is a discussion of the role of international law within the United States and the controversy on the Supreme Court over its role. The different perspectives of the justices over the applicability of international law in deciding constitutional issues will be extensively discussed. Because international law is so controversial in the United States, it has not been very useful for death row inmates and has had limited impact on the practice of the death penalty. Several cases involving attempts by death row inmates to prevent their executions on international law grounds will be used as illustrations. Finally, the chapter concludes with a discussion of how the use of the death penalty by the United States has affected its relations with other nations, specifically their reluctance to extradite suspects to the United States without assurances that the death penalty will not be utilized.

International Law and the Death Penalty

The death penalty is on the decline around the world. Although the death penalty was utilized frequently by the Nuremberg Tribunal established after World War II to prosecute Nazi officials for the atrocities they committed during the war, more recent international tribunals do not apply the death penalty. The International Criminal Court does not allow defendants to be sentenced to death. Even the two tribunals established in order to prosecute perpetrators of genocide in Rwanda and Yugoslavia do not permit the death penalty. In 2007, the United Nations General Assembly for the first time endorsed a moratorium on executions.[1] Most importantly, more than two-thirds of the world's nations have either abolished capital punishment or no longer impose it as a criminal sanction. That figure includes almost the entire continent of Europe. In Europe, abolition has been achieved through Optional

---

1   U.N. General Assembly, Moratorium on the Use of the Death Penalty, U.N. Doc. A/C.3/62/L29 (Nov. 1, 2007).

Protocols 6[2] and 13[3] to the European Human Rights Convention. In addition, the Council of Europe has made membership conditional on the abolition of capital punishment. Because Belarus is the only European nation that has retained the death penalty, it cannot become a member of the Council of Europe. In Central America, only Belize retains the death penalty and in South America, the death penalty is retained only in Guyana. Capital punishment, however, is still widely practiced in certain areas of the world, including China and Japan, the Middle East, in many African nations, parts of the Caribbean, and of course in the United States.

The worldwide movement away from the death penalty has occurred despite the fact that international law does not prohibit its use. The International Covenant on Civil and Political Rights[4] (ICCPR) is one of the leading human rights treaties. Almost every nation in the world has signed and ratified the Covenant. Its provisions are considered binding international law even in those nations that have not ratified the Covenant because its provisions have been so widely adopted and practiced by the nations of the world that they have also become customary law. Article 6 of the ICCPR specifically addresses capital punishment. Section 1 states that "Every human being has the inherent right to life. This right shall be protected by law. No one shall be arbitrarily deprived of his life." This section, however, has never been interpreted as a per se prohibition on the use of the death penalty. It only prohibits the arbitrary taking of life. Furthermore, Section 2 provides that a "sentence of death may be imposed only for the most serious crimes," which implies that the death penalty can be imposed for serious crimes. According to the comments to Section 2, "the death penalty should be a quite exceptional measure,"[5] limited to homicide.

Several nations have imposed or attempt to impose capital punishment on non-homicide offenders, in violation of international law. For instance, 32 nations, including the United States, retain the death penalty for persons who commit drug offenses not involving murder or violence. Drug offenses include drug trafficking, cultivation, manufacturing, and/or importing or exporting drugs. Six of these 32 nations execute drug offenders in high numbers on an

---

2   Optional Protocol 6 prohibits the death penalty during peacetime but permits it for "acts committed in time of war or of imminent threat of war." Protocol No. 6 to the 1950 European Convention for the Protection of Human Rights and Fundamental Freedoms, E.T.S. 114, *entered into force* March 1, 1985.

3   Optional Protocol 13 totally prohibits capital punishment, even during wartime. Protocol No. 13 to the Convention for the Protection of Human Rights and Fundamental Freedoms, Concerning the Abolition of the Death Penalty in all Circumstances, E.T.S. 187, *entered into force* July 1, 2003.

4   International Covenant on Civil and Political Rights, Dec. 16, 1966, 999 U.N.T.S. 171.

5   Human Rights Committee, General Comment No. 6: The Right to Life (Art. 6), U.N. Doc. HR1/GEN/1 (1982) at 5.

annual basis.[6] In the United States, the death penalty can be imposed for drug offenses committed in furtherance of a continuing criminal enterprise involving large quantities. No one has been executed or sentenced to death for such an offense. In 2008, the U.S. Supreme Court ruled that the death penalty could not be imposed in the case of a defendant who rapes but does not cause the death of a child, and stated that "the death penalty should not be expanded to instances where the victim's life was not taken."[7] However, the decision was "limited to crimes against individual persons. We do not address for example, crimes defining and punishing treason, espionage, terrorism, and drug kingpin activity, which are offenses against the State."[8] It is not clear whether the Court would regard drug trafficking as a crime against the state and allow traffickers to be executed.

Individuals are sentenced to death for other crimes which are not serious enough to warrant the death penalty. Iran's penal code prescribes execution by hanging or stoning as the penalty for adultery by married persons, in clear violation of international law. Another example involves Uganda's attempt to make "aggravated homosexuality" a capital offense. Aggravated homosexuality is defined as follows:

A person commits the offence of aggravated homosexuality where the (a) person against whom the offence is committed is below the age of 18 years; (b) offender is a person living with HIV; (c) offender is a parent or guardian of the person against whom the offence is committed; (d) offender is a person in authority over the person against whom the offence is committed; (e) victim of the offence is a person with disability; (f) offender is a serial offender; or (g) offender applies, administers or causes to be used by any man or woman any drug, matter or thing with intent to stupefy, overpower him, or her so as to thereby enable any person to have unlawful carnal connection with any person of the same sex.[9]

This law would punish some consensual homosexual relations. Even the provisions where the offender deserves to be punished, such as sexual acts with minors, do not warrant the death penalty under international law. Only murder, and possibly treason, would be a sufficiently exceptional crime that would justify capital punishment under international law.

Article 6 places other limits on the use of the death penalty. The death penalty cannot be imposed on persons below 18 years of age and is not to be carried out on pregnant women. Article 6 also requires that those sentenced to death be

---

6   China, Iran, Saudi Arabia, Vietnam, Singapore, and Malaysia.

7   *Kennedy v. Louisiana*, 128 S. Ct. 2641, 2659 (2008).

8   *Id.*

9   Information regarding the bill is located at http://www.amnesty.org/en/library/info/AFR59/003/2010/en.

provided with an opportunity to seek a pardon or commutation of their sentence. Furthermore, Article 6 makes it clear that nations are free to abolish capital punishment, and the comments indicate that abolition is "desirable."[10] The Second Optional Protocol to the International Covenant on Civil and Political Rights does require abolition of capital punishment but it has not been widely adopted and its provisions are not considered customary international law.[11]

International law also provides criminal defendants with procedural rights which would also be applicable to defendants facing death. Criminal defendants are entitled to the presumption of innocence, a public trial, the opportunity to confront witnesses, the privilege against self-incrimination, the right to be represented by counsel even if indigent, and equal protection of the laws. Although international law requires that a criminal defendant be tried before an impartial tribunal, it does not require a trial before a jury. Furthermore, everyone convicted of a crime has the right to appeal his conviction to a higher tribunal. Capital punishment can be lawfully applied only after a fair trial during which these rights have been provided.

Numerous human rights treaties prohibit "torture or cruel, inhuman or degrading treatment or punishment."[12] The prohibition of such treatment is so widespread around the world that it is also prohibited under customary law. However, this provision has never been interpreted under international law as prohibiting nations from imposing the death penalty. The United States explicitly stated so in its reservations to the Torture Convention:

> I. The Senate's advice and consent is subject to the following reservations:
>
> ...
>
> (4) That the United States understands that international law does not prohibit the death penalty, and does not consider this Convention to restrict or prohibit the United States from applying the death penalty consistent with the Fifth, Eighth, and/ or Fourteenth Amendments to the Constitution of the United States, including any constitutional period of confinement prior to the imposition of the death penalty.

Although the death penalty is not considered a violation of the international prohibition on torture and inhumane or degrading treatment or punishment, this provision has been used to limit the death penalty. Some nations have broadly

---

10   *Supra*, note 5.

11   Second Optional Protocol to the International Covenant on Civil and Political Rights, Aiming at the Abolition of the Death Penalty, *opened for signature* Dec. 15, 1989, 29 I.L.M. 1464.

12   Article 7 of the International Covenant on Civil and Political Rights, Dec. 16, 1966, 999 U.N.T.S. 171; Article 5 of the Universal Declaration of Human Rights, Dec. 10, 1948, U.N. G.A. Res. 217 (III 1948); Convention Against Torture And Other Cruel, Inhuman, Or Degrading Treatment Or Punishment, Dec. 10, 1984, 23 I.L.M. 1027 (1984), as modified, 24 I.L.M. 535 (1985); Article 3 of the European Convention For the Protection of Human Rights and Fundamental Freedoms, Nov. 4, 1950, 312 U.N.T.S. 221.

interpreted similar provisions in their domestic constitutions to prohibit capital punishment. For instance, South Africa's highest court found that the death penalty violated its constitutional prohibition on cruel, inhuman, or degrading punishments.[13] Furthermore, the European Court of Human Rights found that death row conditions in the United States violated the prohibition on torture or inhuman or degrading treatment or punishment provision of the European Convention. In *Soering v. United Kingdom*,[14] a West German attending the University of Virginia escaped to the United Kingdom after he and his girlfriend killed her parents. Virginia sought Soering's extradition so that he could be tried, and the state's intention was to seek the death penalty. The European Court of Human Rights held that because of the conditions he would face on Virginia's death row, including the long delay in carrying out executions in the United States and the mental anguish that results therefrom, there was the risk that Soering would be subject to torture or inhumane treatment were he to be extradited. As a result, the Court held that the United Kingdom could not extradite Soering to the United States to face the death penalty. Soering was subsequently extradited after Virginia gave assurances that it would not seek the death penalty.

The international law prohibition on torture and cruel, inhuman, or degrading treatment or punishment further limits the manner in which the death penalty may be carried out. The United Nations Human Rights Committee held that "when imposing capital punishment, the execution of the sentence ... must be carried out in such a way as to cause the least possible physical and mental suffering."[15] Charles Ng had been extradited by Canada to the United States to be tried for murder, and he faced a possible death sentence by lethal gas. He argued before the Committee that his execution by lethal gas would constitute cruel and unusual punishment, in violation of international law. The Committee noted that "gas asphyxiation may cause prolonged suffering and agony and does not result in death as swiftly as possible, as asphyxiation by cyanide gas may take over 10 minutes."[16] Therefore, the Committee held that "execution by gas asphyxiation ... would not meet the test of 'least possible physical and mental suffering' and constitutes cruel and inhuman treatment."[17]

The prohibition on torture and cruel, inhuman, degrading treatment or punishment places further limits on the manner in which the death penalty can be imposed. In Japan, executions are carried out in total secrecy. The inmate is never informed of the date of his execution. He only learns moments before his execution is to be carried out. He is only given enough time to write a final letter and receive last rites. His family is not informed until after the inmate has been

---

13 *State v. Makwanyane*, (3) SALR 391 (CC, 1995).
14 161 Eur. Ct. H.R. (ser. A).
15 *Ng v. Canada*, Comm. No. 469/1991, U.N. Doc. A/49/40, vol. II, at 189 para. 16.2 (1983).
16 *Id*. at para. 16.3.
17 *Id*. at para. 16.4.

executed, and they are given 24 hours to collect his body. The United Nations Human Rights Commission has condemned Japan's secretive executions. Certain other methods of executing inmates would also violate the ban on cruel and inhuman punishment. In Iran, inmates are sometimes stoned to death; in Saudi Arabia they are beheaded. In China, Iran, and Saudi Arabia, political opponents of the government have been executed. Singapore's mandatory death penalty would also violate the prohibition on cruel treatment as it does not allow for the consideration of mitigating circumstances.

Another limitation is the prohibition on juvenile executions. Both the International Covenant on Civil and Political Rights and the Convention on the Rights of the Child, ratified by every nation in the world except the United States and Somalia, expressly prohibit capital punishment for crimes committed by persons under 18 years of age. The prohibition on executing juveniles has become so widespread that it is also considered to be part of customary law. Iran and Saudi Arabia are the only nations in the world known to violate the prohibition against executing juveniles.

International Law in the United States

Under Article VI of the United States Constitution, treaties are "the supreme Law of the Land and the Judges in every state shall be bound thereby."[18] The Supreme Court has held that a treaty is on par with a statute enacted by the United States Congress[19] and is superior to any contradictory state law.[20] The Court, however, has limited the enforceability of treaties. The Court has held that a treaty is only enforceable if it is self-executing. A treaty is self-executing as long as it does not require separate "implementing legislation."[21] Customary international law is also binding in U.S. courts but only in the absence of a treaty or federal law on the subject.[22]

Although the Constitution and the United States Supreme Court have made it clear that international law is binding and enforceable in U.S. courts under certain conditions, international law has long been a controversial subject in the United States. John Bolton, the former U.S. Ambassador to the United Nations, once declared: "International law is not law; it is a series of political and moral arrangements that stand or fall on their own merits and anything else is simply theology and superstition masquerading as law."[23] Bolton believes that "It is a big

---

18   U.S. Const. art. VI.

19   *Whitney v. Robertson*, 124 U.S. 190, 194 (1888).

20   *Crosby v. National Foreign Trade Council*, 530 U.S. 363 (2000).

21   *Foster v. Neilson*, 27 U.S. 253, 314 (1829).

22   *The Paquette Habana*, 175 U.S. 677, 700 (1900).

23   J. Bolton, *Is There Really "Law" in International Affairs*, 10 Transnat'l L. & Contemp. Probs. I, 48 (2000).

mistake for us to grant any validity to international law even when it may seem in our short-term interest to do so – because over the long term, the goal of those who think international law really means anything are those who want to constrict the United States."[24] President Barack Obama on the other hand has confirmed the United States' commitment to international law:

> On my first day in office, I prohibited – without exception or equivocation – the use of torture by the United States of America. I ordered the prison at Guantanamo Bay closed, and we are doing the hard work of forging a framework to combat extremism within the rule of law ... The world must stand together to demonstrate that international law is not an empty promise and that treaties will be enforced.[25]

Interviews with former State Department Legal Advisors have confirmed that international law has long played an important role in U.S. foreign policy and has often constrained the President's policy preferences.[26] Despite the fact that international law has played an important role in shaping U.S. foreign policy, death row inmates have been unsuccessful in asserting international law in court, even in cases in which a clear violation has occurred. I will discuss below several attempts by death row inmates to use international law in order to prevent their executions.

Most importantly, the debate in the United States over the role of international law has also occurred at the Supreme Court. There is no disagreement among the justices that when Congress explicitly authorizes the courts to apply international law, they are bound to do so. For instance, the Alien Tort Statute provides that "the district courts shall have original jurisdiction of any civil action by an alien for a tort only, committed in violation of the law of nations or a treaty of the United States."[27] The justices would agree that in order to resolve a claim brought under this statute, courts must consult the "law of nations." A spirited debate, however, has occurred over the extent to which the courts should apply international law when Congress is not so explicit, and over the extent to which the Supreme Court should consult foreign sources of law to interpret the U.S. Constitution. For instance, in deciding whether a particular punishment violates the Eighth Amendment's prohibition on cruel and unusual punishments, should the Court take into account foreign judicial

---

24 S. Power, *Boltonism*, The New Yorker, March 21, 2005.

25 *Text, Obama's Speech to the United Nations General Assembly*, N.Y. Times, September 23, 2009, available at http://www.nytimes.com/2009/09/24/us/politics/24prexy. html?pagewanted=all.

26 M. Scharf and P. Williams, *Shaping Foreign Policy in Times of Crisis: The Role of International Law and the State Department Legal Advisor* (Cambridge and New York: Cambridge University Press, 2010).

27 28 U.S.C. § 1350.

decisions interpreting a similar provision of its constitution or treaties that outlaw the specific practice? An argument for doing so is as follows.

My point is simple: those who advocate the use of international law in U.S. constitutional interpretation are not mere "international majoritarians" who believe that American constitutional liberties should be determined by a worldwide vote. Rather, transnationalists suggest that particular provisions of our Constitution should be construed with decent respect for international and foreign comparative law. When phrases like "due process of law," "equal protection," and "cruel and unusual punishments" are illuminated by parallel rules, empirical evidence, or community standards found in other mature legal systems, that evidence should not simply be ignored. Wise American judges did not do so at the beginning of the Republic, and there is no warrant for them to start now.

Additional arguments for consulting foreign sources of law can be made. First, we live in an increasingly interconnected world and it is therefore appropriate to consult foreign sources when resolving common legal problems. Second, it is common practice within the United States legal system to consult court decisions in other jurisdictions for assistance in constitutional interpretation. No one would object if the California Supreme Court, in interpreting a provision of its state constitution, consulted and considered a decision by the Alabama Supreme Court interpreting a similar provision of its constitution, even though theses two states are culturally and politically very distinct.

Proponents of consulting international law and practice believe that it is especially important to do so when deciding whether a particular punishment is cruel and unusual in violation of the Eighth Amendment. For instance, when the Court considered whether a sentence of life imprisonment without the possibility of parole for a juvenile who does not commit murder was cruel and unusual punishment, the Court noted that no other nation in the world imposed such a harsh sentence on juvenile offenders. In its view, the fact that no other nation in the world imposed such a sentence, while not dispositive, is evidence that it violates the Eighth Amendment. As the Court explained:

> The Court has treated the laws and practices of other nations and international agreements as relevant to the Eighth Amendment not because those norms are binding or controlling but because the judgment of the world's nations that a particular sentencing practice is inconsistent with basic principles of decency demonstrates that the Court's rationale has respected reasoning to support it.[28]

Justice Scalia has been the leader on the Court in articulating the opposite view:

> We emphasize that it is *American* conceptions of decency that are dispositive, rejecting the contention of petitioners and their various *amici* ... that the sentencing practices of other countries are relevant. While "[t]he practices of

---

28   *Graham v. Florida,* 130 S.Ct. 2011, 2034 (2010).

other nations, particularly other democracies can be relevant to determining whether a practice uniform among our people is not merely an historical accident but rather so implicit in the concept of ordered liberty" that it occupies a place not merely in our mores, but text permitting, our Constitution as well, "they cannot serve to establish the first Eighth Amendment prerequisite, that the practice is accepted among our people."[29]

The debate over the use of foreign law and practices in interpreting the Constitution came to a head in *Roper v. Simmons*.[30] In *Roper*, the Supreme Court had to decide whether it was cruel and unusual punishment for a state to execute a juvenile offender. The Court held that the execution of juvenile offenders violated the Eighth Amendment. In determining whether the execution of juveniles was cruel and unusual, the Court's decision rested primarily on the fact that the practice had become disfavored in most states within the United States. The Court also indicated that the execution of juveniles was cruel and unusual because it did not serve the purposes of deterrence and retribution. The Court also added that "it is proper that we acknowledge the overwhelming weight of international opinion against the juvenile death penalty, resting in large part on the understanding that the instability and emotional imbalance of young people may often be a factor in the crime."[31] The Court discussed the international consensus against executing juveniles:

> As respondent and a number of *amici* emphasize, Article 37 of the United Nations Convention on the Rights of the Child, which every country of the world has ratified save for the United States and Somalia, contains an express prohibition on capital punishment for crimes committed by juveniles under 18 … Respondent and his *amici* have submitted and petitioner does not contest, that only seven countries other than the United States have executed juvenile offenders since 1990: Iran, Pakistan, Saudi Arabia, Yemen, Nigeria, the Democratic Republic of Congo and China. Since then each of these countries has either abolished capital punishment for juveniles or made public disavowal of the practice. In sum, it is fair to say that the United States now stands alone in a world that has turned its face against the death penalty.[32]

In dissent, Justice Scalia accused the majority of ignoring the views of U.S. citizens in determining whether juvenile executions were cruel and unusual. Rather, according to Justice Scalia, "the views of other countries and the so-called international community take center stage."[33] In his view:

---

29   *Stanford v. Kentucky*, 492 U.S. 361, 369–70 n. 1 (1989) (emphasis in original).
30   543 U.S. 551 (2005).
31   *Id.* at 578.
32   *Id.* at 575.
33   *Id* at 622 (Scalia, J., dissenting).

[T]he basic premise of the Court's argument – that American law should conform to the laws of the rest of the world – ought to be rejected out of hand ... I do not believe that approval by "other nations and peoples" should buttress our commitment to American principles any more than (what should logically follow) disapproval by "other nations and peoples" should weaken the commitment.[34]

He accused the majority of having a double standard with respect to the views of the international community. According to Justice Scalia, the majority cites foreign sources when those sources support the result they wish to reach but ignores such sources when they are in conflict with the majority's desired result. He provides two examples: 1) separation of church and state; and 2) abortion. Regarding the separation of church and state, he asserts that even those nations committed to religious neutrality like the United States do not prohibit direct government payments to religious schools. On abortion, he indicated that the United States is one of only six nations that allow abortion on demand until the point of viability.

Justice Kennedy is correct that U.S. courts have consulted foreign sources of law throughout its history. The practice has become controversial because only recently has the Court used foreign sources of law to support controversial decisions such as banning the juvenile death penalty, as it did in *Roper*, or overturning laws against sodomy,[35] or upholding affirmative action.[36] In response to these decisions, a few members of Congress sought to restrain the Court from using international law in interpreting the Constitution. Although this proposed legislation had no plausible chance of passing and was probably unconstitutional, it reflects the division in the United States over the use of international law. This division has likely impacted the courts in rejecting claims by capital defendants based on international law.

International Law Claims Rejected by U.S. Courts

Death row inmates have used international law in claiming that their rights to consular notification under the Vienna Convention on Consular Relations was violated; that international law prohibits the execution of juveniles; and that their extended confinement on death row constitutes cruel and inhuman treatment, in violation of international law. Although foreign courts have been receptive to these arguments, courts in the United States have rejected each of these claims.

---

34   *Id.* at 624.
35   *Lawrence v. Texas*, 539 U.S. 558, 572, 576–7 (2003).
36   *Grutter v. Bollinger*, 539 U.S. 306, 344 (2003).

Foreign Nationals

The United States, along with 172 other nations, is a party to the Vienna Convention on Consular Relations. Article 36 of the Convention is designed to "facilitat[e] the exercise of consular functions relating to the sending State" by facilitating communication and access between a foreign national who has been arrested and that individual's diplomatic personnel in the host country.[37] It provides that "consular officers shall be free to communicate with nationals of the sending State and to have access to them."[38] Article 36 further provides that:

> if he so requests, the competent authorities of the receiving State shall, without delay, inform the consular post of the sending State if, within its consular district, a national of that State is arrested or committed to prison or to custody pending trial or is detained in any other manner.[39]

Furthermore, "[a]ny communication addressed to the consular post by the person arrested, in prison, custody or detention shall also be forwarded by the said authorities without delay."[40] State authorities are required to "inform the person concerned without delay of his rights under [Article 35]."[41] Under Article 36 consular officers "have the right to visit a national of the sending State who is in prison, custody or detention, to converse and correspond with him and to arrange for his legal representation."[42] Thus, any non-citizen arrested in the United States must be informed by the arresting authorities that they have the right to contact their nation's consulate and the consulate must be allowed free access to their citizen.

Article 36 is important because many foreign nationals are unfamiliar with the local criminal justice system. Frequently there are language and cultural barriers which prevent foreign suspects from fully understanding their rights. Therefore, it is crucial that the foreign national have access to their government to insure that they are properly informed of their rights. For instance, whether a suspect has to answer police questions varies tremendously around the world. In Paraguay, a suspect may receive a sentence reduction if he confesses. On the other hand, in the United States, a suspect's incriminating statements will be used against him. The suspect's consulate may also assist him in obtaining legal assistance. In death penalty cases, the consulate may be able to assist the inmate in obtaining mitigation evidence. There may be witnesses, documents, or medical and school

---

37   Vienna Convention on Consular Relations and Optional Protocol on Disputes, Apr. 24, 1963. 21 U.S.T. 77. 100, 596 U.N.T.S. 292.

38   *Id.* at 101, 596 U.N.T.S. at 292.

39   *Id.*

40   *Id.*

41   *Id.*

42   *Id.*

records that would assist the jury in determining that death is not warranted which are located in the suspect's home country, and the consulate can assist him in obtaining this information.

Until recently, the United States was also a party to the Optional Protocol to the Vienna Convention, which provides that '[d]isputes arising out of the interpretation or application of the [Vienna] Convention shall lie within the compulsory jurisdiction of the International Court of Justice."[43] Thus, according to the U.S. Constitution, both the Vienna Convention and the Optional Protocol are the law of the United States. Because only nation-states can be parties in the International Court of Justice, individuals have had to seek recourse for violations in U.S. courts.

Non-compliance with the Article 36 notification requirements has been a persistent problem. This problem will only intensify as the number of non-citizens in U.S. prisons increases. Voluminous litigation in U.S. courts and in international tribunals has resulted from state officials' failure to provide foreign nationals with the notification required by Article 36. In most instances, state officials do not deny that they failed to provide the required notification. Jose Medellin's experience, for instance, was fairly typical. After he was apprehended by Houston officials for the murder of two teenagers, Medellin told the arresting officers in Texas that he was born in Laredo, Mexico. He also told the booking authorities that he was not a United States citizen. Medellin, however, "was arrested, detained, tried, convicted, and sentenced to death without ever being informed that he could contact the Mexican counsel."[44] Most of the litigation in U.S. courts centered on four issues: 1) whether the Convention creates individually enforceable rights; 2) whether the non-citizen must object at trial to preserve the issue for appeal; 3) whether the foreign national must prove that he was prejudiced by the failure to provide notification; and 4) the appropriate remedy for an Article 36 violation.

In *Sanchez-Llamas v. Oregon*,[45] a Mexican and a Honduran immigrant sought to enforce Article 36 after the local law enforcement officials failed to provide the required notification. Although the Supreme Court refused to address the issue of whether the Vienna Convention is individually enforceable, the Court expressed its doubts that judicial remedies were intended by the parties to the Convention.[46] Furthermore, there is a presumption that international treaties do not create rights that are privately enforceable in U.S. courts. The Supreme Court explained the rationale for this presumption as follows:

---

43   Optional Protocol Concerning the Compulsory Settlement of Disputes art. I, Apr. 24, 1963, 21 U.N.T.S. 488. On March 7, 2005, the United States announced that it would no longer be a party to the Optional Protocol.

44   *Medellin v. Dretke*, 544 U.S. 660, 675 (2005) (O'Connor, J., dissenting).

45   548 U.S. 331 (2006).

46   *Id.* at 343.

A treaty is primarily a compact between nations. It depends for the enforcement of its provisions on the interest and the honor of the governments which are parties to it. If these fail, its infraction becomes the subject of international negotiations and reclamations, so far as the injured party chooses to seek redress, which may in the end be enforced by actual war. It is obvious that with all this the judicial courts have nothing to do and can give no redress.[47]

Several lower courts have addressed the issue and have held that the Vienna Convention cannot be enforced by an individual.[48] They have refused to allow individuals to enforce the treaty for three reasons. First, they have based their conclusion on the language in the Vienna Convention's Preamble, which states: "[T]he purpose of such privileges and immunities is *not to benefit individuals* but to ensure the efficient performance of functions by consular posts on behalf of their respective States."[49] Second, the lower courts are reluctant to allow individual enforcement of treaties for fear of interfering in a nation's foreign affairs.[50] Third, the lower courts have given deference to the view of the State Department that the Convention is not judicially enforceable, but rather that the remedies for violations of the Convention are diplomatic, political, or exist between states under international law.[51]

Many foreign nationals have been unsuccessful in pursuing a judicial remedy for the violation of the consular notification provision because they failed to timely raise the issue. There is a general rule requiring that criminal defendants raise objections at trial before an appellate court will consider any assertions of error. In *Sanchez-Llamas*, a Honduran national was charged with murder but was never told of his right to contact the Honduran consulate by either the local law enforcement officials or his attorney. He received a 30-year sentence but did not raise the issue of the failure to receive the required notification until he attempted to have his conviction overturned during his state habeas proceedings. The Honduran consulate executed an affidavit in support of his appeal in which it stated "it would have endeavored to help Mr. Bustillo in his defense"[52] had it learned of his detention prior to trial. The state court denied relief based on procedural default for not raising the issue earlier. The U.S. Supreme Court held that because the procedural default doctrine applies to violations of the United States Constitution, it should likewise apply to violations of the Vienna Convention.

---

47 *Head Money Cases*, 112 U.S. 580, 598 (1884).

48 See, e.g., *United States v. Emuegbunam*, 268 F.3d 377, 391 (6th Cir. 2001); *Cauthern v. State*, 145 S.W.3d 571, 626 (Tenn. Crim. App. 2004); *Kasi v. Commonwealth*, 508 S.E.2d 57, 64 (Va. 1998).

49 *Emuegbunam*, 268 F.3d at 392 (quoting Vienna Convention, 21 U.S.T. at 79, 596 U.N.T.S. at 262.

50 *Emuegbunam*, 268 F.3d at 394.

51 *Id.* at 392.

52 *Sanchez-Llamas v. Oregon*, 548 U.S. 331, 341 (2006).

The Supreme Court addressed the issue of whether a violation of the Vienna Convention required the suppression of any evidence obtained from the suspect. The second defendant in *Sanchez-Llamas*, a citizen of Mexico, was arrested after shooting a police officer. *Miranda* warnings were given to him in both English and Spanish. However, he was not told of his right to contact the Mexican consulate for assistance. He made incriminating statements to the police that resulted in his conviction, but before trial he moved to suppress these statements as a result of the violation of Article 36. He asked the Supreme Court to overturn the lower court's determination that suppression of his confession was not warranted and to suppress his incriminating statements as a remedy for the Article 36 violation. The Supreme Court refused to do so. The Vienna Convention doe not prescribe a remedy for Article 36 violations; and, according to the Court, because most nations have rejected the exclusionary rule, they could not have intended suppression to be the remedy. Furthermore, the Court argued that suppression is not necessary because:

> Finally, suppression is not the only means of vindicating Vienna Convention rights. A defendant can raise an Article 36 claim as part of a broader challenge to the voluntariness of his statements to the police. If he raises an Article 36 violation at trial, a court can make appropriate accommodations to ensure that the defendant secures, to the extent possible, the benefits of consular assistance. Of course, diplomatic avenues – the primary means of enforcing the Convention – also remain open.[53]

Thus, even in the unlikely event that the Supreme Court eventually recognizes that the Vienna Convention is individually enforceable, any remedy for a violation would be practically non-existent. Therefore, because foreign defendants were unable to obtain a satisfactory resolution in U.S. courts, their nations decided to seek redress in the International Court of Justice (ICJ) pursuant to the Optional Protocol. The ICJ has considered three significant cases regarding the United States' obligations under the Vienna Convention.

Paraguay v. U.S.[54] Angel Francisco Breard was under suspicion for murder and attempted rape. During a search of Breard's apartment, the Arlington, Virginia, police found his Paraguayan passport and therefore knew that he was a Paraguayan national. The Arlington police, however, did not inform Breard that he was entitled to contact the Paraguayan consulate; nor did they notify Paraguayan consulate officials of Breard's arrest. After he was indicted, Virginia officials offered Breard a life sentence if he would agree to plead guilty. Because Paraguay does not permit plea-bargaining, and in fact makes such deals null and void, Breard rejected

---

53   *Id.* at 350.

54   Vienna Convention on Consular Relations (Para. v. U.S.), 1998 I.C.J. 426, 427 (Discontinuance Order of Nov. 10).

the offer.[55] He decided instead to testify and to confess his crime to the jury. In Paraguay, "[t]he principal means to obtain leniency ... would be to confess to and denounce the criminal acts charged and appeal to the mercy of the court."[56] The jury convicted Breard and the court sentenced him to death.

Approximately three years later, Paraguayan officials learned for the first time of Breard's imprisonment and pending execution. They informed Breard of his rights to consular notification under the Vienna Convention and explained to him the differences between the U.S. and Paraguayan legal systems. By this time Breard was well into the appellate process. He raised for the first time, in his federal habeas petition, a claim based upon the failure of Virginia officials to notify him of his rights to consular access. The federal courts held that because the claim had not been raised in state court, it was procedurally defaulted. Paraguay sought to prevent Breard's execution in the ICJ. It was successful in convincing the ICJ to issue an order that the U.S. "take all measures at its disposal to ensure that Angel Francisco Breard is not executed pending the final decision in these proceedings."[57] The U.S. Supreme Court affirmed the lower court's application of the procedural default doctrine and held that the ICJ's order was not legally binding in U.S. courts.[58] The Supreme Court suggested that the only means of recourse for Breard was a reprieve from the Governor of Virginia. The U.S. Secretary of State wrote to the Governor of Virginia advising him that the ICJ's order was non-binding, but she requested a delay of Breard's execution. The Virginia Governor refused to do so and Breard was executed. Paraguay subsequently withdrew its complaint from the ICJ.

Germany v. U.S.[59] Walter and Karl LaGrand were German nationals who lived most of their lives in the United States. They were both convicted and sentenced to death for their roles in an Arizona bank robbery. Arizona authorities conceded that the LaGrands were convicted and sentenced to death without receiving the consular notification required by Article 36 and that the German consulate had not been notified of their arrests. Arizona authorities further conceded that no notification was given even after its officials became aware that the LaGrands were German nationals and not U.S. citizens. Neither LaGrand brother objected to the Vienna Convention violation until their cases were on appeal, and thus the U.S. courts applied the procedural default doctrine and refused to consider the merits of their claims. Both LaGrand brothers were subsequently executed, despite diplomatic interventions by the German government and despite a provisional order from the ICJ insisting that Walter LaGrand not be executed pending the disposition of the ICJ proceedings.

---

55 *Id.* at para. 2.6.
56 *Id.* at para. 2.6.
57 *Id.* at para. 2.32.
58 *Breard v. Greene*, 523 U.S. 371, 374 (1998).
59 LaGrand Case (F.R.G. v. U.S.), 2001 I.C.J. 466, 475 (June 27).

Germany subsequently complained to the ICJ that, as a result of the Vienna Convention violations, it was deprived of the opportunity to provide assistance to its nationals. Even though both LaGrand brothers were executed during the proceedings, Germany, unlike Paraguay, sought redress for the violations. Specifically, it sought to prevent the U.S. from raising the procedural default doctrine in the future with respect to any Vienna Convention violation and an assurance from the U.S. that it would not repeat its actions in the future. The main contention of the U.S. was "that rights of consular notification and access under the Vienna Convention are rights of States, and not of individuals,"[60] even though individuals may benefit from these rights. The ICJ held that "it would be incumbent upon the United States to allow the review and reconsideration of the conviction and sentence by taking account of the violation of the rights set forth in the Convention."[61] In addition, the ICJ rejected the U.S. claim that the Convention does not confer individual rights.

Mexico v. U.S.[62] This was the most important of the three decisions. Mexico has long sought to provide consular assistance to its nationals residing in the United States. In 1942, Mexico and the U.S. entered into a bilateral consular agreement as a result of the "frequent inter-state travel of their respective citizens." In 1965, Mexico ratified the Vienna Convention in order to supplement its bilateral agreements. In 1986, Mexico developed the Program of Legal Consultation and Defense for Mexicans Abroad in order to provide legal assistance to its nationals charged with capital offenses. Despite these efforts, Mexico's efforts to assist its nationals and to ensure compliance with the Vienna Convention have met with limited success. As a result, Mexico sought the assistance of the ICJ.

In 2003, Mexico commenced proceedings against the United States on behalf of 54 of its nationals who had been sentenced to death in the U.S., primarily but not exclusively in Texas. Mexico complained that these individuals were arrested, detained, tried, convicted, and sentenced to death without being allowed to exercise their rights under Article 36. The ICJ agreed with Mexico that the U.S. had breached its obligations to Mexico under the Vienna Convention. Specifically, the ICJ found the following violations of the Convention:

1. failing to inform, without delay, the Mexican nationals of their rights under the Convention;
2. failing to inform, without delay, the Mexican consulate of the detention of their nationals, thereby denying Mexico the opportunity to render assistance to its nationals;

---

60   *Id.* at 493–4.
61   *Id.* at 514.
62   *Avena and Other Mexican Nationals (Mex. v. U.S.)* (Judgment of Mar. 31, 2004), available at http://www.icj-cij.org/docket/files/128/8188.pdf.

3. depriving Mexico of its rights to communicate with, and have access to, its nationals in a timely manner;

4. deriving Mexico of the right to obtain legal representation for its citizens in a timely fashion;

5. failing to review and reconsider the convictions and sentences of three Mexican nationals awaiting execution.[63]

Mexico sought to have these convictions and sentences overturned and any statements or other evidence obtained from its nationals prior to receiving consular notification excluded from any criminal proceedings subsequently brought against them. The ICJ rejected Mexico's request that their convictions and sentences be vacated. It agreed with the U.S. that there had to be a determination whether the Vienna Convention violation prejudiced the defendants. Most significantly, however, it agreed with Mexico that the inmates were entitled to a reconsideration of their Vienna Convention claims. Although it left the choice of means to the United States, the ICJ rejected the U.S. position that the executive clemency process would provide sufficient review. Furthermore, the ICJ held that U.S. courts should be precluded from applying the procedural default doctrine during the review of these claims.

The top two law enforcement officials in Texas reacted negatively to the ICJ's decision in *Avena*. Governor Rick Perry's spokesman stated that "[o]bviously the governor respects the world court's right to have an opinion but the fact remains they have no standing and no jurisdiction in the state of Texas."[64] A spokesman for the Texas Attorney General proclaimed that "[w]e do not believe the World Court has jurisdiction in these matters."[65] Most of the reaction outside of Texas has not been nearly as negative. In fact, there was a grudging acknowledgement that the decision demands compliance. For instance, in an Oklahoma case involving a Mexican national sentenced to death without receiving the required notification, the Oklahoma Court of Criminal Appeals held that it was bound by the ICJ's decision. The Oklahoma court granted a stay of execution and ordered an evidentiary hearing to determine whether the inmate was prejudiced by the denial of his rights. After the court determined that he had been prejudiced, the Governor of Oklahoma subsequently commuted his sentence to life imprisonment without the possibility of parole as a result of the *Avena* decision.[66] The Arkansas Attorney General's office dropped its effort to execute a Mexican national and

---

63   *Id.* paras. 106, 152.

64   P.R. Hughes, *U.S. Told to Review Case of Mexicans Sentenced to Death*, Houston Chronicle Apr. 1, 2004, at A1 (quoting Robert Black, spokesman for Governor Rick Perry).

65   Dane Schiller and Maro Robbins, *Mexico Wins in World Court*, San Antonio Express-News, Apr. 1, 2004, at 1A (quoting Paco Felici, spokesman for the Texas Attorney General).

66   *Triple Play in Oklahoma: Foreign National Gets Stay, New Hearing and Clemency* (May 2004), available at http://www.deathpenaltyinfo.org/article.php?scid=31&did=579.

the *Avena* decision provided the primary rationale for doing so.[67] Furthermore, California enacted a law requiring obligatory advisement of consular rights upon incarceration and the provision of lists of imprisoned nationals to consulates upon request.[68]

The most significant reaction was that of the President of the United States. Recognizing the nation's obligation to comply with the ICJ's judgment under Article 94 of the United Nations Charter,[69] President George W. Bush issued the following directive:

> I have determined, pursuant to the authority vested in me as President by the Constitution and the laws of the United States of America, that the United States will discharge its international obligations under the decision of the International Court of Justice … by having state courts give effect to the decision in accordance with general principles of comity in cases filed by the 51 Mexican nationals addressed in that decision.[70]

Given President Bush's complicated relationship with the international community, this order was a surprise to many. There are probably several explanations for the order. First and foremost, the United States has an interest in a strong relationship with Mexico. The two nations share a border; there is a strong economic relationship between the two nations, as evidenced by the North American Free Trade Agreement; and Mexico's cooperation is essential to U.S. efforts to fight terrorism, curtail illegal immigration, and combat drug trafficking. Therefore, the U.S. risked severely damaging its relationship with Mexico if it failed to comply with the ICJ's decision. President Bush's order can further be explained by the fact that the U.S. and most nations have an interest in ensuring that international law is complied with. More specifically, given the frequency with which Americans travel abroad, full compliance with the Vienna Convention is in the country's interest. Furthermore, because the United States has been a frequent litigator before the ICJ, high-level and uniform compliance with ICJ decisions is essential and this case provided the U.S. with an opportunity to stress the importance of compliance. Finally, President Bush may have had a selfish reason for complying

---

67   *ICJ Decision Prompts Settlement in Arkansas Case* (Aug. 2004), available at http://www.deathpenaltyinfo.org/article.php?scid=31&did=579.

68   *New California Law Enhances Prisoners' Consular Rights* (Oct. 2004), available at http://www.deathpenaltyinfo.org/article.php?scid=31&did=579.

69   U.N. Charter art. 94(1) provides that "[e]ach member of the United Nations undertakes to comply with the decision of the International Court of Justice in any case to which it is a party."

70   Press Release, George W. Bush, President of the United States, Memorandum for the Attorney General (Feb. 28, 2005), available at http://www.whitehouse.gov/news/releases/2005/02/20050228-18.html.

with the ICJ's order since by doing so he would greatly expand the power of the President.

The case for President Bush's authority to issue such an order is strong. First, the Vienna Convention and Optional Protocol, both ratified by the United States Senate, are the supreme law of the land and trump state law. The order was issued pursuant to the President's duty to "take Care that the Laws be faithfully executed."[71] In addition, the courts have recognized the plenary power of the President to conduct foreign affairs, especially to remedy violations of international law by the United States.[72] Pursuant to this power, the courts have been willing to allow presidents to settle disputes with foreign nations as long as Congress has acquiesced in allowing them to do so. For instance, in *Dames & Moore v. Regan,*[73] President Jimmy Carter was allowed:

> to terminate all legal proceedings in United States courts involving claims of United States persons and institutions against Iran and its state enterprises, to nullify all attachments and judgments obtained therein, to prohibit all further litigation based on such claims, and to bring about the termination of such claims through binding arbitration.[74]

President Carter was allowed to interfere in pending judicial proceedings in order to obtain the release of U.S. hostages being held by Iranian militants with the support of the Iranian government. His actions were upheld by the Supreme Court because:

> the settlement of claims has been determined to be a necessary incident to the resolution of a major foreign policy dispute between our country and another, and where, as here, we can conclude that Congress acquiesced in the President's action, we are not prepared to say that the President lacks the power to settle such claims.[75]

Given the fact that President Bush was enforcing two treaties which Congress ratified and therefore made federal law, that the courts – including the Supreme Court – have traditionally deferred to Presidents in conducting foreign relations especially when Congress has authorized the action taken by the President, and the fact that state courts are obligated to enforce federal law, his order seemed to be lawful. Texas officials, however, challenged the President's authority to

---

71   U.S. Const. Art. II, § 3.
72   *United States v. Curtiss-Wright Export Corp.*, 299 U.S. 304, 319–20 (1936).
73   453 U.S. 654 (1981).
74   *Id.* at 665.
75   *Id.* at 688.

Most Deserving of Death

enforce the ICJ's judgment which required the Supreme Court to resolve the issue in *Medellin v. Texas*.[76]

Jose Medellin was a Mexican national who had lived in the United States since he was a child. He had been convicted and sentenced to death for the brutal murder of two teenagers during a gang initiation in Texas. When the police apprehended Medellin, they gave him *Miranda* warnings but failed to inform him of his rights under the Vienna Convention to notify the Mexican consulate of his detention. His lawyers failed to object to the Vienna Convention violation either at trial or on direct appeal. He raised the Vienna Convention violation for the first time in his state habeas petition. The state courts held that the claim had been procedurally defaulted as a result of his failure to object earlier. When he raised the claim in federal court, it agreed with the state courts that Medellin had procedurally defaulted the claim. Medellin was one of the defendants at issue in Mexico's case against the United States. After the ICJ's decision in *Avena* and President Bush's order, Medellin again sought review in the Texas state court. The Texas court again rejected Medellin's Vienna Convention claim. The Texas court held, as it had previously, that the claim had been procedurally defaulted. The Texas court disregarded both the ICJ's decision in *Avena* and President Bush's order on the grounds that neither could displace Texas's procedural default rules.[77] After Medellin petitioned the Supreme Court, the Court agreed to decide whether the ICJ's decision in *Avena* was binding on state courts and whether the President had the authority to make the decision binding.

Medellin argued that the Supremacy clause makes the decision in *Avena* the law of the land and therefore trumps Texas's procedural default rules. The Supreme Court broke from its prior precedents granting the President broad authority to conduct foreign affairs especially when Congress has authorized or at least acquiesced in the President's actions. The Court held that the President's order did not trump state law even though he was acting pursuant to two treaties, the Vienna Convention on Consular Relations and the Optional Protocol, that Congress had ratified. The Court acknowledged that the *Avena* decision created an international obligation. However, according to the Court, "not all international law obligations automatically constitute binding federal law enforceable in United States courts."[78] The Court held that although the Optional Protocol created an international obligation for the United States, the treaty is non-self-executing because the textual provisions of the treaty do not indicate that the President and Senate intended for the agreement to have domestic effect. As Justice Breyer pointed out in dissent, it would be unnecessary to include an explicit provision in a multilateral treaty stating that it is self-executing given the fact that some nations automatically incorporate international law into their domestic law. Justice Breyer points out that the decision in *Medellin* calls into question many treaties to which

76   552 U.S. 491 (2008).
77   *Ex parte Medellin*, 223 S.W.3d 315, 322–3 (Tex. Crim. App. 2006).
78   *Medellin v. Texas*, 552 U.S. 491, 504 (2008).

the United States is a party which contain no express language recognizing it to be self-executing: "[i]n a world where commerce, trade, and travel have become ever more international, that is a step in the wrong direction."[79]

The Court also refused to enforce the decision in *Avena* on the grounds that although the United States agreed in the Optional Protocol to submit disputes to the ICJ, there is no language in the treaty making nations bound by the ICJ's decisions interpreting the agreement. According to the Supreme Court, decisions of the ICJ are only enforceable through the United Nations Charter absent the clear intent of the President and Congress to make ICJ decisions domestically enforceable. Article 94 provides that "[e]ach Member of the United Nations undertakes to comply with the decision of the [ICJ] in any case to which it is a party." According to the Court, Article 94 does not bind nation-states to ICJ decisions. Article 94 only requires nation-states to seek domestic compliance with ICJ decisions. Shortly after the Court's rejection of Medellin's Vienna Convention claim, he was executed.

As a result of the Court's decision in *Medellin*, in order for a decision of the ICJ to have binding effect in the United States, it was not enough that Congress ratified a treaty in which it agreed to the jurisdiction of the ICJ. The President and Senate would have to be clear in their intent to bind the United States to decisions of the ICJ and the Court was certainly aware that in the present political environment, that would almost never occur. Thus, although the Vienna Convention confers rights upon any foreign national detained in the United States, the Court has left these individuals without any judicially enforceable remedy for a violation of these rights.

Juvenile Executions

Before the United States Supreme Court ruled that the death penalty could not be imposed on juveniles, several death row inmates who were juveniles when their crimes were committed made claims based on international law. For instance, in *Beazley v. Johnson*,[80] Napoleon Beazley was convicted of murdering the father of a federal appellate judge when he was 17. Texas law at the time provided that if a person was at least 17 when he committed a capital offense, he could receive the death penalty. Beazley claimed that because he was a juvenile when the crime was committed, his execution would violate international law and, as a result of the Supremacy clause, United States law. Beazley's claim was based on Article 6(5) of the International Covenant on Civil and Political Rights (ICCPR), which prohibits the imposition of the death penalty on juveniles. In 1992, although the United States Senate ratified the ICCPR, it attached various reservations, understandings, and declarations. With respect to Article 6(5)'s prohibition on the execution of

---

79   *Id.* at 562.
80   242 F.3d 248 (5th Cir. 2001).

juvenile offenders, the United States Senate attached the following pertinent reservation and declaration:

> That the United States reserves the right, subject to its Constitutional constraints, to impose capital punishment on any person (other than a pregnant woman) duly convicted under existing or future laws permitting the imposition of capital punishment, including such punishment for crimes committed by persons below eighteen years of age ...
>
> That the United States declares that the provisions of Articles 1 through 27 of the [ICCPR] are not self-executing.[81]

Under international law, a nation is allowed to ratify a treaty and to attach reservations exempting it from certain provisions of the treaty. If other parties to the treaty are dissatisfied with the reservations, they may present a diplomatic protest or may decline to recognize themselves as being in a treaty relationship with the reserving nation. Furthermore, the fact that the United States had declared that Article 6(5) was not self-executing was designed to prevent the treaty from being enforced in U.S. courts – although that is ultimately a matter for the courts to decide. Beazley argued that the United States reservation to Article 6(5) and the declaration regarding self-execution was not compatible with the ICCPR and was therefore void. In support of his position, he cited the United Nations Human Rights Committee's General Comment on reservations to the ICCPR:

> The Covenant neither prohibits reservations nor mentions any type of permitted reservation ... where a reservation is not prohibited by the treaty or falls within the specified permitted categories, a State may make a reservation provided it is not incompatible with the object and purpose of the treaty ... Reservations that offend peremptory norms would not be compatible with the object and purpose of the Covenant ... Accordingly, a State may not reserve the right ... to execute children ... the normal consequence of an unacceptable reservation is not that the Covenant will not be in effect at all for a reserving party. Rather, such a reservation will generally be severable, in the sense that the Covenant will be operative for the reserving party without benefit of the reservation.[82]

The Fifth Circuit Court of Appeals found the United States' reservation to be valid despite the comment of the Human Rights Committee and rejected his claim. Beazley was executed shortly thereafter.

---

81   138 Cong. Rec. S4781-01, S4783-84 (daily ed. April 2, 1992).

82   General Comment 24, *General Comment on Issues Relating to Reservations Made Upon Ratification or Accession to the Covenant or the Optional Protocols Thereto, or in Relation to Declarations Under Article 41 of the Covenant*, U.N. GAOR Human Rights Comm. 52d Sess., pp. 5,6,8,18, U.N. Doc. CCPR/C/21/Rev. 1/ Add. 6 (Nov. 1994).

Prolonged Delays in Carrying out Executions

Most death row inmates are not executed until well after their conviction, if at all. Of course much of the delay is a result of the long appellate process. However, it is frequently the case that the inmate is not responsible for the prolonged delay. The delay in carrying out an inmate's execution may be attributable to the misconduct of government officials, for instance, by withholding exculpatory evidence or other constitutional violations. The delay may also be a function of the courts' failure to promptly review and resolve the inmate's appeals. The inordinate delay in carrying out an execution has become known as the "death row phenomenon" and results in an inmate suffering extreme psychological trauma because of his solitary confinement in a small cell for 23 hours a day. The psychological trauma an inmate suffers has been described as follows:

> From the moment he enters the condemned cell, the prisoner is enmeshed in a dehumanizing environment of near hopelessness. He is in a place whether the sole object is to preserve his life so that he may be executed. The condemned prisoner is "the living dead" ... Throughout all this time the condemned prisoner constantly broods over his fate ... The horrifying specter of being [executed] is, if at all, never far from mind.[83]

Although some amount of suffering is an incidental part of processing a condemned inmate's appeals prior to carrying out an execution, such suffering becomes unnecessary – and possibly unconstitutional – when state actors cause a substantial, unwarranted delay. Such long-term gratuitous suffering becomes a separate form of punishment, which may be equivalent to or greater than the actual execution.

The practice of forcing a condemned man to wait an inordinate amount of time before execution was condemned by English common law. In 1752, the British Parliament enacted an "Act for better preventing the horrid Crime of Murder," which provided that all persons convicted of murder should be executed two days after sentencing.[84] Common law in America followed the English common law practice of swift executions. Colonial New York, for example, executed convicted felons within a few days of sentencing. Similarly, in colonial New England, "capital offenders were put to death without moral qualms but they were dispatched swiftly without unnecessary suffering."[85] Many framers shared the view that executions should be carried out swiftly. Thomas Jefferson wrote that "whenever sentence of death shall have been pronounced against any person for treason or murder,

---

83   *Catholic Comm'n for Justice & Peace in Zimb. v. Attorney Gen.*, No. S.C. 73/93 (Zimb. June 24, 1993) (reported in 14 Hum. Rts. L. J. 323 (1993)).

84   *The Murder Act*, 1751, 25 Geo. 2, ch. 37 (Eng.).

85   E. McManus, *Law and Liberty in Early New England* 182 (Amherst: Univ. Mass. Press, 1993).

execution shall be done on the next day but one after such sentence, unless it be Sunday, and then on Monday following."[86] In a 1777 letter, George Washington stated that the execution of a soldier "better be done quickly and in a[s] public [a] manner as possible."[87] Supreme Court Justice James Wilson, another leading framer, wrote that the principles of utility and of justice require that the commission of a crime should be followed by speedy infliction of the punishment."[88]

Death row inmates have argued that inordinate delay in carrying out an execution is cruel and constitutes torture. Several foreign tribunals have been receptive to this argument. Most notably, the British Privy Council – the highest judicial body in the United Kingdom – held that Jamaica could not execute an inmate 14 years after sentencing him to death.[89] The Privy Council concluded that it was an "inhuman act to keep a man facing the agony of execution over a long extended period of time."[90] It held that any delay of more than five years was "inhuman or degrading punishment or other treatment" unless "due entirely to the fault of the accused."[91] The Zimbabwean Supreme Court held that delays of five or six years were inordinate and constituted "torture or ... inhuman or degrading punishment or other such treatment." The Supreme Court of India has held that judges must take account of delay when deciding whether to impose the death penalty.[92] Finally, as discussed earlier, the European Court of Human Rights held that the United Kingdom could not extradite a defendant to the United States to face the death penalty because of the risk that he would be subject to a long delay before he was executed.[93]

In a case involving a Texas inmate who spent 17 years on death row, Justice Stevens indicated that he was receptive to the argument that inordinate delay in carrying out an execution violated the Eighth Amendment of the U.S. Constitution.[94] He pointed out that the purpose of retribution has been served by the severe punishment already inflicted. He also added that there was no additional deterrent effect in executing someone who has spent so much time on death row. Justice

---

86   Thomas Jefferson, *A Bill for Proportioning Crimes and Punishments* (1779), reprinted in *The Complete Jefferson* 90, 95 (S. Padover ed., New York: distr. by Duell, Sloan & Pearce 1943).

87   Letter to Colonel George Gibson, March 11, 1778, vol. XI, in *The Writings of George Washington from the Original Manuscript Sources* 1745–99 (Washington, D.C.: U.S. Gov't Printing Office 1931–44).

88   Robert Green McCloskey, *The Works of James Wilson* vol. II 628–30 (Cambridge, Mass.: Belknap Press of Harvard Univ. Press, 1967).

89   *Pratt v. Attorney General of Jamaica* [1994] 2 A.C. 1, 4 All E.R. 769 (P.C. 1993) (en banc).

90   *Id.* at 29.

91   *Id.*

92   *Sher Singh v. State of Punjab*, A.I.R. 1983 S.C. 465.

93   European Court of Human Rights: *Soering v. United Kingdom*, 11 Eur. Ct. H.R. (Ser. A), 439, 478, P111 (1989).

94   *Lackey v. Texas*, 514 U.S. 1045 (1998) (memorandum of Justice Stevens respecting the denial of certiorari).

Stevens believed that carrying out an execution after an inmate has spent so much time on death row is nothing more than the "pointless and needless extinction of life with only marginal contributions to any discernible social or public purposes."[95]

While I was representing a Texas death row inmate, Justice Stevens issued his memorandum. Larry Wayne White was incarcerated on death row for 17 years. Although he exercised his right to pursue an appeal during this time, most of the delay in carrying out his sentence was attributable to the state. For instance, his appeal was before the Texas Court of Criminal Appeals for five years before that court rendered a decision. Therefore, I accepted Justice Stevens's invitation to pursue a claim that Texas had forfeited its right to execute White after such a prolonged delay in the lower courts since his case seemed like a model for such a claim. The lower courts were not at all receptive to the claim. The Fifth Circuit held that the delay was White's fault because he could have been executed earlier but chose instead to pursue his appeals.[96] The Supreme Court refused to hear White's case and he was subsequently executed.

Not only have the lower courts been unreceptive to claims of inordinate delay in carrying out executions. Justice Stevens has been unable to convince any of his colleagues besides Justice Breyer to grant certiorari and consider the merits of such a claim. The closest the Court came to considering the issue involved the cases of a Florida death row inmate who spent more than 25 years on death row and a Nebraska inmate who spent more than 19 years imprisoned on death row.[97] In both cases, a primary cause of the delay was the state's defective death penalty procedures which caused both inmates' sentences to be overturned. Although the Court denied certiorari, Justices Thomas and Breyer engaged in an extensive debate over the issue. According to Justice Thomas, claims based on the delay in carrying out an inmate's execution should be rejected. First, according to Justice Thomas, these defendants availed themselves of the extensive death penalty appeals process and therefore have no basis for complaining that their executions were taking too long. Second, Justice Thomas believes that in the event the Supreme Court were to recognize such a claim, lower courts may give short shrift to the inmates' other claims to avoid being accused of unreasonably delaying the case. Third, Justice Thomas believes that an Eighth Amendment claim based on inordinate delay will cause even longer delays because most inmates will make such claims. In response, Justice Breyer repeated the argument of Justice Stevens that a long delay in carrying out an execution serves neither the retributive or deterrent function of capital punishment. Justice Breyer believes that an Eighth Amendment claim should be available to an inmate whose confinement was prolonged, as in these cases, by the government's deliberate conduct or negligence.

---

95   *Id.* at 1046, quoting *Furman v. Georgia*, 408 U.S. 238, 312 (1972).
96   *White v. Johnson*, 79 F.3d 432, 439 (5th Cir. 1996).
97   *Knight v. Florida*, 528 U.S. 990 (1999).

Extradition and the Death Penalty

As a result of the international disapproval of capital punishment, many extradition treaties contain provisions prohibiting the extradition of a criminal suspect who would face the death penalty. Fairly typical is Article 6 of the United States–Argentina extradition treaty:

> When the offense for which extradition is requested is punishable by death under the laws in the Requesting State, and the laws in the Requested State do not permit the death penalty for that offense, surrender of the person sought may be refused unless the Requesting State provides assurances that the death penalty shall not be imposed, or, if imposed, shall not be executed.[98]

In *Ng v. Canada,* the Human Rights Committee held that a nation is not required to refuse extradition or to seek assurances under this treaty provision.[99] However, because the United States has the death penalty while many of its allies in Europe, Canada, and Mexico do not, these nations typically refuse to extradite without assurances from the U.S. that the death penalty will not be imposed. Some nations will even refuse to cooperate in the investigation of a suspect if the death penalty is being sought. For instance, Germany refused to turn over its intelligence files in the case of Zacarias Moussaoui, the only participant in the September 11 airplane destruction of the World Trade Center and Pentagon to be prosecuted, because the United States was seeking a death sentence in Moussaoui's case.

Conclusion

The United States is a party to most multilateral human rights treaties. However, these treaties were not signed and ratified by the U.S. in order to confer rights upon its citizens as the framers of these treaties intended. Rather, they were signed for public relations purposes in order to improve the nation's image abroad. The courts have gone along by refusing to hold the United States to the commitments it made in these treaties. Although Article VI of the U.S. Constitution makes treaties the supreme law of the land, the courts have refused to enforce international law in death penalty cases and are likely to continue to do so for the foreseeable future.

---

98   United States–Argentina Extradition Treaty available at http://www.oas.org/juridico/mla/en/traites/en_traites-ext-usa-arg.pdf.

99   Comm. No. 469/1991, U.N. Doc. A/49/40, vol. II, at 189 para. 15.6 (1993).

Chapter 8
Methods of Execution

The execution process has become fairly uniform throughout the United States. As a result of the Antiterrorism and Effective Death Penalty Act (AEDPA), discussed in Chapter 6, most inmates will only have one round of appeals, barring an exceptional circumstance. Typically the inmate's execution is scheduled after his appeals have been exhausted. Shortly before the inmate's execution, he is placed on suicide watch. On the day of his execution, he is given a last meal of his choice. He is allowed to spend his last day with his family and with his attorney, often hoping that a court somewhere will provide him with a miracle last-minute stay of execution. The inmate is allowed to have "guests" attend his execution and the victim's family members and the prosecutor are also allowed to attend, along with a member of the media. After he is executed, the family can retrieve his body and he is finally allowed to leave the prison grounds. For the many inmates who have no family ties or whose family cannot afford burial expenses, they are buried on prison grounds.

What has also become uniform is the method of executing the inmate. Every state now utilizes lethal injection as its primary method of execution, although a few provide some inmates with a choice of another method. Lethal injection has not always been the primary execution method. For much of the nation's history, hanging was the predominant method of executing those condemned to die. Hanging gradually gave way to electrocution but other methods were also used, including lethal gas and the firing squad. Although the overwhelming number of executions today are by lethal injection, some inmates choose another method if allowed to in order to make a point about what they believe to be the barbarity of capital punishment. A recurring question has been whether particular methods of execution are consistent with the Eighth Amendment to the Constitution, which states: "Excessive bail shall not be required, nor excessive fines imposed, nor cruel and unusual punishment inflicted." Inmates have challenged each of these methods on grounds that the method of execution constitutes cruel and unusual punishment. This chapter will describe each method still in force and the litigation that has ensued as a result. Because the basis of the legal challenges is the Eighth Amendment's Cruel and Unusual Punishments Clause, I will begin with a review of the Supreme Court's Eighth Amendment jurisprudence.

The Eighth Amendment's prohibition on cruel and unusual punishments originated in the English Bill of Rights of 1689. The measure was adopted in response to the Stuart regime's frequent use of torture and other barbaric measures against English subjects. In 1791, the United States Congress adopted the Eighth Amendment for ratification. However, it was not until 1962 that the Supreme Court applied the Eighth Amendment to the states through the Fourteenth Amendment. In interpreting whether the amendment's prohibition on cruel and unusual punishment is violated, the courts first perform a historical analysis. Any practice that was prohibited when the Eighth Amendment was adopted is also prohibited now. When the Eighth Amendment was adopted, it prohibited some of the more gruesome methods of execution – such as burning at the stake, crucifixion, breaking on the wheel, disemboweling while alive, drawing and quartering, and public dissection. None of the current methods of execution were prohibited at the time of the Eighth Amendment's adoption and therefore would not be outlawed based on historical analysis.

The Court does not confine itself to historical analysis. To determine whether modern punishments are cruel and unusual, the Court employs an "evolving standards of decency" analysis. This test is necessary because "time ... brings into existence new conditions and purposes. Therefore, a principle to be vital must be capable of wider application than the mischief which gave it birth."[1] For that reason, current claims of cruel and unusual punishment must be assessed "in light of contemporary human knowledge."[2] With respect to execution methods, the Court has held that "[p]unishments are cruel when they involve torture or a lingering death ... something more than the mere extinguishment of life."[3] In determining the constitutionality of an execution method, the Court considers: 1) whether the method involves "the unnecessary and wanton infliction of pain;"[4] 2) the method must ensure "nothing less than"[5] human dignity (for example, "a minimizing of physical violence during execution");[6] 3) the risk of "unnecessary and wanton infliction of pain;"[7] and 4) "evolving standards of decency" as measured by "objective factors to the maximum extent possible,"[8] such as legislation enacted by elected representatives or public attitudes. The Supreme Court has held that a painless execution is not possible and that a minimal amount of pain is acceptable. As a result, the Court has never found any method of execution to be unconstitutionally cruel and unusual punishment.

Descriptions of the different methods of execution follow. Every state that has retained the death penalty uses lethal injection as its primary method of execution. However, a few states continue to provide the inmate with the option of being executed by a different method. For instance, in the State of Washington some inmates are allowed to choose to be executed by lethal injection or hanging. In the

---

1   *Weems v. United States*, 217 U.S. 349, 373 (1910).

2   *Robinson v. California*, 370 U.S. 660, 666 (1962).

3   *In re Kemmler*, 136 U.S. 436, 447 (1890).

4   *Gregg v. Georgia*, 428 U.S. 153, 173 (1976); *Louisiana ex rel. Francis v. Resweber*, 329 U.S. 49, 463 (1947).

5   *Trop v. Dulles*, 356 U.S. 86, 100 (1958).

6   *Glass v. Louisiana*, 471 U.S. 1080, 1085 (1985) (Brennan, J., dissenting).

7   *Farmer v. Brennan*, 511 U.S. 825, 842 (1994).

8   *Stanford v. Kentucky*, 492 U.S. 361, 369 (1989).

event that the inmate refuses to choose, the inmate is hanged. Utah provides some inmates with the option of being executed by lethal injection or firing squad. Why do these states provide inmates with an option? In order to avoid any constitutional problems as a result of a change. Defendants sentenced to die by a certain method might argue that they are "entitled" to be executed by that method, or that their due process rights were violated by the change in methods, or that the change was an admission by the state of the cruelty of the previous method. Providing the inmate an option therefore avoids any legal challenges the inmate might raise to the method the state uses to execute him.

Hanging

Hanging was the predominant method of lawfully executing prisoners in England and was adopted by the American colonists.[9] Hanging basically involved dropping the inmate from a height with a noose around his neck. Hanging was the preferred method of execution because "[i]t required no equipment beyond a rope and a high structure sturdy enough to support the weight of a human body. It called for no expertise apart from the ability to tie a knot. In most cases it caused little damage to the exterior of the corpse."[10] The purpose of hanging was to deter future crime and as a result hangings occurred outdoors, often before thousands of spectators. The hanging was a small part of the ceremony which included a parade, a sermon or two, and a dramatic speech by the condemned person. In fact hangings became popular spectacles. Several reasons have been given to explain why so many would attend such a gruesome event. First, hangings were a form of violent entertainment and this type of entertainment has always been popular. Second, because of the sympathy they engendered for the condemned, hangings were a way of symbolically reintegrating the condemned person into society. The condemned was once again seen as human and as part of the community. Third, by watching a hanging, the spectators were able to signify their disapproval of the crime and the criminal. Hanging was eventually replaced by electrocution as the predominant method of execution in the United States. The states of New Hampshire and Washington, however, continue to provide some inmates with the option of being hanged.

Inmates have challenged hanging on cruel and unusual punishment grounds. In *Campbell v. Wood*,[11] a Washington state inmate refused to make a choice between hanging and lethal injection, and therefore was to be hanged. He alleged that hanging violated the Eighth Amendment on several grounds. Because hanging

---

9   Many African Americans were lynched in the South whenever they were accused of raping, murdering, or even stealing from a white person.

10   S. Banner, *The Death Penalty: An American History*, 44 (Cambridge, Mass.: Harvard Univ. Press, 2002).

11   18 F.3d 662 (9th Cir. 1994).

was acceptable when the Bill of Rights was adopted, it did not violate the Eighth Amendment under a historical analysis. The Court then had to determine whether hanging comported with contemporary standards of decency. Campbell argued that although hanging historically had been endorsed by the American people, this was no longer the case, as evidenced by the fact that at the time there were only two states (Washington and Montana) that continued to employ it. The court held that when determining whether an execution method was constitutional, the focus should not be on the number of states that employed the method in question but rather on the amount of pain that may or may not attend the practice. The Ninth Circuit held that hanging, as carried out in Washington, "results in rapid unconsciousness and death"[12] and was not therefore cruel and unusual punishment. Campbell argued that hanging carried a risk of decapitation or asphyxiation but the court held that the risk was too slight to make hanging unconstitutional. The Supreme Court has never ruled on the constitutionality of hanging.

Electrocution

Execution by hanging failed to convey the message intended. Rather, "[t]he execution ceremony, by focusing attention on the qualities of the person being hanged, produced as much pity as condemnation."[13] The sympathy that was engendered spurred movements toward a total abolition of capital punishment. The search began for an execution method that would minimize the sometimes sympathetic nature of hangings and also be more humane. The New York legislature appointed a commission to investigate and report "the most humane and practical method known to modern science of carrying into effect the sentence of death in capital cases."[14] The commission reported in favor of execution by electricity. The legislature adopted the commission's recommendation and replaced hanging with electrocution; and other states followed. Executions would be carried out by the most advanced and lethal technology available. Death by electricity would be fast, painless, and humane. Unlike hangings, electrocutions were not open to the public. Thus, the shift to electricity also caused a shift in the predominant purpose behind executions, from deterrent to retributive instead. The fact that executions would be inflicted by electricity and not in public had the added advantage that if anything went wrong, it was not on display for everyone to see.

Electrocution involves strapping the inmate to a chair with belts that cross the chest, groin, legs, and arms. The inmate is first given a jolt of electricity of between 500 and 2,000 volts, which lasts for approximately 30 seconds. After New York adopted electrocution, William Kemmler was scheduled to be the first person executed by electricity, for murdering his girlfriend. A year of litigation

---

12   *Id.* at 684.

13   Banner, *The Death Penalty: An American History* 148.

14   *In re Kemmler*, 136 U.S. 436, 444 (1890).

ensued as he challenged his execution on cruel and unusual punishment grounds. He was supported by the Westinghouse Company because the company was concerned that people would get the impression that electricity was dangerous. The New York state courts held hearings and concluded that electrocution was not more painful than hanging. The Supreme Court rejected Kemmler's challenge and deferred to the state courts' conclusion that death by electrocution was not cruel. The Court did hold that "[p]unishments are cruel when they involve torture or a lingering death ... [S]omething more than the mere extinguishment of life."[15] This legal conclusion remains viable.

Kemmler's execution was carried out but ended in disaster. A newspaper account of the execution of William Kemmler is as follows:

> After the first convulsion there was not the slightest movement of Kemmler's body ... Then the eyes that had been momentarily turned from Kemmler's body returned to it and gazed with horror on what they saw. The men rose from their chairs impulsively and groaned at the agony they felt. "Great God! He is alive!" someone said: "Turn on the current," said another ...
>
> Again came that click as before, and again the body of the unconscious wretch in the chair became as rigid as one of bronze. It was awful, and the witnesses were so horrified by the ghastly sight that they could not take their eyes off it. The dynamo did not seem to run smoothly. The current could be heard sharply snapping. Blood began to appear on the face of the wretch in the chair. It stood on the face like sweat ...
>
> An awful odor began to permeate the death chamber, and then, as though to cap the climax of this fearful sight, it was seen that the hair under and around the electrode on the head and the flesh under and around the electrode at the base of the spine was singeing. The stench was unbearable.[16]

After the execution of Kemmler, electrocution became a popular means of execution in other states despite continued mishaps and botches. The Supreme Court's decision in *In re Kemmler* settled the constitutionality of electrocution. However, inmates condemned to die by electrocution raised other claims. In *Malloy v. South Carolina*,[17] an argument was made that the switch from hanging to electrocution enhanced the punishment for murder and thus was a violation of the ex post fact clause of the Constitution. The Court held that the switch did not increase the punishment for murder but merely changed its mode. Louisiana's first attempt to electrocute Willie Francis failed after the electric chair had malfunctioned.[18] Francis argued that it would be cruel and unusual punishment for the state to attempt to

---

15 *Id.* at 447.

16 D. Denno, *Is Electrocution an Unconstitutional Method of Execution? The Engineering of Death Over the Century*, 35 Wm. & Mary L. Rev. 551, 600, n. 322 (1994).

17 237 U.S. 180, 185 (1915).

18 *Louisiana ex rel. Francis v. Resweber*, 329 U.S. 459 (1947).

execute him again. The Court held that the Eighth Amendment prohibited only the "infliction of unnecessary pain,"[19] and the justices assumed that state officials performed "their duties in a careful and humane manner."[20] Justice Frankfurter did acknowledge that a series of abortive attempts at electrocution would raise a different question.[21]

The states were unable to eliminate the problems that electrocution caused, even after the passage of time and improvements in technology. Botched electrocutions continued after the modern era of capital punishment began in 1976.[22] There have been at least 18 botched electrocutions since 1976. As a result of a number of botched electrocutions in Florida, where inmates had been burned and bled during their executions,[23] the Supreme Court granted certiorari to review the constitutionality of electrocution.[24] Florida immediately called a special session of its legislature and changed its method of execution from electrocution to lethal injection, which mooted the case before the Court. However, the remaining states that used the electric chair saw the writing on the wall and abandoned it in favor of lethal injection. The coup de grace to the electric chair occurred when Nebraska's Supreme Court ruled that its use was forbidden under its state constitution.[25] The Nebraska Supreme Court held that electrocution inflicts "intense pain and agonizing suffering," and that "condemned prisoners must not be tortured to death, regardless of their crimes."[26]

Gas Chamber

Even though death by electrocution had been adopted by many states it remained controversial. As a result some states sought a more humane method of execution.

---

19   *Id.* at 464.

20   *Id.* at 462.

21   *Id.* at 471.

22   D. Denno, *Execution and the Forgotten Eighth Amendment*, in America's Experiment with Capital Punishment, 572–3 (J.R. Acker, R.M. Bohm, and C.S. Lanier eds (Durham, N.C.: Carolina Academic Press 1998)).

23   During Pedro Medina's March 25, 1997 electrocution, "Blue and orange flames up to a foot long shot from the right side of Mr. Medina's head and flickered for 6 to 10 seconds, filling the execution chamber with smoke." D. Denno, *Getting to Death: Are Executions Constitutional?* 82 *Iowa Law Review* 319, 361 (1997). On July 8, 1999, blood from Allen Lee Davis's nose poured onto the collar of his white shirt and blood spread across his chest. Florida Supreme Court Justice Leander Shaw described Davis's execution and noted, "the color photos of Davis depict a man who – for all appearances – was brutally tortured to death by the citizens of Florida." *Provenzano v. Moore*, 744 So.2d 413, 440 (Fla. 1999) (Shaw, J., dissenting).

24   *Bryan v. Moore*, 528 U.S. 960 (1999).

25   *Nebraska v. Mata*, 745 N.W.2d 229, 279–80 (Neb. 2008).

26   *Id.*

In 1921, Nevada became the first state to use the gas chamber. This method of execution involved placing the condemned person in an airtight chamber and releasing into the chamber a poisonous gas. After Nevada conducted what was thought to be several painless executions, other Western and Southern states adopted the gas chamber as well. The gas chamber became a Western and Southern phenomenon as no other regions used lethal gas to carry out their executions. The gas chamber, however, was not a smashing success: "[l]ike the electric chair, the gas chamber sometimes inflicted pain, and when it did, the results were just as troubling to watch."[27] Because it inflicted pain, several inmates challenged the gas chamber on Eighth Amendment grounds. In California, the gas chamber had been the principal means of execution. The U.S. Court of Appeals for the Ninth Circuit agreed with the findings of a district court that:

> (1) inmates are likely to be conscious for anywhere from fifteen seconds to one minute from the time that the gas strikes their face; (2) there is a substantial risk that consciousness may persist for up to several minutes; (3) during this period of consciousness, the condemned inmate is likely to suffer intense physical pain; and (4) the cause of death by cyanide gas was a "substantially similar experience to asphyxiation" … [and] that asphyxiation would be an impermissibly cruel method of execution.[28]

The Ninth Circuit held that California's use of lethal gas constituted cruel and unusual punishment because "such horrible pain, combined with the risk that such pain will last for several minutes by itself is enough to violate the Eighth Amendment."[29] Two other federal circuits, however, reached different conclusions regarding the constitutionality of the gas chamber.[30] The California legislature subsequently changed the state's method of execution to lethal injection. The Supreme Court vacated the judgment of the Ninth Circuit and remanded the case for reconsideration in light of the changed statute. The Supreme Court has never rendered a decision regarding the constitutionality of the gas chamber.

Firing Squad

Utah has used a firing squad as its primary method of execution throughout its history. The use of a firing squad in Utah is a consequence of the Mormon doctrine of blood atonement, the concept that some sins are so heinous that the offender can

---

27 Banner, *The Death Penalty: An American History* 200.

28 *Fierro v. Gomez*, 77 F.3d 301, 308 (9th Cir. 1996), vacated on other grounds, 519 U.S. 918 (1996).

29 *Id.* at 308.

30 *Gray v. Lucas*, 710 F.2d 1048 (5th Cir. 1983); *Hunt v. Nuth*, 57 F.3d 1327 (4th Cir. 1995).

atone only by literally shedding his blood. The execution is carried out by placing a target over the condemned person's heart. Some of the guns are loaded with live bullets and others with blanks, in a pattern not known to the shooters so that no one would know whether he was actually an executioner. In 1878, Utah's use of the firing squad was challenged in the Supreme Court on grounds that it was cruel and unusual punishment. The Supreme Court permitted the execution of Wallace Wilkerson by firing squad in the Utah territories.[31] In assessing whether execution by firing squad was cruel and unusual punishment, the Court pointed to the fact that firing squads were routinely used to execute military officers. However, despite the Supreme Court's approval of death by firing squad, there was still some dissent about the process, as evidence by one of the daily newspapers:

> The execution of Wallace Wilkerson at Provo yesterday affords another illustration of the brutal exhibitions of inquisitorial torture that have of late disgraced ... the country and which have in some states so shocked the natural sensibilities of the people that extreme punishment has been abrogated from pure disgust excited by the sickening spectacle of rotten ropes, ignorantly or carelessly adjusted nooses or inexperienced marksmen. These disgusting scenes are invariably ascribed to accidental causes, but they have become so horrifyingly frequent that some other method of judicial murder should be adopted. The French guillotine never fails. The swift falling knife flashes in the light, a dull thud is heard and all is over. It is eminently more merciful than our bungling atrocities, and the ends of justice are fully secured.[32]

More recent decisions have also rejected claims that the firing squad is cruel and unusual punishment.[33]

Lethal Injection

Oklahoma was the first state to adopt lethal injection, in 1977, and Texas was the first state to carry out an execution by lethal injection, in 1982. Today lethal injection is used by every death penalty state and the federal government. Lethal injection has become the predominant execution method because of the belief that it is the most humane method possible. In general, the inmate is strapped to a gurney in an execution chamber. A catheter is inserted into a vein and a non-lethal solution is injected in order to prevent clogging. After the death warrant is read and the inmate is provided an opportunity to make a last statement, a lethal mixture is injected by one or more executioners or, depending on the state, by a

---

31   *Wilkerson v. State of Utah*, 99 U.S. 130, 134–5 (1878).
32   L.K. Gillespie, *The Unforgiven: Utah's Executed Men* 13 (Salt Lake City: Signature Books, 1991) (citing Daily Ogden Junction, May 17, 1879).
33   *Andrews v. Shulsen*, 802 F.2d 1256, 1275 n. 16 (10th Cir. 1986).

machine. The lethal mixture consists of three chemicals. The first is a non-lethal dose of sodium thiopental, which is a frequently used anesthetic for surgery. The purpose of sodium thiopental is to induce a deep sleep and loss of consciousness in about 20 seconds. The American producer of sodium thiopental has stopped manufacturing the drug and another sedative is being used, pentobarbital. The next drug that is administered is pancuronium bromide, also known as Pavulon, a total muscle relaxant. It stops the inmate from breathing by paralyzing the diaphragm and lungs. This is done to prevent any involuntary movements, such as reflexes or seizures, from occurring. The last chemical used in the lethal injection process is potassium chloride, a drug most frequently used during heart bypass surgery. Potassium chloride induces cardiac arrest and stops the inmate's heartbeat permanently. Despite the serene appearance that witnesses often describe of a lethal injection, there is ample evidence that inmates often experience pain and suffering prior to dying. Even the American Association of Veterinary Medicine indicated that it did not recommend the chemicals used in lethal injections of humans for the euthanasia of animals.[34] Some experts contend that lethal injection "is the most commonly 'botched' method of execution in the United States."[35]

An execution by lethal injection can be botched for several reasons. There is general agreement that, if applied properly, the chemicals will cause a humane death.[36] However, inmates differ in their physiological constitutions as well as in their drug tolerance and drug use histories. Therefore, some may need a far higher dosage of sodium thiopental than others in order to lose consciousness and sensation. Furthermore, sodium thiopental wears off quickly. Inmates can experience substantial pain and suffering if they receive an inadequate dosage of sodium thiopental or in the event that the drug wears off while they are being injected with the second and third chemicals.

Problems also occur when the drugs are not administered by medical professionals. In order to minimize an animal's suffering when it is being euthanized, the Humane Society firmly states that the chemicals must be injected by "well trained and caring personnel."[37] As the Humane Society recognizes, problems can occur when the drugs are not administered by medical personnel. The law, however, does not require physicians to be involved in administering the death penalty. Rather, the involvement of physicians in executions is left up to the medical profession. The American Medical Association (AMA), based on the Hippocratic principle that a physician should do no harm, has taken the position that "[a] physician, as a member of a profession dedicated to preserving

---

34   Am. Veterinary Med. Ass'n, *2000 Report of the AVMA Panel on Euthanasia*, 2185 Am. Veterinary Med. Ass'n 669, 680 (2001).

35   *Sims. v. State*, 754 So.2d 657, 667 n. 19 (Fla. 2000) (quoting the expert testimony of Professor Michael Radelet).

36   *Baze v. Rees*, 553 U.S. 35, 40 (2008).

37   Humane Society of the U.S., *General Statement Regarding Euthanasia Methods for Dogs and Cats*, Shelter Sense, Sept. 1994 at 11–12.

life when there is hope of doing so, should not participate in a legally authorized execution."[38] The AMA defines physician participation as follows:

> Physician participation in an execution includes, but is not limited to, the following actions: prescribing or administering tranquilizers and other psychotropic agents and medications that are part of the execution procedure; monitoring vital signs on site or remotely (including monitoring electrocardiograms); attending or observing an execution as a physician; and rendering of technical advice regarding execution.[39]

Furthermore, the head of ethics at the AMA has reportedly opined that "[e]ven helping to design a more humane protocol would disregard the AMA code."[40]

Despite the AMA's pronouncements, there is a spirited debate over whether physicians should participate in the execution process. On the one hand, the participation of doctors in the execution process may prevent some of the mishaps from occurring and, as they frequently do in the case of terminally ill patients, ensure that the condemned inmate's death is as smooth and painless as possible. Proponents of physician participation in executions would further note that in some jurisdictions, doctors are allowed to provide drugs to terminally ill patients for the sole purpose of ending their life. Oregon's Death with Dignity Act, for instance, allows doctors to dispense or prescribe a lethal dose of drugs upon the request of a terminally ill patient. On the other hand, a doctor's participation in the execution process may sanitize or humanize executions, as three doctors explained:

> Lethal injection looks more like therapy than punishment. It involves a traditional and familiar therapeutic modality, intravenous general anesthesia, typically with Pentothal and a muscle relaxant. The only difference is that the "patient," once "put to sleep," is not recovered. By wrapping punishment in a therapeutic cloak, the whole process leading to that final moment feels less aversive to those who are required to participate and is therefore more bearable.[41]

One could also cite Nazi Germany as an example of the danger of allowing physicians to participate in state-sponsored executions.

Other medical professionals have taken a similar position. The American Nurses Association (ANA) takes the position that participation in an execution "is

38   AMA, *Code of Medical Ethics, Policy E-2.06 Capital Punishment* (2000), available at http://www.ama-assn.org/ama1/pub/upload/mm/369/e206capitalpunish.pdf.

39   *Id.*

40   E. Marris, *Will Medics' Qualms Kill the Death Penalty?* 441 Nature 8–9 (May 4, 2006).

41   J.D. Gorman et al., *The Case Against Lethal Injection*, 115 Virginia Medical 576 (1988).

a breach of the ethical traditions of nursing, and the *Code for Nurses.*"[42] According to the ANA, a nurse must not "take part in assessment, supervision or monitoring of the procedure or the prisoner; procuring, prescribing, or preparing medications or solutions; inserting the intravenous catheter; injecting the lethal solution; and attending or witnessing the execution as a nurse."[43] The National Association of Emergency Medical Technicians (NAEMT) holds that "[p]articipation in capital punishment is inconsistent with the ethical precepts and goals of the [Emergency Medical Services] profession."[44] Medical professionals would be able to adjust the dosage of sodium thiopental according to the needs of the inmate. Because of the failure of medical personnel to administer the drugs, prison employees must do so. This increases the likelihood that the proper dosage of chemicals will not be administered and that the inmate will suffer as a result.

A second problem that stems from the absence of medical professionals during the execution process is the amount of discretion provided to prison officials. Most states do not specify the quantity of lethal injection chemicals to be used during an execution.[45] As a result, the decision as to quantity is left to prison officials. This often results in too little sodium thiopental being administered and the inmate being conscious when the other drugs are administered. Another problem arises due to the fact that many inmates suffer diabetes and/or obesity, are/were heavy drug users and their veins are damaged by drug use, and that some inmates are extremely muscular. Each of these conditions may make it difficult to locate a suitable vein for injection and may result in the chemicals not being properly injected – resulting in the chemicals flowing away from the inmate's heart, thereby hindering their absorption and increasing the likelihood that the inmate will experience pain. Finally, because the inmate is paralyzed after pancuronium bromide is injected, the inmate is unable to verbalize or, through bodily movements, express any pain that he may experience prior to his death.

Professor Deborah Denno has described many of the botched lethal injections since 1976. For instance, Bert Leroy Hunter, "in a violent reaction to the drugs, ... lost consciousness and his body convulsed against his restraints during what one witness called a 'violent and agonizing death.'"[46] Scott Dawn Carpenter "gasped and shook for three minutes following the injection. He was pronounced dead eight minutes later."[47] There were reports that Robyn Lee Parks "violently gagged and bucked in his chair after the drugs were administered. One witness

---

42   ANA, *Position Statement: Nurses' Participation in Capital Punishment* (1994).

43   *Id.*

44   NAEMT, *Position Statement on EMT and Paramedic Participation in Capital Punishment* (June 9, 2006).

45   D. Denno, *When Legislatures Delegate Death: The Troubling Paradox Behind State Uses of Electrocution and Lethal Injection and What it Says About Us*, 63 Ohio St. L. J. 63, 149 (2002).

46   *Id.* at 141.

47   *Id.* at 140.

said that his death looked 'painful and inhumane.'"[48] It took Arkansas officials "almost an hour for a team of eight to find a suitable vein" on Ricky Ray Rector's arm. "Eventually, Rector himself assisted in finding the vein."[49] Stephen McCoy "choked and heaved" in a violent reaction to the drugs which Texas prison officials attributed to a weak dosage.[50] Two minutes into Raymond Landry's execution in Texas, "after a lengthy search for an adequate vein, the syringe came out of Landry's vein, 'spewing deadly chemicals toward startled witnesses.'"[51] Texas officials were unable to find a vein, which caused Elliot Rod Johnson's execution to take nearly an hour.[52] According to a witness, Thomas Andy Barefoot "emitted a 'terrible gasp,' [and] Barefoot's heart was still beating after the prison medical examiner had declared him dead."[53] The *St. Petersburg Times* reported on Florida's execution of Angel Diaz. Diaz's execution took 34 minutes, nearly three times as long as usual. Correction officials acknowledged that 34 minutes was an unusually long time. During the 34 minutes that it took for him to be executed, "Diaz squinted his eyes and tightened his jaw as if in pain. Twenty-six minutes into the procedure, Diaz's body suddenly jolted." According to one witness, "[i]t looked like Mr. Diaz was in a lot of pain ... [h]e was gasping for air for 11 minutes." Prior to his execution, Diaz clung to his innocence in his final statement: "The state of Florida is killing an innocent person," he said.[54]

Because so many lethal injections have been botched, death row inmates began to bring claims alleging that execution by lethal injection inflicts cruel and unusual punishment. Instead of causing an instantaneous, relatively pain-free death, these inmates alleged and produced expert testimony indicating that many inmates suffered for an extended period of time prior to their deaths. Many lower courts were receptive to these arguments. Twenty-nine executions had been stayed in 11 states due to lethal injection challenges. Some of these challenges exposed deep problems in the way in which many states were administering lethal injections. In Tennessee, for instance, a federal judge found that the state's protocols did not adequately ensure that inmates were properly anesthetized, which could "result in a terrifying, excruciating death."[55]

The Supreme Court could no longer avoid the issue and would have to decide for the first time in over 100 years whether a state's method of execution violated

---

48   *Id.*

49   *Id.*

50   *Id.* at 139.

51   D. Denno, *Lethally Humane? The Evolution of Execution Methods in the United States,* in America's Experiment with Capital Punishment: Reflections on the Past, Present, and Future of the Ultimate Penal Sanction, 693, 740 (James R. Acker et al. eds., 2d ed. 2003).

52   *Id.*

53   *Id.*

54   C. Tisch and C. Krueger, *Second Dose Needed To Kill Inmate,* St. Petersburg Times, December 14, 2006.

55   *Harbison v. Little,* 511 F. Supp.2d 287, 883 (M.D. Tenn. 2007).

the Eighth Amendment. The Court agreed to decide whether Kentucky's lethal injection procedure complied with the Constitution by granting certiorari in *Baze v. Rees*. Kentucky seemed like an odd state for a review of the lethal injection procedures since it had only executed two offenders since 1976, and only one by lethal injection. Kentucky, like 30 of the 36 states that have adopted lethal injection, used the three-drug combination. Prison personnel mix the drugs, load them into syringes, and administer them. A physician is present to assist in any effort to revive the prisoner in the event of a last-minute stay of execution but by statute is prohibited from participating in the "conduct of an execution" except to certify the cause of death. An execution team administers the drugs remotely from a central room through 5 feet of intravenous (IV) tubing. If the warden and deputy warden determine through visual inspection that the prisoner is not unconscious within 60 seconds following the delivery of the sodium thiopental, a new 3-mg dose of sodium thiopental is administered before injecting the pancuronium and potassium chloride. The inmates in *Baze* argued that there was a significant risk that these procedures would not be followed – in particular that the sodium thiopental would not be properly administered – resulting in severe pain when the other chemicals are administered. They proposed an alternative procedure consisting only of sodium thiopental, and dispensing with pancuronium and potassium chloride, along with additional monitoring by trained personnel to ensure that the sodium thiopental was properly administered.

Although seven of the nine justices agreed that Kentucky's lethal injection protocol was constitutional, only three justices could agree on a specific standard that executions by lethal injection must meet. Chief Justice Roberts's opinion, which was joined by Justices Kennedy and Alito, rejected the unnecessary risk standard proposed by the inmates. Their opinion adopted instead a "substantial risk of harm standard." To succeed, an inmate must demonstrate that there is a substantial risk that he will suffer severe pain as a result of a state's lethal injection procedures. In addition, the inmate must proffer a "feasible, readily implemented" alternative as part of his affirmative case. Their opinion concluded that Kentucky's procedures did not pose a substantial risk of severe pain to inmates. Justice Thomas, joined by Justice Scalia, would hold that a method of execution "violates the Eighth Amendment only if it is deliberately designed to inflict pain." He listed methods of execution that were designed to terrorize the criminal and therefore would be unconstitutional under this standard: burning at the stake, gibbeting ("hanging the condemned in an iron cage so that his body would decompose in public view"), public dissection, disemboweling alive, breaking on the wheel, flaying alive, crucifixion, rendering asunder with horses, and mutilating and scourging to death. Because lethal injection was adopted in order to make executions more humane, it could not be unconstitutional under his standard. Under Justice Thomas's and Scalia's standard, no matter how painful an execution by lethal injection might be or how sloppy the procedures for carrying it out, it would never violate the Constitution because its purpose is not to deliberately inflict pain on the prisoner. Justice Thomas believes that judges do not have the institutional capacity to resolve whether the pain associated with an execution is too severe and intolerable. In dissent, Justice Ginsburg urged the Court to determine whether lethal injections "pose an untoward, readily avoidable risk of inflicting severe and unnecessary pain." If measures are readily available which would materially increase the likelihood that the inmate will not suffer pain, a state's failure to adopt these measures would be unconstitutional. Justice Ginsburg suggested that there were several measures that were readily available to Kentucky officials to minimize the risk that the inmate would suffer pain. For example, Kentucky relied exclusively on the warden's visual inspection to determine whether the inmate was conscious after receiving an injection of sodium thiopental. There were other measures that could be easily employed to check for consciousness that were utilized by other states. Someone could call the inmate's name, shake him, brush his eyelids to test for reflex, or apply a noxious stimulant to gauge his response. Furthermore, because the inmate is connected to an electrocardiogram (ECG/EKG), his blood pressure and heart rate could be monitored. A drop in either would signal that the drug has entered his bloodstream.

Because of the justices' failure to agree on a standard for future challenges to lethal injection, the litigation over the constitutionality of lethal injection is likely to continue. As Justice Stevens noted, "[w]hen we granted certiorari in this case, I assumed that our decision would bring the debate about lethal injection to a close. It now seems clear it will not."[56] Justice Thomas added: "[f]ar from putting an end to abusive litigation in this area ... today's decision is sure to engender more litigation."[57]

Conclusion

The Supreme Court has upheld the firing squad, electrocution, and, more recently, lethal injections against constitutional challenges. Those seeking to end the death penalty by having the Court declare the methods of carrying it out unconstitutional have been thwarted in their efforts and will have to find another mechanism for accomplishing their objective.

---

56   *Baze v. Rees,* 553 U.S. 35, 71 (2008).
57   *Id.* at 105.

Chapter 9
Judges and Capital Punishment

Introduction

Judges are an integral part of the death penalty process. Trial judges preside over capital murder trials. Appellate judges must review death sentences for errors. Supreme Court justices also play an important role. They are typically presented with a condemned inmate's final appeal prior to his execution. They also determine the constitutionality of death penalty statutes and procedures. As a result of their unique and important role in the "machinery of death," an interesting and important question has arisen regarding the obligations of judges who are opposed to capital punishment. By comparison, potential jurors who are opposed to capital punishment are not allowed to serve as jurors in death penalty cases. What should judges do when their moral beliefs conflict with the duties of the judicial office? This section examines the very unique role of judges in the death penalty process and some of the complex issues raised when a judge personally opposes capital punishment. As will be discussed, Justice Scalia believes that these judges should resign from the bench. This is probably too drastic and unnecessary. Most judges have strong moral beliefs about some of the issues that they will be required to rule on during their careers. It is therefore not possible or desirable to populate the judiciary with judges who lack strong moral convictions about some of the issues upon which they will be required to rule. Furthermore, there are sufficient safeguards to prevent judges from "ignoring duly enacted, constitutional laws and sabotaging death penalty cases," as Justice Scalia suggests they might. First, individuals with strong moral objections to capital punishment are not likely to be selected to serve as judges. Second, judges are constrained in their ability to enact personal policy preferences. For instance, a trial judge's rulings are reviewed by appellate courts and appellate judges must build a consensus for their positions. Third, there is a long history of judges enforcing laws that they find morally objectionable, beginning with fugitive slave laws.

The Views of Justice Scalia

In a rare moment, Justice Scalia shared his thoughts on the subject of judges and capital punishment at the University of Chicago's Religion and the Death Penalty

Conference.[1] In his view, the death penalty passes constitutional muster since "it was clearly permitted when the Eighth Amendment was adopted ... And so it is clearly permitted today."[2] He believes that if the death penalty is abolished or reformed in the future, this movement should come from the legislative branch and not from "the nine lawyers who sit on the Supreme Court of the United States."[3] Justice Scalia's position on the death penalty runs counter to that of his faith, the beliefs of the Pope and the Catholic Church.

During his remarks, Justice Scalia explained why, although a devout Catholic, he does not accept the Church's position on the issue. Although he believes that the Pope and other church leaders' views on the death penalty are entitled to "thoughtful and respectful consideration,"[4] Justice Scalia argues that all practicing Catholics need not accept the Church's position. First, in his view, the Church's position "either ignores or rejects the longstanding church teaching that retribution is a valid purpose, indeed the principle purpose of government punishment."[5] Second, practicing Catholics need not adhere to the Church's position because the death penalty, unlike the prohibitions on birth control and abortion, "is not a moral position that the Church has always – indeed ever before – maintained."[6] Finally, he believes that the Church's position would have "disastrous" consequences for practicing Catholics. According to Justice Scalia, if most practicing Catholics accepted the Church's position on capital punishment, few Catholics would be elected to legislatures; Catholic candidates for Governor would rarely succeed; Catholics would rarely be selected for the bench; and practicing Catholics would be subject to recusal when called for jury duty in capital cases. In fact, he says that the Catholic position on the death penalty, if accepted by practicing Catholics, would require that Catholics retire from public life.

Justice Scalia says that he would resign from the bench if he accepted the Church's position on capital punishment. In his view any judge who believes that the death penalty is immoral should resign from the bench:

> I pause here to emphasize the point that in my view the choice for the judge who believes the death penalty to be immoral is resignation, rather than simply ignoring duly enacted, constitutional laws and sabotaging death penalty cases. He has after all, taken an oath to apply the laws and has been given no power to supplant them with rules of his own. Of course if he feels strongly enough he can

---

    1   Antonin Scalia, *Religion, Politics and the Death Penalty*, Address at University of Chicago Religion and the Death Penalty Conference (Jan. 25, 2002), available at http://pewforum.org/deathpenalty/resources/transcript3.php3.

    2   *Id.*

    3   *Id.*

    4   *Id.*

    5   *Id.*

    6   *Id.*

go beyond mere resignation and lead a political campaign to abolish the death penalty – and if that fails, a revolution. But rewrite laws he cannot do.[7]

According to Justice Scalia, judges who are opposed to capital punishment are obligated to resign, even if they are able to enforce the death penalty, because judges should not enforce laws that they find morally offensive. Is Justice Scalia correct? Should judges with moral and other reservations about the death penalty resign? Are there other choices available to judges wrestling with the conflict between their consciences and the law?

Reasons for Judicial Opposition to Capital Punishment

There are numerous reasons why a judge might oppose capital punishment. The most common are religious objections, concerns about the inherent injustices of capital punishment; the fact that it is gratuitous since it does not deter crime and does nothing more to protect society than incarceration; and the growing number of inmates who have been exonerated in recent years and the danger of executing an innocent person.

Religion

Some judges might have religious objections to capital punishment. Almost every organized religious denomination initially supported the death penalty.[8] That support began to erode during the twentieth century. Today, almost every major Christian denomination has announced its opposition to capital punishment. In addition, the Unitarian Universalist and most conservative and Reform Jewish religious organizations are opposed to the death penalty. Catholic judges might especially be opposed to capital punishment as a result of the vigorous opposition to it by church leaders. Pope John Paul II and the United States Conference of Bishops opposed the death penalty as a result of their belief in the sanctity of human life. The Pope stated that all human life deserves respect, "even [the lives] of criminals and unjust aggressors."[9] According to the Pope, since human life, "from its beginning ... involved the 'creative action of God' and remains forever in

---

7   *Id.*

8   For a history of organized religious denominations and their attitude toward capital punishment, see D. Douglas, *God and the Executioner: The Influence of Western Religion on the Death Penalty*, 9 Wm. & Mary Bill Rts. J. 137, 142–61 (2000); the remarks of Rabbi David Novak, available at http://pewforum.org/deathpenalty/resources/transcript1.php3.

9   T. Berg, *Religious Conservatives and the Death Penalty*, 9 Wm. & Mary Bill Rts. J. 31, 42 (2000).

a special relationship with the Creator, only God is the master of life."[10] Therefore, the government:

> [o]ught not go to the extreme of executing the offender except in cases of absolute necessity; in other words, when it would not be possible otherwise to defend society. Today, however, as a result of steady improvements in the organization of the penal system, such cases are very rare, if not practically non-existent.[11]

The Pope and the Catholic Church have played a major role in the death penalty debate. As execution dates approach, the Pope sometimes intercedes on behalf of death row inmates to the relevant Governor and parole board. The Governor of Missouri honored the Pope's request for mercy and commuted an inmate's death sentence to life imprisonment after meeting with the Pope in 1999.[12] U.S. bishops have also interceded on behalf of death row inmates and have issued a series of statements, beginning in 1980, asserting that "in the conditions of contemporary American society, the legitimate purposes of punishment do not justify the imposition of the death penalty."[13]

Injustices

A major injustice is the fact that racism infects the process. African Americans are sentenced to death at higher rates than their percentage of the general population. They have also been disproportionately executed. Those who kill whites are treated more harshly, whereas those who kill African Americans and other minorities usually do not end up on death row. The courts have not been receptive to claims of racial discrimination in the administration of the death penalty. Furthermore, discriminatory jury selection continues despite the Supreme Court's decision in *Batson v. Kentucky*,[14] primarily because the courts have failed to require more from prosecutors than a perfunctory explanation for striking black jurors. The courts have also shielded prosecutorial decisionmaking from review. Courts have even been willing to tolerate racial discrimination by defense counsel.[15]

Judges are on the front line of the criminal justice system and they see the difference that resources or the lack thereof can make in criminal cases in general and in death penalty cases in particular. The prosecution has almost unlimited

---

10   *Id.*

11   *Id.*

12   *Id.* at 43.

13   *Id.* at 41.

14   469 U.S. 79 (1986).

15   In *Mata v. Johnson*, 99 F.3d 1261, 1270 (5th Cir. 1996), the prosecutor and defense counsel agreed to excuse all prospective minority jurors, thereby ensuring an all-white jury. The court determined that this was a harmless error.

resources: numerous prosecutors, police, forensic laboratories, investigators, experts, and other law enforcement agencies. In order to have any chance at an acquittal or to receive a sentence less than death, a capital defendant needs adequate resources for counsel, experts, and investigators. Most defendants do not have resources anywhere close to the prosecution. In addition, they must rely on appointed counsel or public defenders who are typically underpaid, overworked, and sometimes incompetent.

Exonerations

There have been erroneous executions throughout United States history. According to Professors Hugo Bedau and Michael Radelet, there have been 416 miscarriages of justice related to the death penalty from 1900 to 1990.[16] The reality that individuals have been wrongly executed was brought home by the recent revelations, discussed earlier, that at least two individuals were executed despite the fact that they were innocent. The advent of DNA testing has resulted in the public's recognition of the fallibility of the criminal justice system. As a result, public support for the death penalty has declined. Much of the current opposition to capital punishment – or at the very least the reform movement – may be attributed to the public's concern about the number of individuals who were sentenced to death and later exonerated. There have been over 100 such exonerations since 1976. After 13 death row inmates in Illinois were exonerated, the Republican Governor of Illinois commuted the sentence of every inmate on Illinois's death row.

The concern over executing innocent individuals has spilled over to judges. At least one federal judge declared the federal death penalty unconstitutional because he was concerned that it was "tantamount to foreseeable, state sponsored murder of innocent human beings."[17] He went on to say:

> Traditional trial methods and appellate review will not prevent the conviction of numerous innocent people ... What DNA testing has proved, beyond cavil, is the remarkable degree of fallibility in the basic fact-finding process on which we rely in criminal cases. In each of the 12 cases of DNA-exoneration of death row inmates referenced in Quinones, the defendant had been found guilty by a unanimous jury that concluded that there was proof of his guilt beyond a reasonable doubt; and in each of the 12 cases the conviction had been affirmed on appeal, and collateral challenges rejected, by numerous courts that had carefully scrutinized the evidence and the manner of conviction. Yet, for all this alleged "due process," the result, in each and every one of these cases, was

---

16   M. Radelet et al., *In Spite of Innocence: Erroneous Convictions in Capital Cases* (Boston, Mass.: Northeastern Univ. Press, 1992).

17   *United States v. Quinones*, 205 F. Supp. 2d 256, 268 (S.D.N.Y. 2002), reversed in *United States v. Quinones*, 313 F.3d 49, 69 (2nd. Cir. 2002).

the conviction of an innocent person who, because of the death penalty, would shortly have been executed – some came within days of being so – were it not for the fortuitous development of a new scientific technique that happened to be applicable to their particular cases.[18]

Frustration

Judges across the political spectrum have become frustrated with the entire death penalty process and have voiced their frustrations. The most prominent judge to express himself was Justice Harry Blackmun. Justice Blackmun supported capital punishment during most of his tenure on the Supreme Court. Shortly after joining the Court in 1972, Justice Blackmun dissented when the Court struck down all death penalty statutes then in effect. For more than 20 years, Justice Blackmun attempted to "develop procedural and substantive rules that would lend more than the mere appearance of fairness to the death penalty endeavor."[19] However, during his last year on the Court, he admitted that he and the Court failed in their endeavor to make the death penalty process truly fair:

> Rather than continue to coddle the Court's delusion that the desired level of fairness has been achieved and the need for regulation eviscerated, I feel morally and intellectually obligated simply to concede that the death penalty experiment has failed. It is virtually self-evident to me now that no combination of procedural rules or substantive regulations ever can save the death penalty from its inherent constitutional deficiencies.[20]

Justice Blackmun announced that he would no longer support the death penalty. Other judges have expressed their frustrations as well. Justice Lewis Powell was so frustrated with the entire process that he told his biographer that he regrets having voted to uphold the death penalty.[21] Justice John Paul Stevens found the death penalty to be constitutional in *Gregg v. Georgia*, but 40 years later he wrote:

---

18   *Id.* at 264.

19   *Callins v. Collins*, 510 U.S. 1141, 1145 (1994) (Blackmun, J., dissenting).

20   *Id.*

21   Justice Powell was asked by his biographer whether he would change his vote in any case. He replied:
"Yes, McCleskey v. Kemp."
Do you mean you would now accept the argument from statistics?
"No, I would vote the other way in any capital case."
In any capital case?
"Yes."
Even in Furman v. Georgia?
"Yes. I have come to think that capital punishment should be abolished." See J. Jeffries, Jr., *Justice Lewis F. Powell, Jr.: A Biography* 451 (New York: C. Scribner's Sons, 1994).

I have relied on my own experience in reaching the conclusion that the imposition of the death penalty represents "the pointless and needless extinction of life with only marginal contributions to any discernible social or public purposes. A penalty with such negligible returns to the state [is] patently excessive and cruel and unusual punishment violative of the Eighth Amendment."[22]

Judge Alex Kozinski, a conservative judge on the United States Court of Appeals for the Ninth Circuit, while supporting the death penalty, favors severely restricting it: "Whatever purposes the death penalty is said to serve – deterrence, retribution, assuaging the pain suffered by victims' families – these purposes are not served by the system as it now operates."[23]

Morality

There are those who oppose capital punishment because they believe that it is immoral. Proponents of this view believe that the state is never justified in taking human life, no matter how vile or reprehensible the killer may be. In *Furman v. Georgia,* Justices Brennan and Marshall explained their votes to strike down the death penalty statutes of 35 states on the ground that the death penalty violated human dignity and therefore it also violated the Eighth Amendment. Justice Brennan believed that "the fatal constitutional infirmity of capital punishment is that it treats members of the human race as non-humans, as objects to be toyed with and discarded."[24] Justice Marshall even maintained that, despite the 35 death penalty statutes then in existence, a "fully informed" citizenry would reject capital punishment.[25] Both justices adhered to their views long after the death penalty was determined to be constitutional by their colleagues. For the duration of their careers they voted to overturn every death sentence that came before the court. They were often the only two votes in favor of granting certiorari. In each case in which the full Court refused to consider an inmate's appeal, Justices Brennan and Marshall would dissent and repeat what became their familiar refrain: "Adhering to our views that the death penalty is in all circumstances cruel and unusual punishment prohibited by the Eighth and Fourteenth Amendments, we would grant certiorari and vacate the death sentence in this case."[26] Justice Brennan defended his refusal to accept his colleague's interpretation of the Eighth Amendment: "Yet, in my judgment, when a justice perceives an interpretation of the text to have departed so

---

22   *Baze v. Rees,* 553 U.S. 35, 86 (2008) (Stevens, J., concurring), quoting *Furman v. Georgia,* 408 U.S. 238, 312 (White, J., concurring).

23   A. Kozinski and S. Gallagher, *Death: The Ultimate Run-On Sentence,* 46 Case W. L. Rev. 1, 4 (1995).

24   W. Brennan, Jr., *In Defense of Dissents,* 37 Hastings L. J. 427, 436 (1986).

25   *Furman v. Georgia,* 408 U.S. 238, 362–3 (1972) (Marshall, J., concurring).

26   See e.g., *Smith v. Hopper,* 436 U.S. 950 (1978) (Brennan and Marshall, JJ., dissenting from denial of certiorari).

far from its essential meaning, that justice is bound, by a larger constitutional duty to the community, to expose the departure and point toward a different path."[27]

Should Judges Who Oppose Capital Punishment Resign?

Is Justice Scalia correct that it is impossible for judges opposed to capital punishment to reconcile their beliefs with their judicial duties? This section examines that question and concludes that resignation is too drastic and unnecessary. First, given the judicial selection process, it is unlikely that an individual with strong moral objections to capital punishment would even be selected and be able to survive the confirmation process. Second, even in the event that such an individual is selected and survives the confirmation process, there are restraints that the system places on the exercise of judicial power. Third, judges throughout history have had to enforce laws with which they disagreed on moral grounds. Fourth, any judge unable to enforce death penalty laws can be prevented from presiding over death penalty cases. Finally, judges often have strong moral beliefs – if not about capital punishment, then about other issues they will face while on the bench, such as abortion. It is therefore not possible or even desirable to populate the federal judiciary with judges who lack strong moral convictions.

Judicial Selection Process

The current process for selecting federal and state judges makes it unlikely that an individual with strong moral objections to capital punishment would ever be selected to serve on the bench. Federal judges are important in the death penalty process because they consider the inmate's last round of appeals. They must be selected by the President and confirmed by the United States Senate. One scholar has described the federal confirmation process as a "mess."[28] The selection of federal judges has become extremely contentious and partisan because academic studies have demonstrated that an individual selected for the federal judiciary by a Republican President will decide cases differently than an individual selected by Democratic Presidents.[29] Because federal judges often resolve cases involving such controversial issues as abortion, affirmative action, the rights of the accused, and Church–state relations – in addition to capital punishment – appointments to the federal courts are now one of the principal ideological battlegrounds of American politics.

---

27   Brennan, *In Defense of Dissents*, 437.

28   S. Carter, *The Confirmation Mess: Cleaning Up the Federal Appointments Process* (New York: Basic Books, 1994).

29   R. Carp et al., *The Decision-Making Behavior of George W. Bush's Judicial Appointees: Far-Right, Conservative or Moderate?* Judicature (July–Aug.) 2004.

Prior to 1987, confirmation to the federal bench was almost pro forma. The United States Senate generally acquiesced in the President's selections. For instance, during the twentieth century, only one Supreme Court nominee, John Parker in 1930, was rejected outright by the Senate prior to 1968. Since then, six Supreme Court nominees have been rejected or withdrawn.[30] In the past, as long as a judicial nominee was deemed to be "qualified" and did not have any serious conflicts of interests or ethical problems, confirmation was routine. The ideological rancor over appointments to the federal bench began in 1987 when President Ronald Reagan nominated Robert Bork for a seat on the U.S. Supreme Court. Because Bork had served in key positions in the Nixon and Ford administrations, played a critical role in the Watergate affair by firing the special prosecutor, and had been a law professor and scholar, his views on a wide range of controversial issues were well known. Following a campaign against the nomination by liberal interest groups opposed to Bork on ideological grounds, the nomination was defeated in the United States Senate.

The intense ideological screening continued during the presidency of George W. Bush, especially during the confirmation of Clarence Thomas. Republicans sought revenge for the defeat of Bork and the contentious battle over the Thomas nomination when Bill Clinton became President. Clinton's nominees had to endure long delays before they were confirmed, and many never even received hearings. This intense scrutiny of judicial nominees continued into the presidency of George W. Bush. During his first few months in office, the Bush administration announced that it would end the long practice of seeking the approval of the American Bar Association (ABA) for judicial nominees prior to the submission of their names to the Senate, since the administration believed that the ABA was biased in favor of liberal nominees and had been unfair to conservative nominees, particularly Robert Bork. During Bush's presidency, the Democrats rejected some of his nominees and delayed consideration of many others. The Republican majority in the Senate became so frustrated with the tactics of the Democrats that they threatened to terminate the practice of allowing a minority of Senators to prevent a vote on a judicial nominee; but they eventually backed down, probably once they realized that whenever they are in the minority, they would not be able to filibuster a future Democratic President's judicial nominees. The battle over judicial nominees has continued during the Obama presidency as he has had fewer nominees confirmed than other Presidents. The end to these contentious battles is nowhere in sight.

Given the intense ideological screening that each nominee must endure, it has become increasingly unlikely that individuals with strong moral objections to capital punishment will ever serve on the bench unless they have done a very good job of hiding their beliefs. First, it is unlikely that any President would nominate such an individual given the fact that a majority of the public still supports capital punishment despite its flaws. Second, the Senate is unlikely to confirm any nominee opposed to the death penalty. The case of Ronnie White illustrates

---

30 *Id.* at 73–5.

that even the perception that a nominee opposes capital punishment can be devastating. White was a justice on the Missouri Supreme Court when President Bill Clinton nominated him for a federal district judgeship in Missouri. Stuart Taylor, a respected journalist who covers courts and legal matters, described White as "an honest, skilled and sometimes eloquent jurist, well within the moderate mainstream."[31] During his tenure on the Missouri Supreme Court, Judge White "had voted to uphold 41 (almost 70 percent) of the 59 death sentences he had reviewed. He voted to reverse the other 18, including 10 that were unanimously reversed and just three in which he was the lone dissenter."[32] In fact, "his rate of affirmance was only marginally lower than the 75 percent to 81 percent averages of the five current Missouri Supreme Court judges whom [former Governor] Ashcroft himself appointed when he was governor."[33] This record did not prevent then Senator Ashcroft from claiming that White has a "serious bias against ... the death penalty."[34]

Ashcroft's claim was based on two cases in which Judge White dissented from his colleagues' decision to deny the defendants a new trial. In one of these cases, the trial judge made a satement contrasting minorities with "hard working taxpayers" six days before the trial of a black defendant facing the death penalty. Judge White was understandably concerned that the defendant did not receive a fair trial. In the second case, the defendant had been charged with murdering law enforcement officials and others. He raised an insanity defense. In attempting to prove his insanity, his defense attorney used evidence from the crime scene, which had actually been manufactured by the police. Both Judge White and his colleagues agreed that the defense attorney had conducted an inadequate investigation. The only disagreement between them was whether the poor performance affected the outcome of the case. Judge White believed that it had, while his colleagues concluded that it had not. According to Stuart Taylor of the *National Journal*, Judge White's dissents in these two cases appear to be "plausible, debatable, highly unpopular (especially among police), and (for that reason) courageous."[35] White's reasonable and thoughtful concern that the defendants' rights in these two cases had been violated was distorted during the confirmation process to make it appear as though he opposed capital punishment, and he was denied a seat on the federal bench as a result. If a nominee like Judge White, who has voted to affirm almost 70 percent of the death sentences reviewed by his court, can be denied a seat on the bench because he was perceived as not supporting capital punishment, it is difficult to fathom how anyone even remotely opposed to the death penalty could ever survive the federal confirmation process.

---

31   S. Taylor, Jr., *A Character Assassin Should Not Be Attorney General*, National Journal, January 13, 2001 at 78.

32   *Id.*

33   *Id.*

34   *Id.*

35   *Id.*

Another example of how devastating it is for someone aspiring to a seat on the federal bench to be perceived as being an opponent of capital punishment is President Obama's nomination of Robert Chatigny for a seat on the United States Court of Appeals for the Second Circuit. Chatigny was a federal district court judge when he was presented with the appeal of Connecticut serial killer Michael Ross, nicknamed the "Roadside Strangler."[36] Ross had been sentenced to death for the killing of four teenage girls. He decided to suspend his appeals. Judge Chatigny questioned whether Ross was mentally competent to make the decision to waive his appeals. The United States Supreme Court has held that a finding of competence is a requirement before an inmate is allowed to waive his appeals. Because Chatigny questioned Ross's competence, Ross's execution had to be delayed. Connecticut prosecutors filed an ethics complaint in the Second Circuit as a result of Chatigny's actions in the Ross case. The Second Circuit cleared Chatigny and found that his actions were appropriate:

> It is clear the judge's concern was to repair what he perceived as a breakdown in the adversarial process, resulting from an attorney's insistence on adhering to his client's expressed desire to waive judicial review and consent to his execution, in spite of indications that the client might be without competence to make such a waiver.[37]

Although Chatigny was cleared by the Second Circuit of any improprieties and in fact was found to have acted appropriately in questioning Ross's competence to be executed, Senate Republicans used the controversy to block his nomination to the Second Circuit.

The likelihood of an individual with strong moral objections to capital punishment being selected for a seat on a state judiciary is even more remote. That is because, in many states, judges are elected to the bench. A public that supports capital punishment is unlikely to elect judges whom they perceive as being opposed to it. There have been some high-profile judicial elections in which the issue of capital punishment was prominent. In each instance, the candidate whom the voters perceived to be in support of the death penalty prevailed and the candidate perceived to be opposed lost the election. The voters of Texas elected an individual to its highest criminal court after he campaigned on a pledge to apply the death penalty more frequently, use the harmless error doctrine more often, and apply sanctions for attorneys filing frivolous appeals in death penalty cases.[38] In Tennessee, during her tenure on the Tennessee Supreme Court, Justice Penny

---

36 *State v. Ross,* 849 A.2d 648 (2004).

37 D. Ingram, *Death Penalty Case Holds Up Nominee for 2nd Circuit,* National Journal, March 11, 2000.

38 S. Bright, *The Politics of Capital Punishment: The Sacrifice of Fairness for Executions,* in America's Experiment with Capital Punishment 123 (James R. Acker et al. eds, Durham, N.C.: Carolina Academic Press, 1998).

White concurred in a Tennessee decision entitling a capital defendant to a new sentencing hearing. This was the only capital case before the Tennessee Supreme Court during her 19-month tenure on the Court. The state Republican Party launched a successful campaign to unseat her as a result of her vote in the case.[39] Mississippi voters did not retain Supreme Court Justice James Robertson after he applied a United States Supreme Court precedent prohibiting the execution of defendants convicted of rape.[40] Finally, the voters of California refused to retain Justice Rose Bird and two other members of the California Supreme Court as a result of their votes in capital cases.[41] I am unaware of any nominee for either the federal or state bench who disclosed any opposition to capital punishment prior to being confirmed. They certainly are aware that doing so would be fatal to their candidacy.

Checks on Judicial Power

Although a death penalty abolitionist is not likely to be selected for judicial office, that does not mean that he or she could not evolve into one once on the bench. For instance, Justice Harry Blackmun voted to uphold the death penalty but subsequently changed his position. Justice Scalia was concerned that anti-death penalty judges could use their position to sabotage the death penalty. There are constraints on a judge's ability to thwart the imposition of capital punishment. Trial judges will find three major constraints on their powers where the death penalty is concerned. First, most capital trials occur in states where the trial judges are elected or otherwise must face the electorate at some point during their careers in a retention election. Since most judges want to be reelected or retained, they are unlikely to attempt to sabotage a law which has public support. Second, trial judges are constrained by the Supreme Court's decision in *Ring v. Arizona*.[42] In *Ring,* the Court held that because capital defendants have a right to be tried by a jury, the judge cannot unilaterally impose the death penalty. Furthermore, in most states the judge cannot overturn a decision of the jury to impose death. Finally, trial judges are constrained by the fact that the appellate courts can overturn their decisions. A good example is provided by the actions of a Harris County, Texas judge and the appellate court's response. John Edward Green was the defendant in a pending capital murder case. After the state gave notice of its intent to seek the death penalty, he filed a motion asserting that the Texas death penalty procedure was unconstitutional because "its application has created a substantial risk that

---

39   K. Williams, *The Deregulation of the Death Penalty,* 40 Santa Clara L. Rev. 677, 724 (2000).

40   *Id.*

41   *Id.*

42   536 U.S. 584 (2002).

innocent people have been and will be, convicted and executed."[43] As a result, he argued that neither he nor anyone else could be executed by the state of Texas. The trial judge commenced an evidentiary hearing on Green's motion. After two days of testimony had been taken, the prosecution challenged the trial judge's authority to conduct the hearing and filed an appeal. The appellate court ordered the trial judge to discontinue the hearing, even though several witnesses had already testified. The appellate court held that the trial judge had exceeded his authority. According to the appellate court, the question of whether the Texas death penalty should be abolished because the risk of executing innocent individuals was too high is a matter for legislative debate, not for the trial judge to decide:

> These are indeed weighty public policy issues, greatly deserving of considerable debate by the appropriate people in the appropriate forum, and at the appropriate time. They are issues that opponents of capital punishment have been raising since the mid-nineteenth century. Certainly the Texas legislature is an appropriate forum in which to debate these public policy issues. That is also an appropriate forum to decide whether to abolish the death penalty in Texas or to enact statutory or constitutional improvements to the current legislative system. The Legislature will be meeting in the very near future and is fully competent to address these issues.[44]

Appellate judges are likewise constrained in their ability to enact personal policy preferences. First, unlike Supreme Court justices, appellate court judges are required to apply Supreme Court precedents whether they like them or not. As an example of how debilitating this requirement is, not even the most conservative lower-court judges in the country have refused to apply the controversial decision permitting abortion. Second, appellate judges serving on multi-member courts are limited in their ability to use their position to enact personal policy preferences by the need to secure consensus. Finally, federal judges reviewing capital cases have been restrained since 1996 by the Antiterrorism and Effective Death Penalty Act (AEDPA). This law has made it more difficult for federal judges to reverse determinations made by state courts in capital cases. The law requires that deference be given both to state courts' findings of fact and to their legal conclusions. As a result, federal judges cannot reverse a state court judgment simply because in their view the state court has erroneously applied federal law. Rather, in order to overturn the factual and legal determinations of state judges in capital cases, the defendant must demonstrate that the state court made a determination that was unreasonable – not simply that the determination was incorrect.

---

43   *State ex rel. Lykos v. Fine,* 330 S.W.3d 904, 906 (Tex. Crim. App. 2011).
44   *Lykos v. Fine,* Nos. AP-76,470 and AP-76,471 (Tx. Crim. App. 2010), available at http://www.cca.courts.state.tx.us/opinions/HTMLopinioninfo.asp?OpinionID=20519.

Judges Enforcing Immoral Laws

Justice Scalia's remarks were probably provoked by the actions of jurists such as Rose Bird, the former Chief Justice of the California Supreme Court. Justice Bird and several of her colleagues were opposed to the death penalty. Justice Bird's Court reviewed 71 death penalty convictions by automatic appeal during her tenure on the court between 1977 and 1986. The conviction or death sentence was upheld in only four of these cases. One scholar characterized the Bird Court's handling of capital cases as follows:

> The approach of the Bird court in reviewing death penalty judgments reflected a norm of reversal, in which the court paid little heed to principles such as abstention, the substantial evidence rule, and the principle of harmless error. Doubts, particularly those involving choice of sentence, were resolved in favor of reversal because of the severity of the final judgment being reviewed.[45]

Justice Scalia appears to have overreacted, however, to judges such as Rose Bird. She and her court were an aberration. Judges are obligated under the Code of Judicial Conduct to "be faithful to the law."[46] Most judges take this obligation seriously. They accept their obligation to be faithful to the law, even when they have strong moral objections to the law in question. History is replete with examples of jurists who have enforced laws that they believe to be unjust: anti-slavery judges enforced fugitive slave laws; anti-death penalty judges have imposed and upheld death sentences; judges opposed to the Vietnam war were able to sentence those who failed to register for the draft; and judges have followed the Federal Sentencing Guidelines, even in cases in which they believed that the guidelines were unjust or too harsh.

Slavery

Judges opposed to slavery, many of whom were committed abolitionists, faced the ultimate dilemma when they were required to enforce the fugitive slave laws. Congress enacted the fugitive slave laws to resolve the "problem" of runaway slaves. The fugitive slave laws empowered the slave owner, his agent, or attorney to seize the fugitive and take him before any federal or state judge or federal commissioners established to assist slave catching. The slave owner had the burden of proving that the person seized was in fact a slave of the claimant. Once this had been done to the satisfaction of the judge, the slave owner would receive authority to remove the prisoner back to his home state. Robert Cover studied the

---

45   G.F. Uelmen, *Review of Death Penalty Judgments by the Supreme Court of California: A Tale of Two Courts*, 23 Loy. L.A. L. Rev. 237, 239 (1989).

46   Code of Jud. Conduct, Canon 3, subd. B.

reaction of anti-slavery judges to the fugitive slave laws.[47] Many judges stated in their judicial opinions that the fugitive slave laws were evil. Nevertheless, Cover found that these judges responded to their dilemma in two ways. First, they stated in their judicial opinions that the fugitive slave laws forced them to decide in favor of slavery. As a result, they exaggerated the mechanical operation of the law, so as to deny themselves any discretion and thereby excuse their failure to act. Second, they claimed that if political or moral values were introduced into the process of adjudication, the authority of the states over all citizens would be eroded.

The experience of Justice Joseph Story provides an excellent illustration of the dilemma that anti-slavery judges faced and how they resolved this dilemma. Justice Story is considered to be one of the greatest jurists ever to serve on the Supreme Court. He was renowned for his passionate anti-slavery stance. In 1819, he publicly advocated for the complete eradication of slavery from the territories, stating that it was against "the spirit of the Constitution, the principles of our free government, the tenor of the Declaration of Independence, and the dictates of humanity and sound policy."[48] In charging a grand jury, Story stated that "the existence of slavery under any shape is so repugnant to the natural rights of man and the dictates of justice, that it seems difficult to find for it any adequate justification."[49] He reminded the grand jury that the constitutions of the United States and of several states declared "that all men are born free and equal, and have certain unalienable rights," and asked them:

> May not the miserable African ask, "Am I not a man and a brother?" We boast of our noble struggle against the encroachment of tyranny, but do we forget that it assumed the mildest form in which authority ever assailed the rights of its subjects; and yet that there are men among us who think it no wrong to condemn the shivering Negro to perpetual slavery.[50]

As for the slave trade, Story said that it "stirs up the worst passions of the human soul," and is "repugnant to the great principles of Christian duty, the dictates of natural religion, the obligations of good faith and morality, and the external maxims of social justice."[51]

In *Prigg v. Pennsylvania*,[52] Justice Story was forced to decide the constitutionality of the fugitive slave laws. In the 1820s, several free states passed what they designated as "personal liberty laws." These laws forbade any assistance

---

47 R. Cover, *Justice Accused: Antislavery and the Judicial Process* (New Haven, Conn.: Yale Univ. Press, 1975).

48 B. Holden-Smith, *Lords of Lash, Loom, and Law: Justice Story, Slavery, and Prigg v. Pennsylvania*, 78 Cornell L. Rev. 1086, 1093 (1993).

49 *Id.* at 1100.

50 *Id.* at 1100–101.

51 *Id.* at 1103.

52 41 U.S. 539 (1842).

on the part of state officers in enforcing the fugitive slave laws. They also made it a criminal act for any person "to take and carry away, by force and violence ... any Negro or mulatto ... to be kept and detained ... as a slave or servant for life."[53] The Supreme Court, in an opinion written by Justice Story, struck down Pennsylvania's personal liberty law as unconstitutional. Furthermore, the Court proclaimed that only the federal government had the authority to legislate with respect to fugitive slaves. The Court also held that no man, acting as principal or agent, could be found guilty of kidnapping for the seizure and return of his own slave. Given Justice Story's strong anti-slavery views, it was probably very difficult for him to uphold a law that he in all likelihood believed to be immoral. In fact, his opinion in *Prigg v. Pennsylvania* has long perplexed historians and legal scholars.[54] His *Prigg* opinion has been criticized as a "highly formalistic abdication of the responsibility to weigh and consider policy and moral implications of constitutional law."[55] Some have attributed the *Prigg* opinion to Story's sense of judicial duty.[56] Story himself has cast the decision as involving morality versus duty. Writing to a friend, he said:

> I shall never hesitate to do my duty as a Judge, under the Constitution and laws of the United States, be the consequences what they may. That Constitution, I have sworn to support, and I cannot forget or repudiate my solemn obligations at pleasure. You know full well that I have ever been opposed to slavery. But I take my standard of duty as a Judge from the Constitution.[57]

In 1843, Story sought to justify the *Prigg* decision to his Harvard Law School class by arguing that:

> There is a clause in the Constitution which gives to the slaveholders the right of reclaiming a fugitive slave from the free States. This clause some people wish to evade, or are willing wholly to disregard. If one part of the country may disregard one part of the Constitution, another section may refuse to obey that part which seems to bear hard upon its interests, and thus the Union will become a "mere rope of sand"; and the Constitution, worse than a dead letter, an apple of

---

53   R. Shaw, *A Legal History of Slavery in the United States*, 237 (New York: Northern Press, 1991).

54   See, e.g., Cover, *Justice Accused* 118; D. Currie, *The Constitution in the Supreme Court, The First Hundred Years: 1789–1888* 245 (Chicago: Univ. of Chicago Press, 1985); C. Eisgruber, *Justice Story, Slavery and the Natural Law Foundations of American Constitutionalism*, 55 U. Chi. L. Rev. 273, 279 (1988).

55   Cover, *Justice Accused* 240.

56   See, e.g., C. Swisher, *The Oliver Wendell Holmes Devise History of the Supreme Court of the United States, Volume V: The Taney Period 1836–64* 541 (New York: Macmillan, 1974).

57   2 *The Life and Letters of Joseph Story* 431 (William Wetmore Story, ed., Boston: Little and Brown, 1851).

discord in our midst, a fruitful source of reproach, bitterness, and hatred, and in the end discord and civil war.[58]

If ever there was a strong case for judicial civil disobedience, slavery provided one. However, the anti-slavery judges' reaction to the fugitive slave laws provides the strongest example of the sense of duty that most judges feel toward the law, even those laws they find morally objectionable. They enforced a law that they abhorred. However, according to Justice Scalia, even though some judges may be able to put aside their personal beliefs and enforce a law which they believe to be immoral, they should not do so. The anti-slavery judges, therefore, should have resigned rather than enforce an immoral law. The judiciary and the nation would have been much worse off without these judges. There were undoubtedly cases in which they made a difference by stringently holding slave owners to their burdens of proof. Their presence on the bench probably ensured that blacks were not cavalierly returned to slavery. It was also important that other judges who may not have shared their anti-slavery views were exposed to the perspectives of the anti-slavery judges. Likewise, the judiciary and the nation would be adversely affected by the resignation of judges who oppose capital punishment. Their presence on the bench can help to ensure that death sentences are meted out fairly. In addition, it is also important that other judges hear the perspectives of anti-death penalty judges. Justice Sandra Day O'Connor, for instance, noted the impact that Justice Thurgood Marshall had on the "way I see the world"[59] and how she was affected by his storytelling – "But over time, as I heard more clearly what Justice Marshall was saying, I realized that behind the anecdotes was a relevant legal point."[60] – and how the Supreme Court benefited from his perspective:

His was the eye of the lawyer who saw the deepest wounds in the social fabric and used law to help heal them. His was the ear of a counselor who understood the vulnerabilities of the accused and established safeguards for their protection. His was the mouth of a man who knew the anguish of the silenced and gave them a voice. At oral arguments and conference meetings, in opinions and dissents, Justice Marshall imparted not only his legal acumen but also his life experiences, constantly pushing and prodding us to respond not only to the persuasiveness of legal argument but also to the power of moral truth.[61]

---

58   As recorded in the journal of Rutherford B. Hayes while a student in Story's class, quoted in Charles R. Williams, 1 *The Life of Rutherford B. Hayes, Nineteenth President of the United States 1834–1860*, at 36–7 (Boston and New York: Houghton Mifflin, 1914).

59   Sandra Day O'Connor, *A Tribute to Justice Thurgood Marshall: Thurgood Marshall: The Influence of a Raconteur*, 44 Stan. L. Rev. 1217, 1220 (1992).

60   *Id.* at 1218.

61   *Id.* at 1217.

Capital Punishment

There is no evidence to support Justice Scalia's assertion that judges who are opposed to capital punishment have been sabotaging the law. To the contrary, they have demonstrated an amazing ability to participate in the process despite their reservations about it. For instance, when he was an appellate court judge, Harry Blackmun wrote that he was "not personally convinced of the rightness of capital punishment."[62] Yet, he dissented when the Supreme Court invalidated every death penalty statute in the United States.[63] He wrote at the time that "I yield to no one in the depth of my distaste, antipathy, and indeed, abhorrence, for the death penalty, with all its aspects of physical distress and fear and moral judgment exercised by finite minds."[64] He added that, while he may personally "rejoice at the Court's result," he dissented because he found the majority's position "difficult to accept or to justify as a matter of history of law, or of constitutional pronouncement."[65] Furthermore, he joined the majority when the Court reinstated capital punishment four years later. Only during the last year of his career on the Court did he permit his decisionmaking to be affected by his personal views on the subject.

Other judges have also demonstrated that they could put aside their personal beliefs regarding the death penalty and enforce the law. Shortly after joining the Court, Justice John Paul Stevens voted with the majority in *Gregg v. Georgia* that the death penalty was constitutional. In 2008, he announced that he had changed his mind regarding the constitutionality of the death penalty writing that:

> I have relied on my own experience in reaching the conclusion that the imposition of the death penalty represents "the pointless and needless extinction of life with only marginal contributions to any discernible social or public purposes. A penalty with such negligible returns to the State [is] patently excessive and cruel and unusual punishment violative of the Eighth Amendment."[66]

In the same opinion, however, he stated that his new view regarding the constitutionality of the death penalty did not "justify a refusal to respect precedents that remain part of our law."[67] As a result, he felt bound by prior precedents of the Court and held that the method of executing inmates by lethal injection did not violate the Eighth Amendment. Judge Robert S. Vance of the United States Court of Appeals for the Eleventh Circuit, which hears cases from three very active death penalty states – Florida, Georgia, and Alabama – said that if he were a legislator, he would vote against the death penalty; if he were governor, he would commute every

---

62   *Maxwell v. Bishop*, 398 F.2d 138, 153–4 (8th Cir. 1968).
63   *Furman v. Georgia*, 408 U.S. 238, 405 (1972) (Blackmun J., dissenting).
64   *Id.* at 405.
65   *Id.* at 414.
66   *Baze v. Rees*, 553 U.S. 35, 86 (2008) (Stevens, J., dissenting).
67   *Id.* at 87.

death sentence; and if he were on the U.S. Supreme Court, he might hold the death penalty unconstitutional.[68] Yet, despite these strong views, he voted to affirm many death sentences during his tenure on the Eleventh Circuit because "he knew that it was not his role to change the system to suit his personal preferences."[69] Justice Gerald Kogan, the former Chief Justice of the Florida Supreme Court, participated as a prosecutor and judge in about 1,200 capital cases, despite being morally opposed to capital punishment. As Ohio prepared to execute Wilford Berry, Ohio Supreme Court Justice Paul E. Pfeifer – who voted to uphold Berry's death sentence and who as a member of the Ohio legislature drafted the state's death penalty statute – stated that "I guess I've come to the conclusion that the state would be better off without [the death penalty]."[70] Judge Gerald Heaney of the United States Court of Appeals for the Eighth Circuit joined the majority in upholding a death sentence but wrote in a concurring opinion "that this nation's administration of capital punishment is irrational, arbitrary, and unfair."[71] Finally, despite upholding the death sentence in question, Judge Lyn Hughes of the Southern District of Texas wrote that the death penalty was "bad policy, and it may be immoral, but it is constitutional."[72]

Other Examples

The Vietnam War and the U.S. sentencing guidelines provide further examples of judges putting their obligation to follow the law above their personal predilections. Many judges who were opposed to the Vietnam War imposed sentences on individuals who had been prosecuted for attempting to avoid the draft by failing to comply with the selective service law.[73] The harsh mandatory sentences required by the federal sentencing guidelines have evoked some negative judicial responses.[74] Most judges, however, grudgingly apply the guidelines, although they sometimes complain about the unjust sentences the guidelines require that they impose.[75]

These illustrations demonstrate the depth of commitment that most judges have to their constitutional duties to enforce the law. Judges generally do not undermine or sabotage laws with which they disagree or find morally objectionable. It is therefore not necessary, as Justice Scalia suggested, that they resign from the bench for that reason. Justice Scalia also suggested that judges with moral convictions against the death penalty should resign rather than participate in the process of enforcing it, even if they could put their own personal beliefs aside.

---

68   R. Lifton and G. Mitchell, *Who Owns Death?* 159–60 (New York: Morrow, 2000).
69   *Id.* at 160.
70   T.C. Brown, *Repeal Death Penalty, Original Sponsor Urges*, Plain Dealer (Cleveland), Feb. 19, 1999 at 1A.
71   *Singleton v. Norris*, 108 F.3d 872, 876 (8th Cir. 1997).
72   *Davis v. Johnson*, 8 F. Supp.2d 897, 907 (S.D. Tex. 1998).
73   See, e.g., *Lawton v. Tarr*, 327 F. Supp. 670, 672 (E.D. N.C. 1971).
74   M. Dubber, *The Pain of Punishment*, 44 Buff. L. Rev. 545, 596–7 (1996).
75   *Id.*

In Justice Scalia's view, judges should not enforce laws that they find morally objectionable. Justice Scalia is correct that it is indeed very difficult to be in the position of having to enforce a law that one finds morally offensive. Justice Story spent much of his life attempting to justify his decision to enforce the fugitive slave laws. Resignation, however, is not the appropriate response in most cases. Given the fact that disputes over morally divisive issues often end up in court, most judges are likely to find themselves in the uncomfortable position of having to enforce a law they find morally objectionable at some point during their tenure on the bench. For instance, there are certainly judges with strong moral beliefs about abortion and same-sex marriage. Should these judges resign from the bench to avoid having to enforce these laws?

It is certainly possible that on occasion there will be judges so morally opposed to capital punishment that they may attempt to sabotage or at least delay the process as long as possible. In all likelihood this happened in the case of Robert Alton Harris. The appellate courts issued four last-minute stays of execution between the evening of April 20 and April 21, 1992. The U.S. Supreme Court vacated these stays and ordered the federal courts not to enter any more stays in Harris's case and he was subsequently executed.[76] Thus, the judicial process was more than adequate in preventing any attempts to obstruct Harris's execution. There is also another less drastic option than resignation available to a judge with strong moral convictions against the death penalty. That option is recusal. For instance, federal law provides that "any justice, judge, or magistrate of the United States shall disqualify himself in any proceeding in which his impartiality might reasonably be questioned."[77] Most states have similar provisions. For instance, a judge in King County, Washington withdrew from a death penalty case, stating that his "personal, individual, religious, moral and philosophical views" would prevent him from signing a death warrant.[78]

Conclusion

Most judges in the United States have excelled in college and law school, were extremely successful lawyers prior to becoming judges, and have been leaders in their communities. As a result, it is reasonable that the vast majority would develop strong views about some of the great issues of the day. This is a good thing. Some of our greatest jurists – including Louis Brandeis, Felix Frankfurter, John Harlan, Thurgood Marshall, William Brennan, and Earl Warren – had strong moral convictions. The Court and our nation would be much worse off had these judges resigned in order to avoid the occasional conflict that arose between their moral beliefs and the law.

---

76   *Vasquez v. Harris*, 503 U.S. 1000 (1992).

77   28 U.S.C. § 455(a) (1993).

78   N. Bartley, *Judge Taken Off Case Over Potential Death Term*, Seattle Times, March 28, 2002, at B1.

Conclusion

At the beginning of the book, I stated that one of my goals was to assess the Supreme Court's success in attempting to limit the death penalty to the worse offenders. It is clear that the Court has not been successful in this endeavor. One of the main proponents of the narrowing approach was Justice John Paul Stevens. He believed that, with the right procedures, it was possible to ensure "even-handed, rational and consistent imposition of the death penalty under law."[1] After retiring from the Court, Justice Stevens wrote that the combination of personnel changes on the Court, along with "regrettable judicial activism," had created a capital punishment system that is biased against African Americans, skewed in favor of conviction, infected with politics, and tinged with hysteria.[2]

Despite the Court's attempt to limit the death penalty since 1976, the manner in which the death penalty is meted out is no fairer now than when the Court first began this endeavor. It continues to be fraught with arbitrariness and racial discrimination. There remains no logical way to separate the cases of those who end up on death row from those who do not. A few examples will illustrate this point. Teresa Lewis began having an affair with Matthew Shallenberger. They decided to kill her husband and stepson in order to collect their life insurance proceeds. Lewis left the door unlocked so that Shallenberger and another man named Fuller, whom Shallenberger recruited to assist him, could enter the home and carry out the murders. After Shallenberger and Fuller shot both her husband and stepson, Lewis initially claimed the murders were committed by an intruder but she later confessed after the authorities suspected her involvement. She cooperated with the authorities and fingered both Shallenberger and Fuller. All three were arrested and charged with capital murder. Fuller received a life sentence in exchange for his testimony against Lewis and Shallenberger. Shallenberger also received a life sentence. Lewis, however, was sentenced to death, despite the fact that she had confessed and cooperated with the authorities and identified the two assailants. Thus, the two individuals who actually carried out the killings and who stood to gain financially from their actions were given life sentences while Lewis was sentenced to death, despite the fact that Shallenberger seemed to have been the mastermind behind the crimes.[3]

---

1   *Jurek v. Texas*, 428 U.S. 262, 276 (1976).

2   J.P. Stevens, *On the Death Sentence*, The New York Review of Books, available at http://www.nybooks.com/articles/archives/2010/dec/23/death-sentence/?pagination=false.

3   According to Fuller, "As between Mrs. Lewis and Shallenberger, Shallenberger was definitely the one in charge of things, not Mrs. Lewis." J. Grisham, *Teresa Lewis Didn't Pull*

No killing would seem more heinous than the murder of a police officer. Juan Leonardo Quintero would seem to be an ideal candidate for the death penalty. During a routine traffic stop, Quintero shot and killed Houston police officer Rodney Johnson four times in the back of the head after being handcuffed and placed in the back of the police patrol car. During the shooting, Quintero hurled racial slurs at Officer Johnson, who was African American. Quintero had previously been deported from the United States for indecency with a child but had illegally reentered the country. He was drunk at the time of the murder and had been convicted previously of driving while intoxicated. Officer Johnson's wife remarked that "if any case warranted the death penalty, this [case] certainly did."[4] The jury, however, did not agree and sentenced Quintero to life. Johnny Ray Conner, whose case is discussed in detail in Chapter 2, panicked while attempting to rob a neighborhood convenience store and killed the store owner. He and many like him are frequently sentenced to death. Is he and killers like him the worst of the worst and deserving of death?

Why do such inconsistencies persist despite the Supreme Court's efforts to limit the death penalty to the worst killers? Although the Court has frequently addressed death penalty issues, there are some important issues the Court has completely avoided. The Court has acknowledged the fact that race continues to play a significant role in determining who should live and who should die; yet it has allowed these racial disparities to persist. There are other issues the Court has addressed inadequately. The Court is well aware that most inmates are on death row because they received substandard legal representation. The standard the Court has created for overturning a death sentence as a result of ineffective assistance of counsel, however, is highly deferential to counsel and so onerous that only the most outrageously deficient representation can satisfy the Court's standard. Furthermore, the Court has created inconsistent commands for the sentencer: on the one hand, attempting to restrict the sentencer's discretion but, on the other hand, requiring that the sentencer have enough discretion to grant mercy. Finally, the Court, along with the United States Congress, has erected procedural barriers that frequently prevent federal courts from considering the merits of an inmate's claim – even a claim of actual innocence.

Some commentators have taken the position that the Supreme Court's role should be minimal, given the fact that the public in most states have elected to have a death penalty. In fact, those who espouse this view believe that the Court has been too involved in regulating the death penalty. Justice Antonin Scalia has made clear his belief that the Court has encumbered the death penalty "with unwarranted

---

The Trigger. Why Is She on Death Row?, Washington Post, September 12, 2010, available at http://www.washingtonpost.com/wp-dyn/content/article/2010/09/10/AR2010091002673.html.

4   B. Rogers and D. Lezon, *Slain Officer's Family Shocked By Life Sentence*, Houston Chronicle, May 20, 2008, available at http://www.chron.com/disp/story.mpl/front/5792183.html.

restrictions neither contained in the text of the Constitution nor reflected in two centuries of practice under it."[5] Justice Scalia believes that the courts should defer to the public's judgment on capital punishment:

> The American people have determined that the good to be derived from capital punishment – in deterrence, and perhaps most of all in the meting out of condign justice for horrible crimes – outweighs the risk of error. It is no proper part of the business of this Court, or of its Justices, to second-guess that judgment, much less to impugn it before the world, and less to frustrate it by imposing judicially invented obstacles to its execution.[6]

Although the Court has been erratic in regulating the death penalty, Justice Scalia is incorrect when he says that the Court has either no role or a very limited one in the process. The Constitution imposes on the Court a fiduciary responsibility to prevent cruel and unusual punishments, as well as to ensure that criminal defendants have, at minimum, a fair trial, due process, and the right to counsel. The Court is also obligated to protect politically powerless minorities. Is there any minority with less political clout than death row inmates, most of whom are poor and many of whom are racial minorities? The Court should defer to the political process when the aggrieved group can vindicate their rights through the political process. However, when the political process is foreclosed, as it is for death row inmates, only the Court can ensure that they are treated fairly.

---

5 *Kansas v. Marsh*, 548 U.S. 163, 187 (2006) (Scalia, J., concurring).
6 *Id.* at 199.

Index

16802965R00130